The High-IQ Bathroom Reader

The High-IQ Bathroom Reader

Brilliant reading for your private moments

The High-IQ Bathroom Reader

ISBN-13: 978-1-60261-021-7
ISBN-10: 1-60261-021-5

Book design by Miles G. Parsons
Contributors: Ella Robinson, Megan Roth, Russ Mitchell, Julie Steward, Anna Cate Little, Heather Stripling, and Holly Smith

Printed in the United States of America

What Is IQ?

IQ, or intelligence quotient, is a score calculated in the process of measuring intelligence.

Hold the bus.

First, what is intelligence? Intelligence is a mental property that encompasses many things. Psychologists like to argue over the true meaning of intelligence, but it is modernly thought to encompass a plethora of related mental capabilities such as:

- Reasoning
- Planning
- Problem solving
- Comprehension of ideas
- Abstract thinking
- Use of language
- Learning and storing knowledge

Intelligence comes from the word *intellegentia,* a Latin verb that translates "to understand." Psychologists argue that intelligence is quite different from both being "smart" and being "clever," as smartness is related to adaptability to environment, and cleverness to the ability to adapt in a creative way.

Back to IQ…

IQ (Intelligence Quotient) was coined in 1912 by German psychologist William Stern.

The score was originally determined by this simplistic formula:

$$100 \times \frac{\text{mental age}}{\text{chronological age}}$$

For example, a five year old whose score was the same as the average ten year old would have an IQ of 200.

Today, IQ is measured using a bell curve with the center value of 100 and a standard deviation of 15 or 16. Standard deviation is the measure of the spread of values in a statistical test or study. Most modern IQ tests measure several areas of intelligence such as short-term memory, verbal knowledge, perceptual speed, and many problem-solving tasks.

Because IQ tests are different, each IQ test is only valid for a particular IQ range. Because of this, IQ tests often are unable to measure abnormally high or abnormally low IQs.

Intelligence of All Flavors

Typically, people find one kind of question easier than others, but researchers have determined that for the most part people who excel in one category do similarly well in the other categories, and if someone does poorly in any one category, he also does poorly in the others. Based on this reasoning, the experts believe there is one general element of intellectual ability that determines other specific cognitive abilities. The best tests, therefore, feature questions from many categories of intellectual ability so that the test isn't weighted toward one specific skill.

What Does an IQ Score Mean?

On most tests, a score between 80 and 115—the median plus or minus 10—is considered average intelligence. A score above 130 is considered exceptional intelligence, and a score below 70 is considered an indication of mental retardation. Like earlier tests, modern IQ tests are adjusted for the age of a child. Children are evaluated in relation to the population at their developmental level.

IQ tests are designed to measure a person's general ability to solve problems and understand concepts. IQ tests measure this general intellectual ability in a number of different ways. They may test:

- Spatial ability – the ability to visualize the relationship of varying shapes
- Mathematical ability – the ability to solve problems and use logic
- Language ability – the ability to complete sentences or recognize words when letters have been rearranged or removed
- Memory ability – the ability to recall things presented either visually or orally

Questions in each of these categories test for a specific cognitive ability, but many psychologists believe they also indicate general intellectual ability.

An IQ score is not forever! Over time, some people experience a change in IQ of as much as 18 points. Researchers attribute the change to the amount of mental exercise a person undergoes. Regularly solving puzzles and playing games such as chess can contribute to IQ maintenance.

Savants

A savant is a person of extraordinary genius. In IQ testing, a person of an IQ above 190–200 is considered to be a savant.

Estimated IQs of well-known savants:

• Leonardo da Vinci	220
• Marilyn vos Savant	186–228
• Johann Wolfgang von Goethe	210

Autistic savants have both autism and savant syndrome.

- **Savant syndrome** describes a condition where a person has a severe developmental handicap and extraordinary mental abilities.
- **Autism** is a mental disorder that is characterized by a lack of development in social interaction, communication, and the display of restricted and repetitive behavior. The symptoms typically begin before the child reaches three years old and are largely attributed to genetics.

Some famous autistic savants have included:

• Matt Savage	US music prodigy
• George Widener	US artist and calculator
• Tom Wiggins	Blind US pianist in the 19th century
• Gottfried Mind	Swiss artist in the 18th century
• Daniel Tammet	UK synesthete and mathematics and language savant

A Name to Drop: Ronald Hoeflin

(Hint: Founder of High IQ Societies)

As a child growing up in St. Louis, Missouri, Ronald Hoeflin memorized pi to 200 places. He received his Ph.D. in philosophy from the New School of Social Research in New York, in addition to studying library science and receiving two bachelor's degrees and two master's degrees.

Hoeflin created the Mega and Titan intelligence tests to provide a measure for people whose IQ is higher than standard tests can evaluate. He has also established several high-IQ societies, including the Top One Percent Society, the One-in-a-Thousand Society, the Prometheus Society, the Epimetheus Society, the Mega Society, and the Omega Society.

High-IQ Societies

Sometimes people with high IQs like to get together and hang out. There are dozens of active high-IQ societies—some meeting together exclusively on the Internet and others holding regular meetings and/or annual conferences. Most of the societies require that a person achieve a certain IQ score to join. Together the organized groups of intellectuals solve problems, exchange ideas, identify and nurture human intelligence, and maintain a motivating intellectual and social environment. The most famous high-IQ societies require a score of 137 and higher.

The Lewis M. Terman Society consists of four high-IQ Societies founded by Ronald K. Hoeflin, Ph.D. These include: Top One Percent Society (99 percent); One-in-a-Thousand Society (99.9 percent), Epimetheus Society (99.997 percent), and Omega Society (99.9999 percent).

High-IQ Societies and Minimum IQ requirements

- Mensa –130
- Intertel –137
- TOPS – 137
- Colloquy – 140
- Cerebrals.com – 144
- ISPE – 150
- Triple Nine – 150
- OATHS – 150
- IQuadrivium – 150
- Glia – 150
- Prometheus – 164
- Ultranet – 164
- Mega – 177
- Pi Society – 177
- Olympiq Society – 180
- Giga Society – 196

High-IQ Societies & Groups with No Specific Test Requirements

- Ancient Cryptography Group – a Mensa special-interest group
- VINCI – for anyone interested in creating and solving novel and unusual puzzles
- National Puzzlers' League – recommended for SERIOUS word puzzle enthusiasts. Founded in 1883, this is the oldest organization of puzzle enthusiasts in the world.
- Science Fiction and Fantasy – a Mensa special-interest group
- Acephalic Swine & Stupid Parrots – a satire/parody-oriented free e-mail discussion list maintained by Richard May. Members of this group must be age 21 or over.

Things to Know About IQ

- Studies have shown that those with a lower IQ are at a higher risk of having brain trauma. One study focused on 520 men who had suffered concussions after their IQs were tested. Results showed that 30.4 percent of these men had abnormal scores, leading researchers to conclude that lower IQ was indeed a risk factor.
- Researchers found that preservatives, coloring, dyes, and artificial flavors affected IQ scores. When these things were removed from the cafeteria menu in a New York school district, researchers found that the scores of 70,000 of the one million students analyzed were two or more points higher.
- Social class, environmental and genetic factors, diet, birth weight, parental IQ, and how often a child is hugged influence a child's IQ.
- Contrary to popular belief, family size and birth order do not influence IQ.
- Feeling rejected has an effect on the human IQ score. Ohio researchers claim IQ can plummet by 25 percent after being rejected. It's harder to think straight after rejection.
- Certain smells may improve the human ability to pass exams. British research indicates students studying for exams could use scent to improve their grades, but also that smells associated with failure can worsen results. The smell of rosemary is also said to enhance mental performance.
- Studies show that on average wine drinkers have a higher IQ than beer drinkers.
- Brain-imaging techniques show that to some extent brain size is related to IQ.

Smart Stuff

Why Are Some People Smarter than Others?

Researchers agree that to some extent intelligence is inherited; however, environment plays a part as well. Environment and the way a child is encouraged through the developing years do have an effect on the way intelligence is presented, but actual brainpower and IQ are strongly determined by genes. The quality of intelligence, a person's ability to express his or her intelligence, is determined by his or her ancestors.

Who's Smarter—Men or Women?

Neither. Although women score higher on tests of memory and verbal skills and men score higher on mathematical and spatial ability, men and women have the same average IQ scores. However, men have a higher variance in IQ scored. There are more men than women with very high or very low IQs.

The Smartest Person in the World

William James Sidis was born in 1898. He learned to read when he was 18 months old and was writing by the time he was three years old. It took him six months to finish a seven-year public school course—he was only six years old at the time. When he enrolled at Harvard University at age 11, he excelled in math. However, after receiving his degree, he worked in low-level positions until he died of a brain hemorrhage at age 46.

Which State Is Smarter?

If you can judge by test scores, three states tied for the highest standardized reading test scores for fourth-grade students in public schools—Connecticut, Massachusetts, and New Hampshire. They each had an average score of 228 out of 500. New Mexico came in last with an average score of 203.

Math Scholars

The Third International Math and Science Study was conducted in 2003. Eighth-grade students in 45 countries were tested in their overall knowledge of math and science. The highest science scores came from Singapore, China, and Japan. In math, Singapore ranked highest, with Hong Kong and Japan coming in second and third.

Students in the US scored in sixth place in science and twelfth place in math.

The Smartest Man in America

Christopher Langan, a California native, is perhaps the smartest man in America. He began talking at six months and taught himself to read before he was four years old. He made a perfect score on the SAT, and he enrolled in two colleges but did not graduate from either. He has worked as a builder, farmer, firefighter, and a bouncer in a bar. He says he has a "double-life strategy" that allows him to divide his time, partly being a regular guy and partly performing equations and working on his Cognitive-Theoretic Model of the universe. Langan is married and owns and operates a horse ranch. His IQ score is said to be around 195.

A Name to Drop: Marilyn vos Savant

(Hint: Highest IQ Ever Recorded)

Born in 1946 in St. Louis, Missouri, Marilyn vos Savant attended Washington University and received an honorary doctorate from the College of New Jersey in 2003.

- She held the distinction of highest IQ from 1986 to 1989 in the Guinness Book of World Records and currently is listed in the Guinness Book of World Records Hall of Fame for highest IQ.
- She works with her husband, Robert Jarvik, assisting him with research regarding cardiovascular disease and serving as Chief Financial Officer for his company, Jarvik Heart.
- Savant has written nonfiction books on a variety of subjects including *The Art of Spelling, The Power of Logical Thinking, The World's Most Famous Math Problem,* and others. She writes the column Ask Marilyn for *Parade* magazine and has written a collection of short stories, a stage play, and two novels.
- Savant's IQ is said to be 228.

The Curvy Figures Add Up

A 2007 US study showed that women with curvy hips and a larger hip-to-waist ratio were more likely to be more intelligent than women without curves. The bigger the difference between the waist and hips, the more likely a woman was to hold a higher IQ. Researchers attributed the results to the fact that most women with curvy hips had fatty omega-3 deposits around their hips, a nutrient that can improve mental ability.

Things to Know About the Brain

- The human brain has about 100 billion neurons. A typical brain cell has from 10,000 to 100,000 connections to other brain cells.
- The human brain is full of nerve cells, but it has no pain receptors. Doctors can operate on the brain while a person is awake and the patient won't feel anything.
- The right side of the human brain controls the left side of the body, and the left side of the brain controls the right side of the body.
- The human brain weight accounts for about 2 percent of body weight. But the brain uses 20 percent of the body's oxygen supply and 20 to 30 percent of the body's energy.
- When a child is born, the brain weighs about a pound. But by age six, the brain weighs three pounds. Learning to stand, talk, and walk creates a web of connections in the human head—two pounds' worth!
- A message for action travels from the human brain to the human muscles as fast as 250 miles per hour.
- Depression shrinks the brain's memory center, and stress causes a decline in mental function and problem-solving capacity.
- A study done at the Medicinal Plant Research Centre (MPRC) at the Universities of Newcastle and Northumbria (Great Britain) in 2003 confirmed sage's ability to improve memory. Sage inhibits the enzyme thought to be responsible for the development of dementia in Alzheimer's patients.

- According to scientific research, the healthiest food for the brain is cranberries. They can also protect brain cells from the free-radical damage that normally occurs over time, and thus preserving cognitive and motor functions.
- Blueberries can improve memory and motor skills.
- Omega-3 fatty acids are believed to help protect the brain from memory loss and cognitive decline related to dementia and Alzheimer's disease.

Genius in a Bottle

There may come a time when it is possible to scarf a pill and increase brainpower. Researchers are studying "cognitive enhancers" that they say may improve mental abilities. These "nootropics" could improve memory, learning, attention, concentration, problem-solving, reasoning, social skills, decision-making, and planning.

Cognitive enhancers already are being used to treat patients exhibiting neurological or mental disorders. However, the beneficial properties of these medications for normal, healthy people have yet to be proven.

Smart drinks, smart power bars, and other "smart" diet supplements are on the market, but there is little evidence to suggest that these products really work. Results from different laboratories show mixed results; some labs show positive effects on memory and learning; other labs show no effects. The long-term safety of these substances has not been adequately tested.

A large portion of the research for cognitive enhancers is focused on the cyclic-AMP response element binding protein (CREB) in the hippocampus of the brain. This part of the brain is said to control the ability to retain long term memories. Although, to date, none of the current drugs has proven to improve memory, Columbia University has performed a study that shows exercise to be effective in improving the area of the brain associated with memory.

A Name to Know: Slobodan Milosevic

From 1989 to 1997 Slobodan Milosevic served as president of Serbia, and from 1997 until 2000, was president of the Federal Republic of Yugoslavia. He led the Serbian Socialist Party from its foundation on.

During the Yugoslav wars of the 1990s and the war in Kosovo in 1999, Milosevic was a key political figure and a highly controversial wartime leader. In 1999, he was indicted for crimes against humanity in Kosovo, for breaching the Geneva Conventions in Bosnia and Croatia, and for genocide in Bosnia.

In 2000, he conceded to the charges. Milosevic was arrested in Yugoslavia on corruption charges and was sent to trial in The Hague. He died before his trial concluded, after spending five years in prison during the deliberations.

- Milosevic began his political career after befriending Ivan Stambolic, whose uncle was the president of the Serbian Executive Council.
- By 1978, Milosevic had become the head of one of Yugoslavia's largest banks, thanks to Stambolic's support.
- In 1986, he was elected chairman of the Belgrade City Committee of the League of Communists, replacing Stambolic, who left to lead the Serbian Communist Party.
- In April 1987, Milosevic became the largest force in the Serbian political scene.
- In Spring 2007, self-titled "vampire hunters" broke into his tomb and put a stake through his heart, in hopes of preventing Milosevic from coming back from the dead as a vampire. It is unknown whether the group actually believed in his propensity to come back and harm others, or if the act was simply a political protest.

The Nobel Prize

The Nobel Prize is an international award administered by the Nobel Foundation in Stockholm, Sweden. The Peace Prize was first awarded in 1901 to International Committee of Red Cross (ICRC) founder Henry Dunant. Since then, the Nobel Prize has been awarded for achievements in physics, chemistry, physiology or medicine, literature, and peace. Each prize consists of a medal, personal diploma, and a cash award. In 1968, Sveriges Riksbank established The Sveriges Riksbank Prize in Economic Sciences, in memory of Alfred Nobel, founder of the Nobel Prize.

The First World War was contradictory of what the peace activists honored by the Nobel Peace Prize had worked so hard to establish. So, the Nobel Committee, located in neutral Norway, decided to award only one prize in 1917 to the ICRC. During the war, the ICRC worked to protect the rights of prisoners of war on all sides, including their rights to contact their families.

Again, little more than 20 years later, the world was embroiled in another war. This time, Germany attacked Norway, and within two months the entire country was occupied. No Peace Prize was awarded until 1944. And it was only appropriate to award the prize again to the ICRC. In the midst of chaos, the ICRC had promoted the "fraternity between nations" that Alfred Nobel had referred to in his will when making provisions for the Noble Peace Prize.

- Since its beginning, 797 people and 20 organizations have been awarded the Nobel Prize. Some have been awarded more than once, but only 34 women have been awarded a Nobel Prize. Marie Curie received two Nobel Prizes, her husband, Pierre, daughter, Irène Joliot-Curie, and son-in-law, Frederic Joliot, also received Nobel Prizes.

- Two Nobel laureates have declined the Nobel Prize: Jean-Paul Sartre in 1964 and Le Duc Tho in 1973. On the other hand, four laureates were forced to decline the Prize. Adolf Hitler forced Richard Kuhn, Adolf Butenandt, and Gerhard Domagk to decline the prize; however they later received the Nobel Prize diploma and medal, but not the prize money. And, in 1958, Boris Pasternak was forced to decline the Nobel Prize in Literature by the Soviet Union.
- The youngest Nobel laureate is Lawrence Bragg, who was 25 years old when he received the Nobel Prize in Physics with his father in 1915.
- The oldest Nobel laureate is Leonid Hurwics, who was 90 years old when he was awarded the Nobel Prize in Economics in 2007.

Nobel Prize Trivia

- Theodor Mommsen, age 85, was the oldest person to win the Nobel Prize in Literature.
- Rudyard Kipling became the youngest when he won the price for literature at age 42.
- Mommsen was born over 134 years before the most recently born laureate, Orhan Pamuk.
- Bertrand Russell, who died at 97, lived longer than any other prizewinner.
- The oldest living laureate is Aleksandr Solzhenitsyn, who was born in 1918.
- The laureate who lived the shortest time afterward was Albert Camus, who died three years after receiving the award at age 46.
- TV and radio personality Gert Fylking began the tradition of shouting "*Äntligen*!" (Swedish for "At last!") when the award winner was announced.
- The first Asian laureate was Rabindranath Tagore.

Women Nobel Laureates

The Nobel Prize has been awarded to 34 women since 1901. One woman, Marie Curie, has been awarded the Nobel Prize two times, first in 1903 (Physics) and again in 1911 (Chemistry).

Physics
1903—Marie Curie
1963—Maria Goeppert-Mayer

Chemistry
1911—Marie Curie
1935—Irène Joliot-Curie
1964—Dorothy Crowfoot Hodgkin

Physiology or Medicine
1947—Gerty Cori
1977—Rosalyn Yalow
1983—Barbara McClintock
1986—Rita Levi-Montalcini
1988—Gertrude B. Elion
1995—Christiane Nüsslein-Volhard
2004—Linda B. Buck

Literature
1909—Selma Lagerlöf
1926—Grazia Deledda
1928—Sigrid Undset
1938—Pearl Buck
1945—Gabriela Mistral
1966—Nelly Sachs
1991—Nadine Gordimer
1993—Toni Morrison

1996—Wislawa Szymborska
2004—Elfriede Jelinek

Peace
1905—Bertha von Suttner
1931—Jane Addams
1946—Emily Greene Balch
1976—Betty Williams
1976—Mairead Corrigan
1979—Mother Teresa
1982—Alva Myrdal
1991—Aung San Suu Kyi
1992—Rigoberta Menchú Tum
1997—Jody Williams
2003—Shirin Ebadi
2004—Wangari Maathai

Noted American Nobel Laureates

1906	Peace, Theodore Roosevelt
1919	Peace, Woodrow Wilson
1931	Peace, Jane Addams
1936	Literature, Eugene O'Neill
1938	Literature, Pearl Buck
1948	Literature, T. S. Eliot
1949	Literature, William Faulkner
1954	Literature, Ernest Hemingway
1964	Peace, Martin Luther King Jr.
1973	Peace, Henry Kissinger
1993	Literature, Toni Morrison
2002	Peace, Jimmy Carter

Quick and Easy Shakespeare

Here is a simple breakdown of William Shakespeare's three most famous tragedies.

- *Romeo and Juliet* – Two families are in the midst of a terrible feud. Children of each family, Romeo and Juliet, fall in love. They marry in secret and violence breaks out amongst the youth of the clans. After a threat of forced marriage, Juliet fakes her own death. She wakes hours later to find that her love has committed suicide in despair over her death. She responds by planting a dagger into her own body.
- *Hamlet* – Prince Hamlet returns home and receives a visit from the ghost of his late father. The spirit informs him that the prince's uncle, Claudius, poisoned his father to marry his mother and take the throne. Determined to avenge his father but uncertain of the truth of the spirit's message, Hamlet feigns insanity and spurns Ophelia, who kills herself in despair. Hamlet finds enough evidence for revenge, but Claudius suspects the prince and plans to poison him. Ophelia's brother, Laertes, challenges Hamlet. With swords and poison everyone dies: Hamlet's mother drinks the poison intended for Hamlet, who stabs Laertes, who stabs Hamlet, who stabs Claudius.
- *Macbeth* – King Duncan is informed that Macbeth defeats an invasion of the rebel Macdonald. The king praises his kinsman for his bravery. Three witches appear before Macbeth and inform him that he will become king. Macbeth tells his wife and the two begin to plot Duncan's murder. The deed is done and Macbeth blames two servants, leading Macduff to suspect him of foul play. Macbeth and his wife fall into madness of guilt. Viewing Macbeth as a tyrant, Macduff plans a rebellion and eventually beheads the murderous king.

The Pulitzer Prize

Joseph Pulitzer died in 1911, leaving $2,000,000 to Columbia University for the establishment of a School of Journalism. He specified that one-fourth of the money should go to prizes or scholarships to encourage quality journalism.

In the beginning, Pulitzer specified only four awards in journalism, four in letters and drama, one for education, and four traveling scholarships. However, he left room in his instructions for growth, and today, 90 years later, there are 21 Pulitzer Prizes, including poetry, music, and photography.

The Pulitzer Prizes are the nation's most prestigious and sought-after awards for journalism, letters, and music. The prizes remain a major incentive for high-quality journalism and have focused worldwide attention on American achievements.

- Each spring for 90 years, the president of Columbia University on the recommendation of the Pulitzer Prize board has announced the awards.
- The first African-American to be awarded a Pulitzer Prize was Gwendolyn Brooks, who was awarded the 1950 Pulitzer Prize in Poetry for "Annie Allen."
- John F. Kennedy was the only US President to be awarded a Pulitzer Prize. He received the Pulitzer Prize in Biography in 1957 for his book *Profiles in Courage.*

Putting the Prize in Pulitzer

Of the 21 Pulitzer categories, 20 include a $10,000 cash award and a certificate. The prize for the Public Service category of the Journalism competition is awarded to a newspaper and, therefore, is a gold medal.

Some Pulitzer Prize Categories

- Public Service
- Breaking News Reporting
- Investigative Reporting
- Explanatory Reporting
- Local Reporting
- Feature Photography
- National Reporting
- Commentary
- International Reporting
- Breaking News Photography
- Feature Writing
- Criticism
- Editorial Cartooning
- Editorial Writing

Joseph Pulitzer

One of the United State's most noted journalists, Joseph Pulitzer was born in Hungary in 1847. At the age of 17, when the Austrian Army turned him down because of his health, he enlisted in the US Union Army.

He served a year in the Lincoln Cavalry along with many other Germans. He later worked his way to St. Louis, where he spent much of his free time at the city's library. Two local newspaper editors often played chess at the library, and they and Pulitzer struck up a friendship.

He was soon offered a job with the German language newspaper *Westliche Post*. In 1872, Pulitzer was offered a controlling interest in the paper. Within six years, he was the owner of the *St. Louis Post-Dispatch* and on his way to becoming a household name.

Another Major Award to Know About

Order of Mapungubwe

As South Africa's highest honor, the Order of Mapungubwe was instituted in 2002. It is awarded at four levels:

- Platinum (OMP), for exceptional and unique achievements
- Gold (OMG), for exceptional achievements
- Silver (OMS), for excellent achievements
- Bronze (OMB), for outstanding achievements

The first recipient of the order (in the Platinum class) was ex-president Nelson Mandela.

The MacArthur Fellowship

Nicknamed the "genius grant," the MacArthur Fellowship is an annual award issued by the MacArthur Foundation. Applicants of any age must show exceptional merit and promise for continued and enhanced creative work in any field. This fellowship does not reward past accomplishment but looks to a person's potential.

The foundation does not accept applications or grant interviews for this fellowship. The awards are based solely on anonymous nominations. The first time that a new MacArthur Fellow knows that he or she has been considered is when the person receives notification of the award.

Two Really Innovative Women

First African-American Woman Millionaire

C. J. Walker was born in Mississippi in 1867 and was an orphan by age seven. She made a living for herself by working first in the cotton fields then as a washerwoman. When she was 20 years old, she moved to St. Louis.

In order to treat her own hair and scalp problems, she began experimenting with various chemicals and creams. Eventually, she created fine hair care items especially for African-American women.

- She employed "Walker Agents," women who would go door to door to sell the hair products. By 1910, her business had grown so much that she opened a factory in Indianapolis, and by 1915, she employed 3,000 people, making her company the largest black-owned business in the United States at the time.

According to the *Guinness Book of World Records*, Walker was the first self-made American woman millionaire who did not inherit her wealth or marry a man who was a millionaire.

At the time of her death, her company and the combination of her personal assets including real estate, furniture, and jewelry were valued at over $1,000,000.

First Woman to Receive a US Patent

African-American Mary Dixon Kies received the first US patent granted to a woman in her own name on May 5, 1809. She had developed an easy method of weaving straw with silk, making a strong fabric to use in making hats and sunbonnets. This was a popular discovery since many women wore bonnets while working in the fields. The straw and silk bonnets were cost effective and sturdy for working in the hot sun.

Kies' invention bolstered New England's hat economy, which had been faltering because of an embargo on imported European goods. Straw bonnets manufactured in Massachusetts alone in 1810 had an estimated value of more than $500,000 or over $4.7 million in today's money. Dolly Madison honored Kies for her innovation.

The first US patent was given to Samuel Hopkins on July 31, 1790 by President George Washington for a method of producing pot ash and pearl ash. Since then more than 6 million patents have been granted.

Pritzker Architecture Prize

Supporting living architects with demonstrated talent, vision, and commitment, the Pritzker Architecture Prize is awarded annually by the Hyatt Foundation. It began in 1979 and is now considered architecture's most prestigious award. The prize also serves to encourage and stimulate greater public awareness of buildings and architectural design.

Pritzker Architecture Prize laureates receive a $100,000 grant, a formal citation certificate, and, since 1987, a bronze medallion. Prior to that, laureates received a limited-edition Henry Moore sculpture. Nominations are open to all nations.

Presidential Medal of Freedom

The nation's highest civilian award, the Presidential Medal of Freedom, recognizes exceptional meritorious service during war or peacetime. President Harry S Truman established a national honors list in 1945 to recognize notable service in World War II. In 1963, President John F. Kennedy increased the honor to include distinguished civilian service during peacetime and changed its name to the Presidential Medal of Freedom.

> The Presidential Medal of Freedom has also been awarded to non-US citizens; the first such recipient was a Canadian spymaster, Sir William Stephenson.

The Spingarn Medal

Joel Elias Spingarn, former chairman of NAACP in 1914, willed $20,000 to the organization to honor the achievements of African Americans.

- The medal calls attention to the existence of distinguished merit and achievement among African Americans and also rewards the achievement of African-American youth.
- The first person to receive this award was Ernest Everett Just, a former professor of biology at Howard University, in 1915.
- Since that time, there has been a recipient each year, except one for 1938.

The Fields Medal

Known as the Nobel Prize for Mathematics, the Fields Medal was presented for the first time in 1936 in Oslo, Norway. Because of war and political upheaval, the Fields Medal was not presented again until 1950. It recognizes work already done and encourages further achievement on the part of the recipients.

- The medal is awarded to two-to-four mathematicians under the age of 40 every four years.
- Jean-Pierre Serre won the Fields Medal in 1954 at the age of 28, making him the youngest winner in history.
- The reward for a Fields Medal is much less than the near $1.5 million awarded with a Nobel Prize. The medal honors a specific body of work produced, rather than a result.

Enrico Fermi Award

One of the oldest and most prestigious science and technology awards given by the US government, the Enrico Fermi Award recognizes scientists of international stature for lifetime achievement in the development, use, control, or production of energy—nuclear, atomic, molecular, and particle interactions and their effects on mankind and the environment.

The award was established in 1956, two years after President Eisenhower and the Atomic Energy Commission honored Enrico Fermi with an award for his lifetime of accomplishments in physics, specifically the development of atomic energy. The first Fermi Award recipients included physicists John von Neumann, Ernest O. Lawrence, Hans Bethe, and Edward Teller.

The Enrico Fermi Award encourages excellence in energy science, and technology;

- shows appreciation to scientists, engineers, and science policymakers who have given unstintingly over their lifetimes to benefit mankind through energy, science, and technology;
- and inspires people of all ages through the example of Enrico Fermi, whose achievements opened new scientific and technological realms, and through the Fermi Award laureates, who continued in his tradition.

The Department of Energy's Office of Science administers the Fermi Award.

A Major Win

A Fermi Award winner receives a citation, a gold medal, and a $375,000 honorarium. In the event the award is given to more than one individual in the same year, the recipients share the honorarium.

A History of Measurement

- Historians believe that pyramid builders issued yardsticks and rulers to the craftsmen so that there would be a standard way of measuring.
- In AD 950, the Anglo-Saxon king, Edgar, established the length of a yard by a rod that he kept stored at Winchester. He said all measurements the length of a yard should be the same length of that one particular rod.
- In the 13th century, Edward I established the Iron Ulna, a master yardstick set in iron that all builders were to use as a standard. Medieval town halls had a yardstick attached to a wall that provided the local standard of measure.
- In 1324, Edward II declared an inch to be three barleycorns, round and dry.
- In ancient Babylon and Egypt, the cubit was the length from a man's elbow to the tip of his middle finger. A man's foot was a common unit of measure, as were the joints on his first finger. Since human feet—and fingers and arms—are not all the same length, without a standard, a builder could end up with several different sizes of stones and bricks and a crooked building.

Today, lengths can be measured by lasers:

Light produced from the electronically excited helium and neon atoms is

Amplified by the

Stimulated

Emission

Radiation produced by housing the laser gain tube between two highly reflective mirrors.

Ancient Stone Structures

There are 97 known pyramids on Earth today. The most notable is the Great Pyramid of Giza. It was built around 2560 BC for the pharaoh Khufu, and has more than 2 million limestone and granite blocks, each weighing about 2.5 tons. The base of the Great Pyramid takes up an area the size of ten football fields, and it is 480 feet tall.

The oldest large stone structure is the step pyramid of Djoser, built around 2630 BC Before this time, Egyptian builders used bricks made out of mud. Originally built with only four steps, two more steps were later added.

The Great Sphinx at Giza is the largest statue of a sphinx, a mythological creature with the head of a man and the body of a lion, in the world. It is also the largest ancient Mediterranean statue. The Great Sphinx is 240 feet long and 66 feet tall. The head is 20 feet wide.

The Seven Wonders of the Ancient World

- Great Pyramid of Giza
- Hanging Gardens of Babylon
- Temple of Artemis at Ephesus
- Statue of Zeus at Olympia
- Mausoleum of Maussolios at Halicarnassus
- Colossus of Rhodes
- Lighthouse of Alexandria

A Name to Drop: Leo Tolstoy

(Hint: Russian Author)

Born on August 28, 1828, in Tula Province, Russia, Leo Nikolayevich Tolstoy moved to Moscow with his family in 1836 so that he and his brothers could attend school. A year later, Tolstoy's father died, and the young Leo was returned to the family estate, Yasnaya Polyana, in Tula Province. He lived there until age 16, when he enrolled at Kazan University to study Arabic, Turkish, Latin, German, English, and French.

Tolstoy dropped out of the university after only a few months; however, during this time he developed an interest in the works of leading authors, including Charles Dickens, Jean Jacques Rousseau, and François-Marie Arouet Voltaire. Although he did not excel as a student, Tolstoy was gifted in learning languages.

- In 1852, *Childhood,* Tolstoy's first book and first of his autobiographical trilogy, was published as a series in the magazine *Sovremennik.* While fighting in the Crimean War, Tolstoy was inspired to write *Sevastopol Sketches,* which was also serialized, this time in *The Contemporary* magazine.
- *Anna Karenina* is considered by many scholars, and popular readers as well, to be the greatest novel ever written. In fact, Tolstoy called it his first real novel. Cleverly weaving fiction and real events, the writer created one of the earliest examples of stream-of-consciousness writing.

The play *The Power of Darkness* was banned in Russia; however, it was the first successful production of a Tolstoy play in the United States. A 1920 English-language Broadway production of the play ran for more than 85 performances.

- Tolstoy's biting commentary was not restricted to fiction. He also wrote numerous nonfiction articles criticizing the government and church. His outspoken judgment led to his excommunication by the Russian Orthodox Church, but it only increased his popularity with the public. By the turn of the century, Tolstoy had a large following of admiring readers.
- In the latter part of his life, Tolstoy turned to pacifism and embraced the teachings of Christianity. He gave up meat, tobacco, alcohol, and eventually his ancestral estate.
- In 1893, he wrote commentary based on the Gospel of Luke. The resulting *The Kingdom of God Is Within You* began a friendship between Tolstoy and Mahatma Gandhi.
- By 1910, Tolstoy had adopted extreme beliefs and alienated the majority of his family. In October, he set out to make a new life for himself. However, only a month later, on November 20, 1910, he died of pneumonia. Thousands of admirers mourned the loss of an accomplished author.
- In January 2007, two of Tolstoy's novels, *Anna Karenina* and *War and Peace,* were named to *Time* magazine's ten greatest novels of all time.

In 1862, at age 34, Tolstoy married Sofia "Sonya" Andreyevna Behrs, with whom he had 12 children. Sonya helped her husband with the business side of writing and managing the estate. She organized his notes, copied out drafts, and handled correspondence. This enabled him to begin writing *War and Peace*, which resulted in six volumes of commentary on the absurdity, hypocrisy, and shallowness of war and aristocratic society. The six volumes were published over a period of six years, between 1863 and 1869.

Ballpark Blast to the Past: The Negro League

Baseball was played in the 1700s, but then it was known as a "gentleman's game," a simple form of recreation for members of rival athletic clubs. In the 1800s, it was no longer a pastime for a select few. Baseball captured the attention of everyone and steadily grew until the game was known as the "national pastime."

In 1868, teams with African-American players were banned from the National Association of Baseball Players. However, when baseball achieved professional status, the professional teams were not bound by those rules, and African Americans became active participants in professional games. Society changed at the turn of the 20th century, as did discrimination among baseball players. African-American players were gradually excluded from all-white leagues, until no black players were allowed to play major league baseball.

The African-American players remained interested in their game and formed all-black teams and all-black leagues. The Cuban Giants came on the scene in 1885 as the first black professional baseball team. But it was not until 35 years later that the first black league, the Negro National League, was organized. Other black leagues were to follow. During their existence, the Negro leagues played 11 World Series and created their own All-Star game, which became one of the biggest African-American sports events in the country.

> "In order to excel, you must be completely dedicated to your chosen sport. You must also be prepared to work hard and be willing to accept constructive criticism. Without one-hundred percent dedication, you won't be able to do this."
>
> Willie Mays

Paper Facts

- Egyptians invented the first paperlike substance in 4000 BC Known as papyrus, it was a woven mat of reeds, pounded together into a thin sheet.
- The word paper comes from the word papyrus.
- In AD 105, paper was made in China using mulberry bark, hemp, rags, and water.
- The first paper mill was established in North America (near Philadelphia) in 1690. At this time, paper was made from old clothes and rags.
- In 1850, a method was devised to make paper from wood pulp.
- Brown paper bags for carrying groceries were invented in 1883. Today more than 10 billion paper bags are used in America each year.
- Although big machinery is now used to make paper, the process is still much the same as it was in AD 105.
- Paper can be made from any plant, but some plants make sturdier and longer-lasting paper than others.
- 17 trees are saved by recycling one ton of paper
- Toilet paper was invented by the Chinese in 875.
- $200 billion is generated by the paper and forest industry each year.
- 28 percent of all trees cut down are for paper products, and for every tree cut down five are planted.

Facts About the Fax

The idea for the fax machine is actually quite old. In 1843, Scottish scientist Alexander Bain patented a method to transmit an electrical signal to indicate whether a given part of a document is black or white. A few years later Frederick Bakewell improved on Bain's idea and made the first public demonstration of a fax transmission at Britain's Great Exhibition in 1851.

Not many people had things they wanted to fax during the 1850s, so Italy's Giovanni Caselli had plenty of time to come up with his pantelegraph, a combination of his own ideas plus those of Bain and Bakewell. To be able to use the pantelegraph, the French government set up the first commercial fax line from Paris to Lyons in 1865. However, people still didn't have much that they wanted to fax.

The pantelegraph gathered dust until the 20th century when Alexander Korn of Germany developed the idea of photoelectric scanning. Newspaper publishers finally caught on to the idea of faxing news stories, and the fax machine has been with us ever since.

The New Fax

An Internet fax allows you to send electronic documents, which are normally sent via e-mail, to fax machines. Instead of using phone lines, it uses the Internet and allows the access of both the Internet and the fax machine.

Profile of a Thinker: John Dewey

Born in 1859, John Dewey attended the University of Vermont in his hometown Burlington. He taught school for two years before enrolling in graduate studies at Johns Hopkins University in Baltimore. He received his Ph.D. in 1884. An outgoing man with strong ideas, Dewey became one of the leading social commentators of the time and wrote frequently for scholarship and for popular publications such as the *New Republic* and *Nation* before his death in 1952.

- He believed knowledge comes about as humans adapt to their environment. And, while teaching at the University of Chicago, he founded and directed a laboratory school, where he applied his developing ideas on teaching.
- Along with Charles Sanders Peirce and William James, Dewey founded the theory of pragmatism. The theory considers important the realist consequences of action in the search for meaning and truth. In other words, pragmatism focuses on the ends of an action as a vital component of truth.
- While a teacher at Columbia University, Dewey wrote articles about the theory of knowledge and metaphysics, many of which were published in two important books: *The Influence of Darwin on Philosophy and Other Essays in Contemporary Thought* (1910) and *Essays in Experimental Logic* (1916). He also wrote *How We Think* and what has been called his most important work, *Democracy and Education*.
- His other significant works include *Logic: The Theory of Inquiry*, *Art as Experience*, and *Knowing and the Known*.

Miniaturization

While working at Texas Instruments in 1958, Jack Kilby was asked to find ways to miniaturize electronic components. His bright idea was to use a semiconductor material, such as silicon, to make tiny electrical parts. He used tiny pieces of silicon to make a circuit in which all the components were integrated. By February 1959, he had an integrated circuit that he called a microchip.

- As Kilby was working on his microchip, Robert Noyce was doing the same sort of thing at Fairchild Semiconductor. He patented his planar integrated circuit five months after Kilby came out with his chip.
- Noyce's integrated circuit was the first to be produced commercially; however, Kilby was the first to patent his chip, so he is known as the inventor of the microchip, and Noyce is called the coinventor.
- In 1967, Kilby invented the first handheld electronic calculator, and in 2000, he was awarded the Nobel Prize for Physics.
- In 1968, Noyce cofounded the little manufacturing company known as Intel.

The forest department of Kerala, India, has put microchips in sandalwood trees to protect them from illegal logging. Reportedly, trade in contraband sandalwood is one of the most lucrative in India.

Hanna-Barbera

William Hanna and Joseph Barbera produced the first animated primetime television show with a half-hour storyline. This cartoon, *The Flintstones,* aired from 1960 to 1966 and became popular with adults as well as children. Actually, *The Flintstones* was produced for adults. A survey had shown that more than 50 percent of the Hanna-Barbera cartoon audience was adults, so the men put their heads together and modeled a cartoon series after the sitcom *The Honeymooners*.

The stone-age family did so well in the ratings that Hanna and Barbera decided to go the opposite direction and introduce a space-age family, *The Jetsons*. It didn't do nearly as well with viewers and ran only one season in primetime. However, it went on to be quite a success in the Saturday morning cartoon lineup.

- Together, William Hanna and Joseph Barbera received many honors during their careers, including seven Oscars and eight Emmy Awards.
- They also have a star on the Hollywood Walk of Fame, received the Jackie Coogan Award for Outstanding Contribution to Youth through Entertainment Youth in Film in 1988, and were elected to the Television Academy Hall of Fame in 1991.

Looney Tunes and *Merrie Melodies* were created by Warner Brothers in the 1930s to feature music from their soundtracks. They served as advertisements for Warner Brothers recordings.

The Internet Race

In the 1950s, the US was in the midst of a space race with the Soviet Union. With the Russian launch of Sputnik in 1957, the US immediately created the Advance Research Projects Agency (ARPA) in order to regain the nation's technological superiority.

Armed with the challenge, ARPA set out to develop a computer network. They created four interface message processors (IMPs) as gateways to let computers enter other systems using telephone lines. By 1971, 23 host computers provided access to other computers, forming a network. Within ten years, there were more than 200 host computers, including several in other countries. The agency's work, first called ARPAnet, is now known as the Internet.

British research scientist Tim Berners-Lee took the network idea a step further. He developed a way to link a set of documents and make them available to other computers around the world. His World Wide Web of information was launched in 1990. He created Uniform Resource Locators (URLs), the Hypertext Transfer Protocol (HTTP), and Hypertext Markup Language (HTML) so that people could use computers to access information in the linked documents.

World's First Website

- The world's first website was http://info.cern.ch. Launched on August 6, 1991, it is still accessible. It first explained the World Wide Web concept and gave users an introduction to getting started with their own websites.
- Today there are more than 150 million websites.

Sir Tim Berners-Lee

Born in 1955, Tim Berners-Lee grew up in London and later graduated from Oxford university in 1976 with a degree in physics.

In 1980, he built a prototype, which he called "Enquire," that would allow researchers to share information using a global system of "hypertext." He presented his idea to combine hypertext with the Internet in 1989—the World Wide Web.

Berners-Lee began work at the Massachusetts Institute of Technology (MIT) in Boston and, in 1994, founded the World Wide Web Consortium at the Laboratory of Computer Science (LCS) at the university. Currently, he serves as director of the consortium and works as a senior research scientist at LCS, now known as the Computer Science and Artificial Intelligence Laboratory.

In 2001, Berners-Lee became a fellow of the Royal Society and was knighted in 2004. He has received numerous other awards and honors.

In addition to his degree from Queen's College in 1976, he has received several honorary degrees:

- Parsons School of Design, New York (D.F.A., 1995)
- Southampton University (D.Sc., 1995)
- Essex University (D.U., 1998)
- Southern Cross University (1998)
- Open University (D.U., 2000)
- Columbia University (D.Law, 2001)
- Oxford University (D.Sc., 2001)
- University of Port Elizabeth (DSc., 2002)
- Lancaster University (D.Sc., 2004)

A Name to Drop: Stephen Hawking

(Hint: Theoretical Physicist)

Born in 1942, in Oxford, England, Stephen Hawking spent his early years in London, where his father worked at the National Institute for Medical Research as a research biologist, and St. Albans. He studied physics at University College in Oxford. After receiving his bachelor's degree, he moved on to Trinity Hall, Cambridge, where he studied theoretical astronomy and cosmology.

- In his mid-20s, Hawking began showing symptoms of amyotrophic lateral sclerosis (also known as Lou Gehrig's disease), a type of neuromuscular disease.

Currently, Hawking is professor of mathematics at the University of Cambridge and a fellow of Gonville and Caius College, Cambridge. His principal fields of research are theoretical cosmology and quantum gravity. Among his many scientific investigations, he has calculated that black holes should thermally create and emit subatomic particles until they exhaust their energy and evaporate. This action is identified as "Hawking radiation." He has studied quantum cosmology, cosmic inflation, the nature of space and time, and other theories relating to the universe.

In 1974, Hawking became one of the youngest fellows of the Royal Society. He has received many other honors, including Commander of the Order of the British Empire, Companion of Honour, and a member of the Board of Sponsors of *The Bulletin of the Atomic Scientists.*

Hawking's Works:

Hawking is perhaps best known for his book *A Brief History of Time,* which was published in 1988. His other popular books include *Black Holes and Baby Universes* (1993), *The Universe in a Nutshell* (2001), and *A Briefer History of Time* (2005). He published a children's science book, *George's Secret Key to the Universe,* in 2007.

- Stephen Hawking played a hologram of himself on an episode of *Star Trek: The Next Generation*.
- Stephen Hawking became the first quadriplegic to float free in zero-gravity in preparation for a suborbital spaceflight in 2009.
- Hawking's *A Brief History of Time* was on the British Sunday *Times* bestseller list for 237 weeks.

Math Stuff

The Golden Ratio

The golden ratio is a formula used by artists, designers, crafters, architects, and engineers to develop projects that are pleasing to the eye.

Simply put, it is the ratio of two sides of a right triangle to the opposite, longer side or hypotenuse. The golden ratio, also called phi, is approximately 1.6180339887498948482.

Like pi, the ratio of the circumference of a circle to its diameter, the digits of the golden ratio go on forever without repeating. Its exact value is:

$$\frac{1 + \sqrt{5}}{2}$$

The Golden Rectangle

A golden rectangle is a rectangle in which the ratio of the length to the width is the golden ratio.

In other words, if one side of a golden rectangle measures 2 feet, the adjacent side will be approximately equal to 2 x 1.62 = 3.24.

Fibonacci Sequence

In the Fibonacci sequence (0, 1, 1, 2, 3, 5, 8, 13, ...), each term is the sum of the two previous terms (for instance, 2+3=5, 3+5=8, ...). As you go farther and farther to the right in this sequence, the ratio of a term to the one before it will get closer and closer to the golden ratio. The Fibonacci sequence is best understood when looking at nature. Take a look at the center of a sunflower, the outside of a pineapple, and the spirals of a seashell. These are visual forms of the Fibonacci sequence.

Loops and Whorls: Fingerprinting

Copying fingerprints—and footprints and handprints—dates back 4,000 years. Ancient prints have been found in Egypt and China. In fact, it was common for the Chinese to use fingerprints as signatures on legal documents such as deeds and loans. Then in the late 17th and early 18th centuries, philosophers began contemplating skin, its surface, and the arrangement of friction ridges on fingers. In the 19th century, Sir William Herschel, an administrator in India, started requiring thumbprints and palm prints on legal documents.

- In 1880, Henry Faulds, a missionary and physician, wrote a paper for *Nature* magazine discussing the unique properties of the loops and whorls of his patients' fingerprints. He noted that cuts and abrasions on fingers did not change the fingerprint pattern. He even asserted that "fingermarks" left on objects by bloody or greasy fingers might lead to identification of criminals.
- The first conviction of a person by means of fingerprint evidence occurred in Argentina in 1892. A woman accused a ranch hand of killing her children, and indeed, investigators found bloody fingerprints on the doorpost of her home. However, upon examination, the fingerprints were not those of the ranch hand but of the mother herself. When confronted, she confessed to the crime.

The National Institute of Standards and Technology developed standards for fingerprint collection. Currently, along with the FBI database, all states and some major cities maintain their own system of criminal fingerprints. These records are shared among law enforcement agencies.

The Bertillon System

Around 1870, the French anthropologist Alphonse Bertillon thought that certain bony parts of a person's body could be measured and reduced to a formula that would uniquely identify only one person. His idea was popular for the day, until 1903, when Will West was convicted and sentenced to the US Penitentiary in Leavenworth, Kansas. There was already another prisoner named William West with the same body measurements. Authorities were quite confused until someone thought to check the men's fingerprints. Indeed, the identical twin brothers with the same body measurements had unique fingerprints. This incident led to the first systematic use of fingerprinting for US criminals.

AFIS: Automatic Fingerprint Identification System

In 1924, an act of Congress established the Identification Division of the FBI, which became the central storehouse for US fingerprint files. By 1946, the FBI had collected 100 million fingerprint cards, and by 1971, 200 million cards. Until the introduction of the Automatic Fingerprint Identification System (AFIS) technology, all of these records were manually maintained. AFIS allowed for the computerization of criminal files, but civil files remained manually maintained.

DNA Fingerprinting

DNA fingerprinting begins by extracting DNA from the cells in a sample of blood, saliva, or other body fluid or tissue. This genetic screening is used in forensic science to match suspects to evidence found at crime scenes. It has also led to several acquittals of formerly convicted suspects.

People other than law enforcement are using DNA tests. Coroners use DNA tests to identify human remains. Family court judges order paternity testing using DNA screens. Physicians match organ donors by using DNA samples. Wildlife conservationists use DNA to study populations of wild animals. Archaeologists use DNA in studying human existence during prehistoric times. At this time, list for the potential use of DNA fingerprinting seems limitless.

A koala's fingerprints and a human's fingerprints are so similar that they could be confused in a criminal investigation.

Going the Extra Mile

Although DNA fingerprinting is close, it is not 100 percent exact. Court trials have questioned not only the scientific principle but also the human factor involved in collecting and processing samples. However, criminals will go long ways to try to ensure that DNA screening doesn't convict them.

The First Catch

In 1988, Colin Pitchfork of Narborough, Leicestershire, England, became the first person to be convicted of a crime because of evidence provided by DNA fingerprinting.

NDNAD

The United Kingdom currently has the most extensive DNA database in the world. As of 2007, the National DNA Database (NDNAD) has well over 4 million records. Given the size of this database, and its rate of growth, civil liberties groups in the UK have begun to raise questions related to the right of privacy. Reportedly, British police are able to take DNA samples of anyone arrested and retain the records even in the event of acquittal.

John Schneeberger, a Canadian physician, was accused of rape in 1992. Police drew blood and compared Schneeberger's DNA with crime-scene evidence and they went through three screenings before realizing that Schneeberger had evaded the DNA tests by surgically inserting a drain into his arm and filling it with someone else's blood and anticoagulants.

Name to Drop: Victor De Leon III a.k.a. L'il Poison

(Hint: Gaming Prodigy)

It doesn't take a genius to pick up an XBox controller and blow an entire day plugged-in. Fans of varying intelligence across the world have embraced the relatively new entertainment. As a result, a dedicated and loyal fan base, which began with youngsters of the late '70s and early '80s, has matured into a demographic that spends billions of dollars annually. Many concerned parents and annoyed spouses loathe the addictive and time-consuming nature of the video games that have stormed into their homes. The proud parents of Victor "L'il Poison" De Leon III of New York, however, are an exception.

L'il Poison, the youngest professional video gamer in the world, might also be the youngest breadwinner outside of Hollywood. Playing his first game of Dreamcast's NBA 2K at age two in 2000, apparently "owned," meaning he was exceptionally good. Currently grossing over six figures, the nine-year-old gamer brings new meaning to the term "young professional."

L'il Poison prepared himself for a professional career in gaming by entering his first Halo competition at age four. He dominated many of the event's competing participants, coming in fourth place overall.

Major League Gaming recruited him in 2005, making him the youngest professional gamer of all time. The organization sponsored a competition which took place in Washington, DC.

Playing against adults, he came in second place in the competition and had earned $2,000 by age seven, losing to his dad, who is aptly known by the handle Poison. The prize placed him in the *2008 Guinness Book of World Records* as the youngest person to be paid to play video games.

A Plot to Know: The Aeneid

Virgil's great epic poem, written in Latin in the first century B.C.E., recounts the legendary exploits of Aeneas, the Trojan heartbreaker who became a founding ancestor of the Roman people. The story is divided into twelve books. The first six focus on Aeneas' voyage to Italy and the last six detail romping war story.

In the first half of the epic, Aeneas and his Trojan cohorts find themselves on the shores of Carthage where beautiful Dido welcomes them with open arms. Aeneas tells her all about the Trojan horse and his flight from Troy. His wife died, and, eventually, so did his dad. By Book IV, Aeneas' exciting, sad tales have won over Dido and she falls for him. Hard. Nevertheless, he has a larger fate to pursue, so he leaves Dido to go to Sicily. She kills herself in grief. Aeneas goes to Hades and sees the future generations of Romans.

In the second half, Aeneas has another chance at love. King Latinus promises his daughter, Lavinia, to Aeneas. However, Prince Turnus has a prior claim on the maiden and he is not about to have her stolen away. Turnus assaults the Trojan camp. Lots of battle scenes follow. Ultimately, as the title of the epic suggests, Aeneas kills Turnus. A nice wedding scene between Aeneas and Lavinia should have followed, but you'll have to imagine that for yourself because Virgil died before he could finish the work.

Black Holes in Space

In 1939, J. Robert Oppenheimer and Hartland Snyder were contemplating the equations of Einstein's general relativity in respect to the universe. They stuck on an idea that if stars collapsed they would form black holes.

Karl Schwarzschild theorized about black holes as early as 1916. Although he didn't call them black holes, he did describe the existence of an extremely dense astrological body whose gravitational force is so strong that nothing, including light, can escape from it.

American scientist John Wheeler coined the term black hole more than 50 years later.

- The first black hole reportedly was discovered in 1962. Named Cygnus X-1, this black hole is about 7,000 light-years from Earth.

Fact: Einstein did not believe in the existence of black holes.

Animals in Space

- A female Samoyed husky named Laika was the first animal to go to space. She was launched by the Soviets in 1957.
- The United States sent two mice, Laska and Benjy, into space in 1958.
- In 1963, the French government launched a cat called Feliette into space.
- A male chimpanzee called Ham was sent into space in 1969 on a United States shuttle mission.

Famous Firsts, Part I

- The first known architect was Imhotep, chief architect to the Egyptian pharaoh Djoser.
- The first paper mill was established in North America (near Philadelphia) in 1690. At this time, paper was made from old clothes and rags.
- The first book published in America was Steven Day's Bay *Psalm Book.*
- Henrietta Johnston, a portrait artist in Charleston in 1707, was the first known professional female artist in America.
- Ivan IV, better known as Ivan the Terrible, was the first Tsar of Russia, beginning his rule in 1547.
- André-Jacques Garnerin was the first person to parachute jump. He dropped from a balloon over Monceau Park in Paris in 1797.
- In 1809, Mary Kies became the first woman to receive a US patent. She received the patent for her idea of weaving straw and silk to make bonnets.
- In 1844, Sir John Alexander McDonald became the first prime minister of Canada.
- Lucy Walker was the first woman to completely climb the Matterhorn in Switzerland in 1871.
- In 1903, Vida Goldstein was the first woman within the British Empire to run for a national office. She ran for senate in Australia.
- Martha Washington was the first woman ever pictured on a US stamp. She was printed on the eight-cent stamp in November 1902.
- In 1904, Maurice Garin was the first official winner of the Tour de France.

The Fermi Problem

Physics teachers (and some folks just out for a little excitement) pose and ponder Fermi problems—a way of making justified guesses about quantities that seem impossible to compute.

Reportedly, Enrico Fermi came up with what people now call a classic Fermi problem—How many piano tuners are there in Chicago? To answer the question, you would multiply a series of estimates that, if correct, would yield the correct answer.

For example:

Take the approximate number of people living in Chicago. (Let's say 5,000,000.)

Then we'll say there are approximately two people living in each household, and approximately one household in 20 has a piano and they have it tuned once a year.

So,

5,000,000 divided by 2 = 2,500,000

1 (piano) divided by 20 (households) = .05

2,500,000 multiplied by .05 = 125,000 (pianos in Chicago)

125,000 multiplied by 1 (tuning per year) = 125,000

Now, it probably takes a piano tuner about two hours to tune a piano, including travel time, and each piano tuner works 8 hours in a day, 5 days in a week, and 50 weeks in a year.

So,

50 multiplied by 5 = 250

250 multiplied by 8 = 2,000

1 (piano tuning) divided by 2 (hours) = .5 (tunings per hour)

2,000 multiplied by .5 = 1,000 piano tunings per year per piano tuner

And, finally,

125,000 divided by 1,000 = 125 piano tuners in Chicago

Now, obviously, this equation has many assumptions, but this is the way Fermi would have gone about calculating his research. He would first find the rough answer (getting a quick, ballpark result) then move on to the more accurate conclusion.

The Fermi Paradox

Enrico Fermi is said to have asked, if we have neighbors in outer space, then where are they? His skepticism showed through when the conversation turned to the extraterrestrial. The apparent contradiction between high estimates of the probability of extraterrestrial life and the lack of contact with such civilizations—simply stated, Where are they?—is known as the Fermi Paradox.

William Faulkner and Clark Gable Go Hunting

During his later years as a writer, the southern novelist William Faulkner worked in Hollywood as a screenwriter of motion pictures. Faulkner, the author of *As I Lay Dying* and *The Sound and the Fury*, who struggled with alcoholic dependency throughout his life, sought to improve his financial standing by writing for the pictures.

Because of his alcoholism, he had limited success in the movie industry, although he did have a few successes worthy of mentioning, including a wrestling picture with Wallace Beery. The time in Hollywood did, however, produce numerous friendships with prominent members of the business, including Humphrey Bogart and Howard Hawkes, the director of *Scarface* (1932) and *Bringing Up Baby* (1938). According to biographer M. Thomas Inge, he also became a companion of one of Hollywood's current leading men, Clark Gable. In his biography, Inge recounts a humorous tale about a hunting expedition during which Gable solicited Faulkner's opinion on the greatest living writers. The writer responded with various living authors and included himself. Gable then asked him if he wrote, and Faulkner responded by asking Gable what he did.

In the 1991 film *Barton Fink*, Joel and Ethan Coen fictionalize both William Faulkner and his peer F. Scott Fitzgerald with the character W. P. Mayhew, an alcoholic writer troubled by writer's block and heartache. Mayhew, like Faulkner, had written wrestling pictures.

Exploding Stars

In Fall 2006, scientists in California and Hawaii watched a star explode. What made this explosion, also called a supernova, special? It occurred in a galaxy 240 million light-years away from Earth and was 100 times greater than other supernovas.

This brightest, most energetic supernova ever recorded is called SN 2006gy. It brightened for 70 days, and at its peak emitted more than 50 billion suns' worth of light. The light observed on Earth from typical supernovas lasts only days or a few weeks.

Supernovas occur when stars collapse, giving into their own gravity. When stars are so large, like the one that resulted in SN 2006gy, they are thought to produce an enormous amount of gamma rays, which are converted into matter and antimatter—mostly electrons and positrons. Typically, the outer layers of a star are stabilized because of gamma radiation. When the gamma radiation weakens, the star begins to fold in on itself, causing a thermonuclear explosion.

Stars as big as the one that resulted in the mega explosion observed in 2006 are somewhat rare. Scientists believe that the Milky Way has only a few of these massive stars. However, they say Eta Carinae, the brightest star in our galaxy, is exhibiting signs of instability. It produces 5 million times more energy than the sun and has been exhibiting signs similar to what researchers think happened to the star that produced SN 2006gy.

Although it may sound a little scary, scientists say if Eta Cariane does explode it is not likely to pose a threat to Earth.

Astronomical Facts

- Earth, Neptune, and Uranus are called blue planets because of the gases in their atmosphere.
- Researchers identify the hottest stars, with a surface temperature of more than 37,000°F, as blue stars. Warm stars (10,000°F) are called white. And cool stars (5,500°F) are called red.
- A red shift occurs when a star's light seen through a spectroscope shifts toward the red area of the spectrum. This means the light is becoming weaker and the star is traveling away from Earth. This phenomenon is the reason scientists believe the universe is expanding.
- Jupiter's red spot is a swirling cloud of gases thought to be red phosphorus.

Spectroscopy

German chemist Robert Bunsen and physicist Gustav Kirchhoff teamed up in 1859 to develop a way to analyze a substance by evaluating the spectrum of light the substance gives off. They called this method spectroscopy. Using their theory of light spectrum, Kirchhoff identified several elements that make up the sun: iron, calcium, magnesium, sodium, nickel, and chromium.

Astronomers use spectroscopy today to calculate the temperature, pressure, density, magnetic fields, and velocity of plants and stars.

One Book Called "Ulysses"

Although listed on the Radcliffe Publishing Course "Top 100 Novels of the 20th Century," and long regarded as one of the most impressive novels ever penned in English, James Joyce's *Ulysses* almost never made it to the United States... legally that is. Shortly after being banned by US customs in 1921, the book became one of the most commonly smuggled texts from Europe. In fact, customs agents were so accustomed to seeing contraband copies of the book that they began ignoring it entirely.

Publishing houses can get away with printing just about anything these days, but less than 80 years ago that wasn't so. A book-burning group known as the New York Society for the Suppression of Vice attempted to suppress anything they deemed immoral. In the early 20th century, the group was responsible for the prohibition of "sensualist" material, including a large selection of what has since become canonized literature. Excerpts of *Ulysses*, printed in *The Little Review* by publishers Kate Heap and Margaret Anderson, caught the attention of the New York Society for the Suppression of Vice and led to obscenity convictions for Heap and Anderson that year, as well as a nationwide banning of the novel. Joyce, ironically now an Irish national hero, had already seen his work blacklisted in Ireland. Regardlessly, the European literary audience devoured Joyce's work and didn't seem to mind the colorful language included in it. Soon it would seem as though American readers didn't mind either.

The literary public in the United States was eager to lay hands on the book, and the unauthorized copies began sliding in uncontested. It became obvious to the American publisher Bennett Cerf of Random House that something had to be done. This probably had more to do with the 1932 acquisition of the much-coveted publishing rights than an idealistic crusade, but nonetheless, a plan was set into motion in 1933. That year, Cerf and his partner, Donald Klopfer, arranged for a copy to be pasted with glowing reviews from European journals and then smuggled into the United States. The two went to the trouble to insist that this copy be seized so that the matter would be brought to trial and gain public attention.

The scheme worked well, and in August of 1933, Judge John M. Woolsey of New York presided over a case that would eventually change American publishing forever. In *United States of America v. One Book Called "Ulysses,"* Woolsey stated that the American public has the right to legally see what an artist creates. Woolsey continued, addressing the language within Joyce's text that the New York Society for the Suppression of Vice found so inflammatory, and concluded that the book was not sensualist and that it is justifiable for a novelist to use the same language his characters would use. Because of one book called *Ulysses,* Woolsey made a decision that set a precedent of freedom of speech that has since become a standard in American publishing.

In an effort to combat censorship, the American Library Association publishes a list of challenged books. Lobbyists and parents contest the books for everything from "religious viewpoints" to "offensive language." Examples of challenged books include J. K. Rowling's *Harry Potter* series and *The Adventures of Huckleberry Finn* by Mark Twain.

Geysers on Saturn's Moon

In 2006, the NASA spacecraft Cassini took pictures of Saturn's moon, Enceladus, that fascinated and baffled scientists. What appeared to be high-speed water fountains were shooting liquid from near-surface pockets of water.

Scientists studied several photos of the phenomena before agreeing that there is evidence to suspect geyserlike activity on Saturn's moon.

NASA scientists were already aware of several moons in the solar system that have liquid-water oceans covered with thick icy crusts. However, on Enceladus the pockets of liquid water are near the surface. Also, evidence of volcanic activity in the universe had already been discovered—on Jupiter's moon, Io, on Earth, and possibly on Neptune's moon, Triton. And now Enceladus is added to the list.

Cassini also sent back data showing that the shooting water was indeed made up of oxygen and hydrogen.

The Red Dwarf

In 2007, scientists discovered a planet outside our solar system that they believe is more like Earth than any other known planet. They say the planet is located, like Earth, not too far and not too close to its star (like Earth's sun), so that liquid surface water might be existent.

The new planet, which seems to be about 50 percent bigger than Earth and about five times more massive, is called Gliese 581 C.

Project Phoenix

In February 1995, the Search for Extraterrestrial Intelligence Institute (SETI) used the world's largest radio telescope in the Southern Hemisphere to search for extraterrestrial civilizations. The Parkes 210-foot radio telescope in New South Wales, Australia, listened for radio signals from another planet. In September 1996, the project moved from Australia to the US, setting up at the National Radio Astronomy Observatory in Green Bank, West Virginia. Observations then moved on to Puerto Rico.

The Phoenix Project computers simultaneously monitored millions of radio channels, examining nearby, sunlike stars. Researchers had picked out specific stars—about 800 of them—that they believed to be most likely to host long-lived planets capable of supporting life. They then assigned 2 billion very narrow channels, 1 Hz wide, to examine for each star.

Because of the ability to detect slowly-drifting signals and the application of near real-time data processing, Project Phoenix was the most comprehensive and sensitive SETI program ever conducted. More than 11,000 hours were spent observing 800 stars with telescopes in Australia, West Virginia, and Puerto Rico; however, no ET signals were detected.

The signal-processing techniques developed for use in Project Phoenix have proven useful in the detection of breast cancer.

The Drake Equation

Developed by Frank Drake in the 1960s, the Drake Equation is a way of estimating the number of civilizations that exist and might be transmitting radio frequencies in our galaxy. The factors of the equation include the number of sunlike stars in our galaxy and the fraction of habitable planets supporting communicating civilizations, along with several other elements of consideration. The result of multiplying these various factors is N, the number of transmitting civilizations. As you might think, many of the factors necessary for the equation are somewhat unknown; therefore, N could range from one (with our civilization being alone in the galaxy) to thousands or even millions. For this reason, the Drake Equation is related to the Fermi Paradox.

The Equation

N = R x fp x ne x fl x fi x fc x L

where:

- **N** is the number of civilizations in our galaxy with which we might expect to be able to communicate
- **R** is the rate of star formation in our galaxy
- **fp** is the fraction of those stars that have planets
- **ne** is the average number of planets that can potentially support life per star that has planets
- **fl** is the fraction of the above that actually go on to develop life
- **fi** is the fraction of the above that actually go on to develop intelligent life
- **fc** is the fraction of the above that are willing and able to communicate
- L is the expected lifetime of such a civilization

Words to Know

- BETA: Billion Channel ExtraTerrestrial Assay—A SETI project supported by the Planetary Society
- Doppler Shift: A change in frequency as a result of the relative motion of the source and the observer
- HRMS: High Resolution Microwave Survey
- IAU: International Astronomical Union
- JPL: Jet Propulsion Laboratory
- MHz: Megahertz, a unit of frequency, 1 million cycles per second
- NRAO: National Radio Astronomy Observatory
- SERENDIP: Search for Extraterrestrial Radio Emission from Nearby Developed Intelligent Populations, an ongoing SETI project conducted by the University of California, Berkeley
- SOFIA: Stratospheric Observatory for Infrared Astronomy

- A light-year is the distance light travels in a year, about six trillion miles.
- Some scientists believe there are numerous black holes, some up to 10 million times larger than the sun. Theoretically, some of the black holes can be found in the centers of energetic galaxies and quasars and are responsible for their enormous energy release.

Controversy in Literature

Harper Lee and Truman Capote

The rumor: The idea that Harper Lee's classic *To Kill a Mockingbird* actually came from the pen of friend and fellow novelist Truman Capote remains a question to many fans of the novel. According to conspiracy theories concerning the text, Capote either cowrote or ghost-wrote the novel.

The truth: Capote, a childhood neighbor and friend of Lee's, was the basis for one of the characters in the book. In a letter to a relative penned in 1959, Capote addresses the idea that he wrote the book, stating that "I did not see Nelle last winter, but the previous year, she showed me as much of the book as she'd written, and I liked it very much." Further information can be found in *A Portrait of Harper Lee* by Charles Shields.

J. K. Rowling and a Gay Headmaster

In October 2007 author, J. K. Rowling stated to a crowd at Carnegie Hall that a character from *Harry Potter,* Albus Dumbledore, is a homosexual. Fierce controversy surrounds the statement about the fictional character's sexuality, a fact that Rowling may have intended when making the announcement. She commented on the furor, stating that "He is my character ... and I have the right to say what I say about him."

Ten Really Smart Animals

Animal experts have varying ideas of which animal is the smartest (other than the human), but they generally agree on the top ten.

- **Chimpanzees** can recognize themselves in a mirror. Scientists believe that chimpanzees are aware of themselves and others. When shown videos of other chimpanzees, the viewers demonstrated recognition and even emotions toward what they were viewing.
- **Baboons** can make analogies.
- **Orangutans** can use tools and show others how to use them. Carel van Schaik, researcher at Duke University, was the first to document wild orangutans' use of tools. Studying the animals in Sumatra, he noted that they devised tools to eat and share food. They used sticks to pry open prickly fruit and scoop out the seeds inside.
- **Prairie dogs** have a language to communicate with each other. According to Northern Arizona University biology professor Con Slobodchikoff, prairie dogs alert other prairie dogs of predators. Studies have indicated that the animals differentiate between types of predators, their size and shape, and even what color they are (or are wearing).
- **Octopi** can open jars, if they are motivated by the contents of food, of course.
- **Dolphins** assist each other in giving birth.
- **Ravens**, **crows**, and **parrots** can solve problems. Some ravens have been noted as being able to count to nine.
- **Pigs** were taught to search out truffles during the Middle Ages. And reportedly, they can be taught to herd other animals such as buffalo.

Highly Intelligent Creatures: Fish?

As it turns out, fish may be more than simple sea creatures. A group of scientists teamed up in 2003 and found that fish were both socially intelligent and manipulative. The studies of three biologists, Calum Brown, Keven Laland, and Jens Krause, found that fish use a number of intelligent tactics in their social relationships, exhibiting tendencies toward tradition and cooperation in dealing with predators and finding food.

Scientists believe that fish are the oldest of major vertebrates and have had ample time to evolve in their behavior patterns. Rivaling other vertebrates, fish are found to be more complex than nonhuman primates, suggesting that judging intelligence by brain volume in animals may be an outdated practice.

Other Animal Facts

- A sperm whale has the largest brain of any animal, weighing between about 17 and 19 pounds. Human brains are about 2.5 to 3 pounds.
- The human brain contains about 100 billion nerve cells or neurons.
- The first ape to learn sign language was the chimpanzee Washoe during the 1960s. Other apes have followed, including Nim Chimpsky, a chimpanzee, and Chantek, an orangutan.

A Plot to Know: The Great Gatsby

They don't call this book great for nothin'. F. Scott Fitzgerald paints a memorable portrait of the Jazz Age in this uncompromising examination of the American Dream. Handsome man of mystery Jay Gatsby lives in a splendid mansion on the north shore of Long Island. Despite his lavish parties and the free-flowing champagne, he is largely reclusive and unhappy. He has achieved fame and fortune, but has not won the heart of his lady love, Daisy. The book begins with Daisy's cousin, Nick, telling the story. He has moved into a small house next door to Gatsby, and he is instantly intrigued by the man. Gatsby begins to open up to Nick, telling him that years ago he and Daisy had an affair, but he was too poor to marry her. She married the philandering, boorish Tom Buchanan instead, and, like Gatsby, she is rich and unhappy. Gatsby persuades Nick to help reunite him with Daisy now that he's wealthy enough for her. They rekindle their romance, but soon Daisy accidentally runs over her husband's mistress, Myrtle. Myrtle's husband blames Gatsby for his wife's death and shoots him. Daisy, shallow to the end, stays with her husband, Tom, and their comfy lifestyle.

F. Scott Fitzgerald coined the term "The Jazz Age" to describe the period from 1918 to 1929. The beginning of the Jazz Age coincides with the close of World War I, and its ending came when the stock market crashed, sending the US into the Great Depression.

Nobel Prize Laureates for Literature for the Last 40 Years

1968 Yasunari Kawabata - Japanese
1969 Samuel Beckett - English/French
1970 Aleksandr Solzhenitsyn - Russian
1971 Pablo Neruda - Spanish
1972 Heinrich Böll - German
1973 Patrick White - English
1974 Eyvind Johnson - Swedish
1974 Harry Martinson - Swedish
1975 Eugenio Montale - Italian
1976 Saul Bellow - English
1977 Vicente Aleixandre - Spanish
1978 Isaac Bashevis Singer - Yiddish
1979 Odysseas Elytis - Greek
1980 Czeslaw Milosz - Polish
1981 Elias Canetti - German
1982 Gabriel García Márquez - Spanish
1983 William Golding - English
1984 Jaroslav Seifert - Czech
1985 Claude Simon - French
1986 Wole Soyinka - English
1987 Joseph Brodsky - Russian/English
1988 Naguib Mahfouz - Arabic
1989 Camilo José Cela - Spanish
1990 Octavio Paz - Spanish
1991 Nadine Gordimer - English
1992 Derek Walcott - English
1993 Toni Morrison - English
1994 Kenzaburo Oe - Japanese
1995 Seamus Heaney - English
1996 Wislawa Szymborska - Polish
1997 Dario Fo - Italian

1998 José Saramago – Portuguese
1999 Günter Grass – German
2000 Gao Xingjian – Chinese
2001 Vidiadhar Surajprasad Naipaul – English
2002 Imre Kertész – Hungarian
2003 J. M. Coetzee – English
2004 Elfriede Jelinek – German
2005 Harold Pinter – English
2006 Orhan Pamuk – Turkish
2007 Doris Lessing – English

Upon winning the Nobel Prize for Literature in 1954, Ernest Hemingway penned these famous words.

"Writing, at its best, is a lonely life. Organizations for writers palliate the writer's loneliness, but I doubt if they improve his writing. He grows in public stature as he sheds his loneliness and often his work deteriorates. For he does his work alone and if he is a good enough writer he must face eternity, or the lack of it, each day.

"For a true writer each book should be a new beginning where he tries again for something that is beyond attainment. He should always try for something that has never been done or that others have tried and failed. Then sometimes, with great luck, he will succeed.

"How simple the writing of literature would be if it were only necessary to write in another way what has been well written. It is because we have had such great writers in the past that a writer is driven far out past where he can go, out to where no one can help him."

The US Navy Marine Animal Program

Believe it or not, the military use of dolphins and other highly intelligent sea mammals has become a common practice.

Because of their unique ability to pick up on sonar signals and detect incoming submarines and mines, sea lions and dolphins can be used for harbor protection, mine clearance, and underwater equipment recovery.

Animal teams have been deployed since the Vietnam War, and are continuously used for many military purposes.

In 1965, the dolphin's intelligence and diving ability led to the creation of a research program at Point Mugu, California. The dolphin was able to use sonar to detect the topography of the ocean floor.

Major development has occurred since the discovery that dolphins and sea lions could be reliable workers even as they were untethered and allowed to explore the open sea.

Dolphins

A dolphin sleeps with only half its brain. Since it must surface to breathe, it sleeps close to the surface of the water. This makes it vulnerable to predators, so it sleeps with half its brain and one eye. During a sleep cycle, a dolphin changes position to allow each side of the brain to rest, sleeping an average of 8 hours a day.

A Name to Drop: Bertrand Russell

(Hint: Analytic Philosophy)

Born on May 18, 1872, in Trelleck, Wales, Bertrand Russell was the grandson of the first Earl Russell, who served as prime minister of England before his grandson's birth. Russell and his brother, Frank, were orphaned at an early age. They lived with their grandmother, who provided the boys with a strict childhood and a variety of governesses and tutors. He enrolled in Trinity College, Cambridge, in 1890 and was elected a fellow in 1895. He married four times and had three children.

- Russell, known as one of the founders of analytic philosophy, had great influence in the fields of both philosophy and mathematics.
- As a prolific and accomplished writer, he set out to change the way philosophical propositions were presented.
- He believed that many of the day's propositions were unclear and oftentimes incoherent.
- Exact language and proper grammar were hallmarks of his understandable propositions and contributed greatly to his success among his colleagues as well as with the general public.

Brain Teaser

What did Russell think was the most essentially philosophical of all questions?
(Answer: Can human beings know anything, and if so, what and how?)

Russell thought that logic and science were the principal tools of the philosopher. Early in his career he approached the principles of mathematics and philosophy with the same elements of logical thinking. This careful approach led him to develop what is now known as Russell's Paradox in 1901, while he was writing *The Principles of Mathematics.*

- Russell is credited with helping to prevent the escalation of nuclear war. Generally, he thought war to be a great evil, but he agreed that in extreme cases, such as Adolf Hitler's campaign to take over Europe, war would be the lesser of the evils. However, as nuclear technology became more straightforward and political leaders became more impulsive, he teamed with Albert Einstein and other prominent scientists to promote atomic energy control.
- He was also instrumental in establishing in 1960 the World Academy of Art and Science to serve as a forum for scholars to join together for discussions of issues important to humankind.

Russell spent about four years, from 1940 to 1944, in the United States. During that time he taught at many of the nation's leading universities including the University of Chicago and the University of California, Los Angeles. He lectured for the Barnes Foundation in Merion, Pennsylvania, for three years before returning to Europe in 1944.

Russell said that only his desire to know more mathematics kept him from suicide.

An Avid Writer

Setting, and often meeting, a goal of 3,000 words a day, Bertrand Russell wrote more than 4,300 publications, most of which are held at McMaster University in Hamilton, Ontario, Canada. *German Social Democracy*, his first book, was published in 1896. This was followed in 1903 with what is called Russell's most important book, *The Principles of Mathematics*. He went on to write three volumes of *Principia Mathematica*, which, combined with the earlier book, made Russell world famous in his field. *A History of Western Philosophy*, published in 1945, offered him a steady income for the remainder of his life; however, he continued to write both scholarly and contemporary articles and books. His three-volume autobiography was published between 1967 and 1969.

Russell was quite popular in many circles, having written mainstream books explaining physics, ethics, and education to the common person. Magazines and newspapers frequently ran stories by or about Russell and his work. He even became a popular television personality in Britain.

Russell's outspoken nature and liberal view often landed him in trouble. During World War I, he was fined, forbidden to lecture, refused a passport, and sentenced to six months in prison for his outspoken political views. Then in 1940, he was offered a teaching position at the City College of New York, but public outrage, mostly because of the views he expounded in his book *Marriage and Morals*, caused the college to withdraw their offer. Again in 1961, Russell (along with his wife this time) was jailed for leading a mass sit-in and promoting civil disobedience in order to publicize his stand on nuclear disarmament.

Russell's Awards

- He was elected a fellow of the Royal Society in 1908, and re-elected as fellow of Trinity College in 1944.
- He received two awards in 1934, the Sylvester Medal of the Royal Society and the de Morgan Medal of the London Mathematical Society.
- In 1950, he was awarded the Nobel Prize for Literature.
- He was the first recipient of the Jerusalem Prize, which acknowledges writers concerned with freedom of the individual in society, in 1963.

Bertrand Russell died in February 1970 at his home in Merionethshire, Wales.

Russell's Paradox

If you create two sets with one set containing all sets and the other set containing no sets, the first set is actually a member of itself. The second, empty, set must not be a member of itself. On the other hand, if you have a set of all sets that do not include themselves, would this set be in itself? It is only if it is not. The same corollary is true of properties.

Other mathematicians were aware of the paradox, but Russell was the first to define it in 1901. He devoted an entire chapter of *Principles of Mathematics* to the paradox, and defined the Theory of Types in an appendix.

New England Transcendentalism

In 1825, the American edition of Samuel Taylor Coleridge's *Aids to Reflection* was published, marking what some scholars say was the impetus of New England transcendentalism. The book brought to light the distinction between reason and understanding. At this same time, Ralph Waldo Emerson and others like him were comparing their religious beliefs to Hindu and Buddhist scriptures.

In September 1836, Emerson, George Ripley, Frederic Henry Hedge, and a few others began discussing Transcendentalist themes. An anonymous pamphlet, *An Essay on Transcendentalism,* stated the most commonly held principles of the group. They also published a magazine, *The Dial,* and several members, including Nathaniel Hawthorne, participated in communal living at Brook Farm in Massachusetts. At the same time, Bronson Alcott, Louisa May Alcott's father, participated in a similar community called Fruitlands.

Transcendentalist Works

- *Representative Men* by Ralph Waldo Emerson
- *The Scarlet Letter* and *The House of Seven Gables* by Nathaniel Hawthorne
- *Moby-Dick* and *Pierre* by Herman Melville
- *Uncle Tom's Cabin* by Harriet Beecher Stowe
- *Walden* by Henry David Thoreau
- *Leaves of Grass* by Walt Whitman

This search for balance between nature and spirituality lasted for little more than five years, as the reality and "realism" of the Civil War pushed ideology aside.

Going to Extremes

Wordsmiths are always fooling around with letters and words and sentences and verses and stories of all kind. One of their favorite ways to fill free time is to concoct pangrams, lipograms, palindromes, and other constrained writing techniques.

Through this kind of "play-with-words," the writer conforms his creation to follow a certain set of rules, such as using all the letters of the alphabet, leaving out a letter of the alphabet, or even making his words read the same from the left as they do from the right.

Many writers, such as members of the French literary group known as *Ouvroir de littérature potentielle,* or "Oulipo," practice constrained writing techniques to increase their creativity and stretch their imagination.

Pangrams

Sentences that use all the letters of the alphabet are called pangrams. The sentence that beginning typists use—The quick brown fox jumps over the lazy dog—is an example. This sentence uses all the letters of the alphabet, and repeats the *e, h, o, r, t,* and *u*. Ideally, each letter of the alphabet should only be used once; however, the fewer the letters in the sentence, the less sense the sentence makes.

The 26 letters of the English alphabet can be combined in 403,290,000,000,000,000,000,000,000 ways.

Lipograms

Writers who wrestle with lipograms leave out a letter, or more. This kind of constrained writing can be sentences, paragraphs, or longer works. The most challenging lipograms attempt to leave out the letter *e*. Many times, in order to follow the rules, the writer must leave out ordinary words, substituting lesser known or cumbersome words.

Ernest Vincent Wright and Georges Perec both wrote novels without using the letter *e*. Wright's *Gadsby* was published in 1939, and Perec's *A Void* (*La Disparition*) was published in 1969. Perec was a member of the French literary group Oulipo. Christian Bok restricted the use of vowels at various times throughout his novel *Eunoia*.

A contemporary fable, *Ella Minnow Pea* by Mark Dunn, although not purely lipogrammatic, certainly challenged the author and works well in delighting the reader. James Thurber's *The Wonderful O* is a similar delight.

Palindromes

The 17th century writer Ben Jonson coined the word *palindrome* to describe a word, phrase, or number that reads the same from the left and from the right. Although they have been around since at least 79 A.D., they are still fun to figure out. Some word sequences form palindromes, such as *fall leaves after leaves fall*.

Some common word palindromes include:

- civic
- did
- kayak
- level
- noon
- radar
- solos
- racecar

And there are sentences:

- Was it a rat I saw?
- Name no one, Man!
- I prefer pi.
- Madam I'm Adam.
- A man, a plan, a canal—Panama

Language purists say that palindromes must make sense, and following that rule, it seems that Giles Selig Hales created the world's longest palindrome in 1980. His palindrome consists of 58,795 letters.

The longest palindrome word in the Oxford English Dictionary is tattarrattat, coined by James Joyce in Ulysses, meaning a knock on the door.

Brain Teaser

What do you call a word that contains another word within itself, in order, and with the same meaning?

Answer: Kangaroo words, of course. Examples of kangaroo words are: masculine, which contains the word male, and observe, which contains the word see.

Literary Feats

- The oldest complete novel in the world was written in Japan in the 11th century. The title is *The Tale of Genji.*
- The youngest author is Dorothy Straight, who wrote *How the World Began* at the ripe old age of four.
- The largest library is the Library of Congress in Washington, DC. It has more than 130 million items (including books, recordings, photographs, maps, and manuscripts) on 532 miles of shelving. It was established in 1800 as a reference library for the US Congress. When the British destroyed it during the War of 1812, Thomas Jefferson helped rebuild the library by selling his personal library.
- The longest novel is *A la recherché du temps perdu* (Remembrance of Things Past) by French author Marcel Proust. It contains an estimated 9,609,000 characters.
- The smallest book is a 1/25-inch square version of *Old King Cole*. The pages are most easily read when turned with a needle.
- The smallest reproduction of a book is the New Testament, King James Version, measuring 0.196 by 0.196 inches. It was reproduced using microlithography technology by scientists at the Massachusetts Institute of Technology in 2001.
- The most translated author is L. Ron Hubbard. His books have been translated into 65 languages.
- The oldest surviving biblical texts are from two silver amulets found under the Scottish Church in Jerusalem in 1979, bearing Numbers 6:22-27 and dated 587 BC
- The world's best-selling book ever is the *Holy Bible* with 6 billion copies sold in more than 2,000 languages and dialects.

- In 1945 various papyrus texts were discovered at Nag Hammadi, Egypt, including Gnostic gospels or secret books (apocryphal) ascribed to Thomas, James, John, Peter, and Paul. They were buried in AD 350, but the originals are thought to have been written in AD 120–150.
- The world's best-selling copyrighted book is the Guinness Book of World Records. Since it was first published in 1955, more than 100 million copies of the book have sold in 37 languages.
- The world's best-selling fiction author is Agatha Christie. Her characters Miss Marple and Inspector Poirot are known around the world. Christie's 78 mystery novels have been translated into 44 languages and have sold approximately 2 billion copies.

Book Trivia

- Agatha Christie wrote romance novels under the pseudonym Mary Westmacott.
- The most valuable book is John James Audubon's four-volume *The Birds of America*. It was sold at auction for $8,802,500.
- The first book published in America was Steven Day's *Bay Psalm Book*. Reportedly, there are only 11 copies of the book still in existence in the US.

Prizes for Literature

- The Nobel Prize for Literature was first awarded in 1901 to French poet René F. A. Sully Prudhomme.
- The Pulitzer Prizes were first awarded in 1917. J. J. Jusserand received the Pulitzer for history writing for *With Americans of Past and Present Days*. In the same year, Laura E. Richards and Maude Howe Elliot won a Pulitzer Prize for their biography of Julia Ward Howe. The first Pulitzer for fiction was given in 1918 to Ernest Poole for the novel *His Family*.
- The National Book Awards were first awarded in 1950. The award for fiction went to Nelson Algren for *The Man with the Golden Arm*. The nonfiction award went to Ralph L. Rusk for his biography of Ralph Waldo Emerson. The poetry award went to William Carlos Williams.

Other noted awards for writers and their books include:

- The Edgar Award for best mystery novel
- The Hugo Award for the best science fiction novel
- The Nebula Award for science fiction/fantasy
- The Newberry Award for best children's book

Academic Regalia

In medieval Europe, men and women wore robes in colors to signify their position and wealth. From this tradition various professions started claiming their own colors and dress. Students and teachers organized into guilds, and eventually the academic robes became distinctive for the bachelors of arts, masters of arts, and doctors.

Through the years, the academic hood became the prominent indicator of a scholar's education. The hood was first a practical element of the scholar's regalia in that it would help the wearer stay warm in the cold, damp schools. Today the hood is purely ornamental. The outside of the hood is black with a two-, three-, or five-inch band of velvet in the color representing the degree received. The hood is lined with the colors of the granting institution.

Academic regalia for universities in the United States were standardized by an Intercollegiate Code in 1895. Each university has its own distinguishing customs. However, academic colors are consistent across the nation. In 1959, the academic costume code was updated to the colors used today.

There are distinctions in the gowns also. The baccalaureate gown has long, pleated front panels and long, pointed sleeves. The master's gown has very long sleeves, with an opening in the front of the sleeves. Doctoral gowns have velvet panels around the neck and down the front of the gown. Three horizontal black velvet bars, or the color representing the wearer's degree, also mark the doctorate.

The Gonfalon

A flag that hangs from a crosspiece or frame is called a gonfalon. It was first used in the medieval republics of Italy as an ensign of state or office. Many universities have adopted the gonfalon as institutional insignias.

Well-Read on Red

- A red flag was a signal for battle in ancient Rome.
- Because red is easily visible, stop signs, stoplights, brake lights, and fire equipment are all painted red.
- The ancient Egyptians painted their bodies with red dye.
- Russian Communists were called "Reds" because the Bolsheviks used a red flag as their symbol when they overthrew the tsar in 1917.
- In South Africa, wearing red means the person is in mourning.
- Red is important in many aspects of Chinese culture. They believe red to bring good luck. It is used as a holiday and wedding color, and Chinese babies are given their names at red-egg ceremonies.
- A "red-letter day" means one of special importance.
- In Greece, eggs are dyed red at Eastertime.
- To "paint the town red" is to celebrate.
- Red is the color most commonly found in national flags.
- In the English War of the Roses, red was the color of the House of Lancaster, which defeated the House of York, symbolized by the color white.
- A person who "sees red" is angry.
- We find "red herrings" in mystery novels as the distraction, something that takes attention away from the real solution.
- A "red eye" is an overnight airplane flight.
- If a business is "in the red," it is losing money.

Going Green

- The Libya national flag is green.
- Ancient Egyptians liked green floors.
- Green was a symbol of victory for ancient Greece.
- Green is the national color of Ireland.
- A "greenback" is slang for a US dollar bill.
- Green means "go."
- The green room of a concert hall or theater is where performers relax before going onstage.
- The "green-eyed monster" is jealousy.
- A newcomer, or novice, is a greenhorn.
- Being "green around the gills" means getting sick.
- A person with a "green thumb" is a good gardener.
- A green, or common, is a town park.
- Green is often considered a healing color, the color of nature.

In ancient times, it was thought that particular colors fended off evil and protected certain sacred places, such as nurseries. Blue, associated with heavenly bodies and spirits, was used to clothe boys, since male children were considered highly valuable to parents. Baby girls were clothed in black until the Middle Ages when pink became associated female children.

All About Yellow

- In Egypt and Burma, yellow signifies mourning.
- In Spain, yellow was the color of clothing worn by executioners.
- In India, yellow is the symbol for a merchant or farmer.
- The French used to paint the doors of traitors and criminals yellow.
- Hindus in India wear yellow to celebrate the festival of spring.
- A person with a "yellow streak" is a coward.
- In Japan during the War of Dynasty in 1357, warriors wore yellow chrysanthemums to pledge their courage.
- A yellow ribbon is a sign of support for soldiers.
- Holistic healers say yellow is the color of peace.
- Yellow is a color of caution, warning, or danger.
- "Yellow journalism" refers to irresponsible and alarmist reporting.

The first known appearance of the word "yellow" in literature can be found in the Old English heroic epic poem *Beowulf.* The anonymous author uses it to describe a shield made from the wood of a yew tree.

The Color White

- A white flag is the universal symbol for truce.
- To wear white in China and Japan means a person is in mourning.
- Ancient Greeks thought that wearing white to bed would ensure pleasant dreams.
- The Egyptian pharaohs of upper Egypt wore white crowns.
- A "white elephant" is a rare, pale elephant sacred to the people of India, Thailand, Burma, and Sri Lanka. In the US, it is a possession that costs more than it is worth.
- To whitewash is to cover up defects or make something seem presentable that isn't.
- A "white knight" is a rescuer.
- A "whiteout" occurs when there is zero visibility during a blizzard.
- A "white sale" is a sale of sheets, towels, and other bed and bath items.
- "White lightning" is slang for moonshine alcohol.
- A white room is a clean room as well as a temperature-controlled, dust-free room for precision instruments.
- Whitewater is the foamy, frothy water in rapids and waterfalls.

Facts on Black

- Black is the symbol of mourning in the US and much of Europe.
- The "Blackshirts" were members of the Italian Fascist party under Mussolini.
- Black often stands for secrecy.
- A "blackhearted" person is evil.
- If a business is "in the black," it is making money.
- A "blacklist" is a list of persons or organizations to be boycotted or punished.
- Black dress is sophisticated and elegant.
- A black belt in karate identifies an expert.
- A black flag in a car race is the signal for a driver to go to the pits.
- Black lung is a coal miner's disease caused by the frequent inhaling of coal dust.
- Blackmail is getting things by threat.
- Black market is illegal trade in goods or money.
- A black sheep is an outcast.
- When you "black out," you temporarily lose consciousness.

Colors seem to pulsate when you look at bright complementary colors next to each other. This is an effect called color fatiguing. The optic nerve is actually sending confused signals to the brain.

The Psychology of Colors

Yellow, orange, and red remind us of heat, while blue, green, and violet make us think of coolness. Researchers have noted that psychological and physiological changes take place in human beings when they are exposed to certain colors. Colors can stimulate, excite, depress, tranquilize, increase appetite, and create a feeling of warmth or coolness. This is known as chromodynamics.

Red has been shown to stimulate the senses and raise the blood pressure, while blue has the opposite effect and calms the mind. People who sit under a red light, as opposed to a blue light, will gamble more and make riskier bets.

Employees often complain of being cold if the office walls are painted blue. If the walls are painted a yellow or orange tone, and the temperature not changed, the workers say they are comfortable.

Seeing Color

The human eye has millions of light-sensitive cells; some are shaped like rods and some like cones. These receptors process light into nerve impulses and send them to the brain. The average human has 120 million rods and 6 million cones in each eye. The cones are responsible for our ability to see color.

About 8 percent of men and less than 1 percent of women are called colorblind. Most people with color deficiencies aren't aware that the colors they perceive as identical appear different to other people.

Many mammals, including birds and fish, perceive the full spectrum. Some insects, especially bees, can see ultraviolet colors invisible to the human eye.

Until recently, researchers thought that dogs didn't see color at all, but studies indicate dogs can tell the difference between red and blue and can even pick out subtle differences in shades.

Neologism: A Word Coined for Coined Words

Neologisms refer to words coined to describe existing situations, theories, sometimes for the purpose of modernizing older terms. New inventions or phenomena often require neoligisms, as there are typically no pre-existing simple terms that can quantify new developments. "E-mail" is an example, as the form of communication was a new concept, and older terminology applied to mail and written communication was inappropriate for the form.

The word neologism was coined in the early 19th century, becoming a neologism itself!

Neologisms can be formed within a number of categories where developments and transitions of thought require new terminology. For example:

In the field of science, the following words can be regarded as neologisms:

- Black hole: coined in 1960
- Prion: coined in 1982
- Radar: coined in 1941

In the field of science-fiction writing, new concepts are created that require matter-of-fact names. Perhaps the most famous is the coining of the word robot in a play by Czech writer Karel Capek titled *Rossum's Universal Robots*. Other examples include:

- Ansible – coined in 1966 by Ursula K. Le Guin in the novel *Rocannon's World.* (An ansible is a machine used for superluminal communication, which is hypothetical, faster-than-light communication.)
- Phaser – coined in the original Star Trek movie. (A phaser is a fictitious weapon that directs lasers.)
- Xenocide – coined by the 1991 book by Orson Scott Card in his famous Ender's Game series. (The term xenocide is now used to describe genocide performed on aliens in science fiction.)

Neologisms in Literature

- "quixotic" – Miguel de Cervantes, *Don Quixote*
- "Serendipity" – Horace Walpole, *The Three Princes of Serendip*
- "moron" – Jean Baptiste Poquelin, *La Princesse d'Elide*
- "vulpine" – Ben Johnson, *Volpone*
- "gargantuan" – Francois Rabelais, *Gargantua*
- "ogre" – Charles Perrault, *Contes*

Johann Wolfgang von Goethe

Born in 1749, in Frankfurt, Germany, Johann Wolfgang von Goethe is most known for his novel *Faust,* a poetic drama that he worked on for nearly 60 years. At the prompting of his father, Goethe finally passed his law exams at age 22 and began practicing law while working on his first novel *The Sorrows of Young Werther* (1774).

Although always more interested in writing and studying nature, in 1775, he was invited to the court of Duke Karl August in Weimar where he worked in several governmental offices, including being a council member and member of the war commission, director of roads and services, and managing the financial affairs of the court. He later became manager of the court theater.

Johann Wolfgang von Goethe died in Weimar in 1832.

Literary great Wolfgang von Goethe was also a student of natural science. He wrote the book *Theory of Colours*, which presented theories contrary to the day but which is said to have influenced the painting of artists such as Mondrian and Kandinsky. He was also fascinated with minerals and mineralogy. Goethite, an iron oxide sometimes used as pigment for paint, is named for him. Found in England and in many US states, including Alabama, Colorado, Georgia, and Michigan, it has also been found on Mars. Because on Earth goethite is found in streams, swamps, and damp caves the discovery of the mineral on Mars has led to some speculation that there might be or might have been water on Mars.

The Alien and Sedition Acts

In 1798, when the US was surely going to war with France, President John Adams encouraged Congress to pass four laws in an effort to strengthen the federal government. These Alien and Sedition Acts were intended to halt political opposition from the Republicans, led by Thomas Jefferson.

- The Naturalization Act required that aliens be residents for 14 years instead of 5 years before they became eligible for US citizenship.
- The Alien Act called for the deportation of aliens who were "dangerous to the peace and safety of the United States" during peacetime.
- The Alien Enemies Act allowed the wartime arrest, imprisonment, and deportation of any alien subject to an enemy power.
- The Sedition Act prohibited any treasonable activity, including the publication of "any false, scandalous, and malicious writing."

As a result of the Sedition Act, 25 men, mostly editors of Republican newspapers, were arrested and their papers forced to shut down. One of them was Benjamin Franklin's grandson, Benjamin Franklin Bache, editor of the *Philadelphia Democrat-Republican Aurora*. Charged with libeling the president, Bache's arrest caused a public outcry against all of the acts.

The great resistance to these acts were partially responsible for the election of Thomas Jefferson to the presidency in 1800. Once elected, Jefferson pardoned those who had been convicted under the Sedition Act, and Congress restored all fines, paid with interest. Congress repealed the Naturalization Act in 1802; the others were allowed to expire.

Skyscrapers

At the beginning of the 20th century, businesses often competed to have the tallest building, a supposed marker of economic success. In New York, the Metropolitan Life Insurance Tower had 50 stories and was 700 feet tall, the Woolworth Building had 58 stories and was 792 feet tall, and the Chrysler Building topped them all with 77 stories and was 1,048 feet tall. Then, a year later, the Empire State Building grew a massive 102 stories and was 1,250 feet tall. It remained the tallest skyscraper for 41 years.

The Empire State Building was built to be a lightning rod. It is struck by lightning 100 times each year.

Shake, Rattle, and Flex

The First Interstate World Center located in Los Angeles, California, is only 26 miles from the San Andreas Fault. However, this 1,018-foot building has been designed to withstand an 8.3 or higher earthquake. The reinforced core is surrounded with lighter columns on the outside. This design makes it flexible so that it can withstand side-to-side shaking without snapping. It is the tallest building ever constructed in an earthquake zone, and the tallest building west of the Mississippi River.

Raining Glass

Quite a disaster struck when builders tried to design the John Hancock Tower in Boston with mirrored glass, which was to cover the entire outside of the structure. Giant slabs of glass, weighing 500 pounds each, shattered when they came crashing off the building. They were eventually successful, as it is now considered the city's most spectacular structure.

- The "father of the skyscraper," the Home Insurance Building in Chicago, was 138 feet tall and had 10 stories. It was demolished in 1931. In 1974, the city jumped back on the bandwagon with the Sears Tower, which has 110 stories and stands 1450 feet high.
- In 1998, the Petronas Towers in Kuala Lumpur, Malaysia, was built with 88 stories and 1,483 feet high.
- Built in 2004, Taipei 101 in Taiwan has 101 stories and is 1,677 feet high, including the 197-foot spire on top.

Top 10 Skyscraper Cities in the World

1. New York City, New York, United States	5,661
2. Toronto, Canada	1,743
3. Chicago, Illinois, United States	1,074
4. Tokyo, Japan	1, 074
5. Vancouver, Canada	583
6. Montréal, Canada	576
7. Los Angeles, California, United States	554
8. Mexico City, Mexico	533
9. Greater London, United Kingdom	519
10. Hong Kong, China	507

Presidential Tidbits

Presidential Bachelors

James Buchanan, president from 1857 to 1861, was a lifelong bachelor. He asked his orphaned niece, Harriet Lane, to be the White House hostess during his term.

Grover Cleveland was a bachelor when he entered the White House in 1885; however, he married Frances Folsom in 1886.

Hail to the Chief

John Quincy Adams was the first president to be honored by "Hail to the Chief." The song was composed by James Sanderson and first played in the US in 1812. The wife of John Tyler (the tenth US president) was the first person to think of having the US Navy band play "Hail to the Chief" to announce the arrival of the president. It became the official musical tribute to the president in 1954.

1600 Pennsylvania Avenue

The White House was not always called the White House. Built for the US president to live in, it has been called the "President's Palace," the "President's House," and the "Executive Mansion." President Theodore Roosevelt officially gave the White House its current name in 1901.

Designed by James Hoban, who was awarded a gold medal for his work, the White House took eight years to construct. It has 132 rooms, 35 bathrooms, and 6 levels. There are also 412 doors, 147 windows, 28 fireplaces, 8 staircases, and 3 elevators.

- The White House requires 570 gallons of paint to cover its outside surface.
- John and Abigail Adams were the first to live in the White House.

- The White House keeps five full-time chefs on staff, who can serve as many as 140 guests for dinner and hors d'oeuvres for more than 1000.
- The White House also provides a tennis court, movie theater, jogging track, and a bowling alley for its residents to use.

While in office...

- James Polk was the first president to have his photograph taken.
- Theodore Roosevelt was the first president to travel outside the country when he visited Panama.
- Franklin Roosevelt was the first president to ride in an airplane.
- William McKinley was the first president to ride in an automobile.

President Harry S Truman was not given a middle name. He once explained, "I was named for Harrison Young. I was given the diminutive Harry and, so that I could have two initials in my given name, the letter S was added. My grandfather Truman's name was Anderson Shippe Truman and my grandfather Young's name was Solomon Young, so I received the S for both of them."

America's First Money

Settlers at the Massachusetts Bay Colony ran out of money and began making their own in 1652. Joseph Jenks used sterling silver, five-sixths the weight of the English coins, to make threepenny pieces, sixpenny pieces, and shillings. Each coin had the same imprint—the word *Massachusetts* and a pine tree on one side, and *New England, Anno 1652* on the other. The only difference was the indication of denomination.

The story goes that England's King Charles II was not pleased when he learned that the colonists were making their own money. However, when he was told that the tree on the coins was the royal oak, where the king sought refuge after his defeat at the Battle of Worcester, he allowed the colonists to make the money as they needed it. In 1690, they began making paper money.

As conflict brewed between the new world and the old, England began putting restrictions on the money that the colonists could make. By 1764, the colonies were forbidden to issue any money.

The First National Bank

The Bank of North America, the first national bank, was established in 1781 in Philadelphia, five years after the American Revolution. Four years later, the dollar was chosen as the US unit of money. When paper bills were first printed, they contained silk fibers, a practice that was discontinued after World War I.

The Origin of the $ Sign

The $ sign is more than likely the result of a combination of the *P* for *peso* with an *S* written over it. The sign was used before the dollar was designated as the US unit of money in 1785.

The US Mint

In 1792, Congress passed the Coinage Act, calling for the creation of a mint, and a year later, 11,178 pennies were in circulation. The first coins were made from copper, gold, and silver. Today's coins are all made of metal alloys.

Scientist David Rittenhouse served as the first director of the US Mint.

Counterfeiting Deterrents

- The United States Secret Service was established in 1865 as a bureau of the Treasury Department to control counterfeiters.
- The Treasury Department began using a security thread and micro-printing for paper money in 1990. The $100 bills were first to carry these security devices, and within three years, all denominations except $1 and $2 had them.
- In 2003, the government began issuing currency with background colors other than green. The 2003 $20 bill was the first to use a color besides green since the Series 1905 $20 Gold Certificate.

What Famous Person Is on the Front of These Bills?

$1

$2

$5

$10

$20

$50

$100

$500

$1,000

$5,000

$10,000

Answers: $1: George Washington; $2: Thomas Jefferson; $5: Abraham Lincoln; $10: Alexander Hamilton; $20: Andrew Jackson; $50: Ulysses Grant; $100: Benjamin Franklin; $500*: William McKinley; $1,000*: Grover Cleveland; $5,000*: James Madison; $10,000*: Salmon Chase.

*no longer produced

> Martha Washington is the only woman whose portrait has been on US paper money. Her portrait was on the $1 Silver Certificate three times—in 1886, 1891, and 1896.

What Image Is on the Back of These Bills?

$1

$2

$5

$10

$20

$50

$100

$500

$1,000

$5,000

$10,000

Answers: $1: the Great Seal of the United States; $2: the signing of the Declaration of Independence; $5: the Lincoln Memorial; $10: the Treasury Building; $20: the White House; $50: the Capitol; $100: Independence Hall. Denominations higher than $100 feature ornate impressions of the numerical value of the note, such as an ornate "500."

The hands of the clock in the steeple of Independence Hall on the reverse of the $100 Federal Reserve Note are set at approximately 4:10.

All About Money

- The Bureau of Engraving and Printing used about 18 tons of ink to print 37 million bills a day in 2006.
- At the onset of the Civil War in 1861, the Treasury Secretary of the Confederacy ordered a suspension of minting coins. Paper notes in denominations of 3 cents, 5 cents, 10 cents, 25 cents, and 50 cents were issued instead. Why? Precious metals rose dramatically in value during the war, so people could melt down coins and exchange it for more than its face value.
- It takes 454 bills to make one pound. A single US bill, regardless of denomination, weighs 1 gram.
- Currency paper is 25 percent linen and 75 percent cotton, with red and blue synthetic fibers of various lengths distributed throughout the paper.
- A paper bill is 2.61 inches wide and 6.14 inches long. It is .0043 inches thick.

How Long Does Your Money Last?

$1 bills stay in circulation about 21 months
$5 bills stay in circulation about 16 months
$10 bills stay in circulation about 18 months
$20 bills stay in circulation about 24 months
$50 bills stay in circulation about 55 months
$100 bills stay in circulation about 89 months

Anagrams

An anagram is formed by rearranging the letters of a word or phrase to produce new words or a phrase. For example, the phrase *A Decimal Point* can be rearranged to say *I'm a Dot in Place,* using every letter in the original phrase.

A person who creates anagrams—and there are such people—is called an anagrammist. While a simple rearrangement of letters to create another word is referred to as an anagram, the goal of most anagrammists is to create a new word or phrase with the letters that actually relates to or reflects on the subject of the original. For instance, the word *army* can be arranged to spell *Mary,* but the anagram does not reflect on the subject of the original word. However, the anagram *dormitory = dirty room* does!

Notable Anagrams

The Morse Code = Here Come Dots
Slot Machines = Cash Lost in 'em
Mother-in-law = Woman Hitler
Semolina = Is No Meal
The Eyes = They See

Some anagrams actually are designed to make a witty response or commentary about the original word, phrase, or person. Here are some examples:

- Frequently Asked Questions = Quit! End One's Flaky Requests
- George Bush = He Bugs Gore

Measuring Hot and Cold

Metals and liquids change when subjected to heat and cold. Thermometers are instruments used to gauge those changes. In a mercury or alcohol thermometer, the liquid expands as it is heated and contracts when it is cooled. Modern thermometers are calibrated in standard temperature units such as Fahrenheit or Celsius.

- Galileo created a basic tool to measure the temperature of water in 1593, allowing temperature variations to be measured for the first time.
- Early thermometers were called thermoscopes. Italian inventor Santorio Santorio was the first to put a numerical scale on the instrument.
- German physicist Daniel Gabriel Fahrenheit invented the alcohol thermometer in 1709. Five years later, he improved his invention by using liquid mercury as the heat indicator.
- Swedish-born Anders Celsius developed the Celsius scale (or centigrade scale) for measuring temperature in 1742. This scale is divided into segments from 0 to 100, with 0 being the freezing point of water and 100 being the boiling point.
- Lord William Thomson Kelvin invented the Kelvin scale in 1848 to measure the extremes of temperature. His scale is based on absolute zero, the temperature when all molecular motion ceases.

0° vs Absolute 0

- 0° Fahrenheit is the temperature derived by mixing equal amounts of snow and common salt.
- Absolute zero is actually -459.6° Fahrenheit and -273.1° Celsius. This is theoretically the lowest temperature possible.
- 0° Kelvin is absolute zero.

What Is Wind Chill?

Wind chill temperature gives us an idea of how cold we are going to feel when we go outside. Why does the wind blowing make us feel cooler? As wind flows across our skin, it takes with it some of our body heat. This decreases the surface temperature of our skin and eventually lowers our internal body temperature.

You can estimate wind chill on a hot summer day, but it is not nearly as dramatic as on a cold day.

If the temperature is 0°F and the wind is blowing at 15 mph, the wind chill is –19°F. At this wind chill temperature, exposed skin can freeze in 30 minutes.

The wind chill factor was formulated in 1945 by Antarctic explorers. They measured how fast water cooled when subjected to varying wind speeds.

In 2001, the National Weather Service issued a revised wind chill table. This one uses numbers derived from testing the heat loss of people subjected to varying wind speeds.

Fahrenheit, Celsius, and Kelvin

- Water freezes at 32° Fahrenheit, 0° Celsius, and 273.15° Kelvin.
- Water boils at 212° Fahrenheit, 100° Celsius, and 373.15° Kelvin
- To convert Fahrenheit to Celsius, subtract 32 and divide by 1.8.
- To convert Celsius to Fahrenheit, multiply by 1.8 and add 32.
- To convert Celsius to Kelvin, add 273.15.

The F-Scale

Theodore Fujita introduced the Fujita Scale in 1971 to categorize tornados by intensity and area. The scale, also known as the F-scale, was divided into six categories:

- F0 (Gale)
- F1 (Weak)
- F2 (Strong)
- F3 (Severe)
- F4 (Devastating)
- F5 (Incredible)

In 2007, the National Weather Service revised the Fujita Scale, relating the damage caused by a tornado to the fastest 1/4-mile wind at the height of a damaged structure. The 2007 Fujita Scale evaluates wind speed in this way:

F Number	Fastest 1/4-mile (mph)	3 Second Gust (mph)
0	40-72	45-77
1	73-112	78-118
2	113-157	119-163
3	158-206	164-210
4	207-260	211-262
5	261 and up	263 and up

Color and Light

Astronomers studied rainbows as early as the 13th century. Roger Bacon wrote about experiments with light shining through crystals and water droplets showing the colors of the rainbow.

Sir Isaac Newton discovered that pure white light, such as sunlight, is composed of the same visible colors. When he directed sunlight through a prism, he found that the light separated into the same progression of colors seen in a rainbow. He identified seven major colors: red, orange, yellow, green, blue, indigo, and violet. He used a second prism to show that each color is composed of a single wavelength and cannot be separated into other colors.

- A double rainbow has reversed colors in the outer bow and a dark Alexander's band between the bows. Alexander's band is the area of unlit sky that lies between the two bows of a double rainbow, which was first described by Alexander of Aphrodisias.
- Sometimes several faint rainbows can be seen on the inner side of the primary rainbow. These are called supernumerary rainbows. Thomas Young, in 1804, was the first to attempt to explain the principles behind supernumerary rainbows. These pastel-colored, alternating rainbows are caused by interference between rays of light following slightly different paths with slightly varying lengths within the raindrops.
- Moonbows or lunar rainbows are often described as white because the human eye cannot easily detect color in low light.

The Science of Strong Winds

Hurricanes, cyclones, and typhoons are the same strong circulating wind over tropical or subtropical waters. It just depends on where they occur as to what you should call it. When these winds reach 74 mph, they are called:

- a hurricane in the North Atlantic Ocean, the Northeast Pacific Ocean east of the dateline, or the South Pacific Ocean east of 160E.
- a typhoon in the Northwest Pacific Ocean west of the dateline
- a severe tropical cyclone in the Southwest Pacific Ocean west of 160E or Southeast Indian Ocean east of 90E
- a severe cyclonic storm in the North Indian Ocean
- a tropical cyclone in the Southwest Indian Ocean

Currently, hurricane names come from a list issued by the World Meteorological Organization. The Atlantic has six lists of names, with one list used each year. After six years, the first list begins again. The lists contain female and male names in alphabetical order. Names beginning with the letters Q, U, X, Y, and Z are never used.

When a very destructive hurricane hits, that hurricane's name is likely to be retired and never used again. Included in retired names are Katrina, Opal, and Camille.

National Institute of Standards and Technology

How do you know you have a gallon of milk? Are you sure your ruler is exactly 12 inches long? You can place your trust in the National Institute of Standards and Technology. This US governmental agency was created in 1901 at the start of the Industrial Revolution to standardize trade practices. In fulfilling this task, they monitor standards of measure, time, and commerce. The NIST also prevents and resolves trade disputes.

Time Tidbits

- The first time zone in the world was established by British railways on December 1, 1847.
- In the US, the four original time zones (Eastern, Central, Mountain, and Pacific) were established on November 18, 1883.
- A year is 365.24219 days.
- Julius Caesar proclaimed every fourth year a Leap Year.
- The chance of being born on Leap Day is about 684 out of one million, or 1 in 1461. Less than 5 million people have their birthday on Leap Day.
- There are about 200,000 people in the US with birthdays on Leap Day.
- In 1582, Pope Gregory XIII made century years leap years if they are divisible by 400 and moved the end of the year back two months to December 31st, so that Easter would occur in the spring.
- Some years are longer than others. Every few years, scientists agree to add or remove a second from a year at midnight on January 1st or July 1st. This is called a leap second. The first leap second was added on June 30, 1972.

Plants Predicting People?

Scientists are often able to study the biology of plants and translate the outcomes in relation to human and animal species. For example, cell division and protein synthesis for plants and animals are fundamentally the same.

- Botanist Gregor Mendel discovered the genetic laws of inheritance while studying peas.
- Likewise, Barbara McClintock discovered what she called "jumping genes" while studying corn.
- Danish botanist Wilhelm Ludvig Johannsen coined the word *gene* in 1901. He also was the first to use the words *phenotype* and *genotype*.

Words to Know

- *Phenotype* is the physical, outward appearance of an organism. It includes the atoms, molecules, macromolecules, cells, structures, metabolism, energy utilization, tissues, organs, reflexes, and behaviors—everything that makes up the observable structure, function, and behavior of a living organism.
- *Genotype* is the internal, coded information that is used to build and maintain a living creature. This language—the genetic code—is found within almost all cells. They are copied when a cell divides or reproduces and are passed from one generation to the next. All the physical parts of an organism are built and maintained by the coded information that is given by the genotype.

Plants: Organic Alarm Systems

Plants have been called our "early warning system." They are often our first indication that something has changed in the environment. Researchers use plants to interpret changes in the earth's environment by:

- Cataloging plant systematics (development) and taxonomy and maintaining accurate records to determine habitat destruction and species extinction.
- Recording plant responses to ultraviolet radiation to monitor problems like the depletion of ozone.
- Reconstructing past climates and predicting future ones by analyzing pollen deposited by plants thousands of years ago.
- Recording and analyzing the timing of plant life cycles to monitor climate changes.

Arabidopsis thaliana, a weedy plant in the mustard family, was one of the first plants to have its genome sequenced.

Medicinal Plants

Many medications are made from plants or synthetic replicas of the plant chemicals.

- Drugs made from fungi, prevent the rejection of transplanted hearts and other organs.
- The active ingredient in aspirin was originally derived from willow bark.
- Paclitaxel, a compound found in the Pacific yew tree, has been found to assist in the treatment of some cancers.

- The rosy periwinkle, meanwhile, yields drugs which help treat diabetes.

Plants also can be used to test the effect of medications on humans and animals. A plant's reaction to a medication can give researchers insight to the actions of those compounds on a human or animal.

Lichens, which are sensitive to atmospheric conditions, have been extensively used as pollution indicators.

As far back as 2000 BC, cannabis, also referred to as marijuana, has been utilized for medicinal purposes. It was used in ancient India to treat gastrointestinal disorders, insomnia, and headaches. The Indians also administered doses of the drug to relieve pain, especially during childbirth. In Egypt, cannabis was used in suppositories to help treat hemorrhoids. Today, medical marijuana is administered to treat a wide range of conditions. It is regarded as an effective antiemetic, which helps diminish the nausea from cancer and AIDS treatments. Cannabis is also used to treat neurological conditions, including epilepsy and multiple sclerosis. It effectively decreases intraocular pressure in patients diagnosed with glaucoma, and it is a proven treatment for many mental illnesses, from depression to bipolar disorder.

The Olympic Games

- The first Olympic Games date back to 776 BC, maybe even earlier. As an honor to the Greek god Zeus, the early Olympic Games were held once every four years in Olympia, Greece.
- The first female to win an Olympic gold medal was Charlotte Cooper from Great Britain. She competed in women's single tennis in 1900, the first year women were allowed to compete in the games.
- The modern torch relay began in 1936, when a torch was lit at the original site of Olympia and carried in relay to Berlin.
- In 1924, the first Winter Olympics were held in Chamonix, France. Only events performed on ice or snow can be a part of the Winter Games. Since 1994, the Winter and Summer Games have alternated even-numbered years. Beijing, China, will host the 2008 Summer Games, and Vancouver, Canada, will host the Winter Games in 2010.

Only one person has won gold medals at both the Winter and Summer Olympic Games. Edward Eagan, from the US, captured the gold for light-heavyweight boxing in 1920 at Antwerp, Belgium, and was on the winning four-man bobsled team at the 1932 games in Lake Placid, New York.

Top Winners

- Four individuals share the distinction of winning the most gold medals in Olympic competition: Paavo Nurmi of Finland, Larisa Latynina of the Soviet Union, Mark Spitz of the US, and Carl Lewis of the US.

- Mark Spitz holds the record for the most gold medals (seven) won at a single Olympics. The woman with the most gold medals in one year is Kristin Otto of East Germany with six.
- Jenny Thompson, with 12 medals, holds the record for the most medals won by an American throughout an Olympic career.
- The oldest person to win an Olympic medal is Oscar Swahn of Sweden. He was awarded a gold medal in the running deer double-shot team event at London, England, in 1908.

Olympic Fencing

Since 1896, fencing has been included in every modern Olympic program. The first games included the men's foil and saber events, and the épée was added in 1900.

Twenty-four years later the women's foil competition was added, and it took another 72 years for the women's épée to be added to the Olympic games.

Fencing judges have a difficult chore in trying first to decide if a hit has been made and then which of the opponents made the first hit. For this reason the electric épée, which scores hits automatically, came into use at the 1936 games. Automatic scoring was introduced for the foil in 1956 and for the saber in 1992.

Opponents in the foils and épée can use only the point of the sword for hits. However, in saber fencing, an opponent can use the point, the cutting edge, or the forward third of the back edge of the sword.

Horse Racing

Triple Crown

The first time the phrase was used in American horse racing was in 1930, when a horse named Gallant Fox won the Kentucky Derby, Preakness, and Belmont races. In 1987, the term was given official status when the three tracks established the Triple Crown Challenge. They offered $5 million to any horse that won the Triple Crown. The challenge was discontinued in 1994.

Though most people think of horse racing when they hear the phrase *Triple Crown*, it first referred to rugby. The British rugby team—English, Irish, Scottish, or Welsh—that defeated all three of its opponents in one season was said to have won the Triple Crown.

Kentucky Derby

Meriwether Lewis Clark Jr. built Churchill Downs in Louisville, Kentucky, and subsequently established the Kentucky Derby, which was first run on May 17, 1875.

By 1920, the derby was running the top race horses from all over the country and was the best-known race in North America.

Today, the Kentucky Derby attracts more than 100,000 spectators and is watched on television by millions more.

Hot-Air Ballooning

A sheep, a rooster, and a duck walked single file into a wooden basket.... This might sound like the beginning of a corny joke, but the story is true.

In 1783, the Montgolfier brothers—Joseph and Étienne — herded the livestock into the basket of their hot-air balloon. The excited animals made history by being the first living creatures to fly with man's help. They flew over Versailles for eight minutes as Louis XVI and Marie Antoinette watched. (No animals were harmed in the making of that experiment.)

Three months prior, the brothers demonstrated their invention in Annonay, France. This first time was without living creatures. With two successful flights under their belts, they courageously offered to send aloft Pilatre de Rozier and Marquis d'Arlandes. The two men stayed up for 25 minutes and flew five miles over France. Then in another few months (when they had had time to build a bigger basket) they sent seven people to view the city of Lyons from above.

The two brothers were so excited with their success that they became a little too over-zealous and claimed to have discovered a new gas. They, of course, called it Montgolfier gas. This new lighter-than-air gas turned out to be simply air. But they did discover that just plain air when heated becomes more buoyant. Although it was not a new gas, it was still a discovery that they could be proud of.

Not to be outdone, physicist Jacques Charles developed his own balloon using hydrogen gas to keep it afloat. About 400,000 people watched as Charles and Aine Robert made the first hydrogen-powered flight on December 1, 1783. They traveled 27 miles in about two hours.

Soon ballooning became a popular leisure activity. In 1898, the Aero Club of France was founded, and the International Aeronautical Federation (IAF) was formed shortly thereafter.

Hot-Air Balloons: A Timeline

- In 1785, the first hot-air balloon crossed the English Channel.
- In 1906, James Gordon Bennett, publisher of the *New York Herald,* offered a prize for an annual international balloon race to be conducted by the IAF.
- In 1961, Edward Yost made ballooning affordable for the masses by developing a hot-air balloon made of nylon and using a propane heater to control inflation. In that same year, the Balloon Federation of America was founded to regulate local and regional meets.
- In 1978, the first hot-air balloon (fueled with helium) crossed the Atlantic Ocean.
- In 1996, several teams began the world's first around-the-world balloon race.

British scientist Henry Cavendish discovered hydrogen gas when he added sulphuric acid to metal shavings.

Airplane Racing

After the Wright brothers introduced flight, people had trouble keeping their feet on the ground. Less than six years after the first flight, pilots were racing airplanes in Rheims, France. Prizes were awarded for the highest altitude, longest flight, most passengers carried, and the fastest one-, two-, and three-lap flights over a 10-kilometer (6.2-mile) course.

The first US air meet took place the next year in Los Angeles, where Glenn H. Curtiss set a world record of 55 mph for a plane carrying one passenger. In October 1910, dozens of planes and pilots from Europe and the US flew in the second international air meet in Elmont, New York.

Prizewinning Flights

- Orville Wright won the Michelin Cup in 1908 for the longest flight between sunrise and sundown of a single day.
- Louis Bleriot of France flew across the English Channel in 1909.
- The first seaplane races over open water were held in 1913.
- Charles A. Lindbergh claimed a $25,000 prize in 1927 for a solo, nonstop flight from New York to France.

An Honorable Mention

Cal Rodgers flew the first successful US transcontinental flight in 1911. It took him 49 days, and he crashed 19 times. Had he been a bit faster and completed the flight in 30 days, he would have won the William Randolph Hearst Prize of $50,000.

The History of Blue

- Public servants wore blue in ancient Rome. Today, police officers and other public servants wear blue.
- In Iran, blue is the color of mourning.
- Superstition says witches dislike blue.
- A person who is "true blue" is loyal.
- Brides carry something blue on their wedding day.
- A room painted blue is said to be relaxing.
- Something "out of the blue" is a surprise.
- A bluebook is a list of socially prominent people (also a list of automobiles values).
- First prize is a blue ribbon.
- A "blue blood" is a person of noble descent.
- "Into the blue" means into the unknown.
- The "blues" is a style of music derived from southern African-American secular songs. It influenced the development of rock, R&B, and country music.
- "Blue laws" are used to enforce moral standards.
- A blue ribbon panel is a group of especially qualified people.

The English term "the blues," which describes feelings of depression or sadness, comes from the fact that the color blue is often associated with rain. In Greek mythology, when Zeus became upset, he would send rain to Earth, symbolizing tears.

The Purposes of Purple

- Cleopatra was a fan of purple. It is said that she had her servants soak 20,000 purpura snails for 10 days to get dye for her clothing.
- In Thailand, purple is a sign of mourning.
- A "purple heart" is a US military decoration for soldiers wounded or killed in battle.
- Purple is the color of royalty.
- Purple robes symbolize authority and rank.
- "Purple speech" is profane talk.
- "Purple prose" is writing that is full of exaggerated literary effects and ornamentation.
- Leonardo da Vinci believed that the power of meditation increases 10 times when done in the purple light of stained glass.
- Purple helps develop the imagination.
- Richard Wagner composed his operas in a room with shades of violet, his color of inspiration.

The word purple is derived from the Old English word *purpul*, which comes from the Greek word, *porphyra*. Porphyra is the name of a dye that was produced in ancient times from the mucus of the spiny dye-murex, a type of sea snail.

Croquet

The origin of croquet, or, as the French called it, *paille-maille,* has been traced back to the 14th century. In the 16th century, the Scots started playing the game to help them practice for their most important sport, golf. In the 17th century, the name was shortened to pall mall. And, in the 19th century, a French doctor took the game and called it an outdoor exercise. His exercise, which he named croquet, became popular in spas throughout southern France.

The "exercise" quickly spread to Ireland and England. The Wimbledon All England Croquet Club was established in 1868, and for almost ten years, the game was played by the British elite. However, in 1877, when lawn tennis became all the rage, the croquet courts at Wimbledon were converted to tennis courts, and the club was renamed the Wimbledon All England Lawn Tennis and Croquet Club.

In the US, croquet was played at the Newport Croquet Club as early as 1865. The National Croquet Association was founded in 1882, when it held its first national tournament.

It didn't take long for Americans to put their own touches to the game. They made special croquet courts with hard, packed clay, changed the wickets to be narrower, and used rubber balls and short mallets. In 1904, to go along with a new set of rules, Americans called their sport roque (they took off the *c* and the *t* from *croquet*).

After World War II, people of all ages across the nation began playing croquet in their backyards.

Croquet made it to the Olympics twice, once in 1900, when only French players participated, and again in 1904, when only US players participated.

Really Old Things: Photography

Joseph Nicéphore Niépce is said to have made the first successful photograph in 1826. He exposed pewter coated with a chemical substance to eight hours of sunlight. The chemical reaction to the sun produced a permanent image of a building and tree. Because the earth and sun were moving over the course of the eight hours, the picture is somewhat blurred. This photograph is on display at the University of Texas, Austin.

1727: Professor J. Schulze mixed chalk, nitric acid, and silver. He noticed a darkening effect on the mixture when it was exposed to sunlight. He had accidentally created the very first photosensitive compound.

1826: Nicéphore Niépce created a permanent image using photosensitive paper.

1834: Henry Fox Talbot created permanent negatives by using paper soaked in silver chloride and fixed with a salt solution.

1861: James Clerk-Maxwell, a Scottish physicist, demonstrated color photography in an experiment that involved three black and white photographs taken through a red, green, or blue filter.

1888: The first Kodak camera was produced. It contained a 20-foot roll of paper and could produce 100 circular photographs, all 2.5 inches in diameter.

The word *photography* comes from the Greek words meaning "light" and "writing." Sir John Herschel is credited as being the first to use the term in 1839; however, photography historian Robert Leggat says that astronomer Johann von Maedler used the term in a lecture before the Royal Society a few month's ahead of Herschel.

Daguerreotypes

Louis Daguerre discovered a way of projecting an image onto glass plates and reduced the exposure time from eight hours to 10 to 15 minutes. He also found that the image could be made permanent by immersing it in salt. He called this process, which took the world by storm, the daguerreotype.

Some people thought the daguerreotype was an instrument of the devil. They believed no manmade machine should attempt to fix an image created by God. Others thought the invention would put an end to painting and artists would be without jobs. However, one of the features of daguerreotypes was the ability to color them. Many artists of the day took on jobs hand-painting the photographs.

Autochrome to Kodachrome

Auguste and Louis Lumière made photography plates that could reproduce color in 1907. The pastel colors made photographs look dark, but the novelty was still received well by consumers. The Lumières called their process autochrome.

Almost 30 years earlier, Louis Ducas du Hauron came up with an idea of coating film with thin layers of dye. When processed, the photographs would be in full color. The only drawback was that the emulsions in the late 1800s were not perfected enough for the process to be accurately tested until the 1930s. The Eastman Kodak company produced a film based on Hauron's idea in 1935 and called it Kodachrome.

When Thomas Edison saw Eastman's cellulose film, he thought of a way to use it to make motion picture film for his Kinograph and Kineoscope.

Technicolor

By 1929, Technicolor, a company founded by three friends, two of whom were graduates of the Massachusetts Institute of Technology, was actively developing a full-color film process. The Depression affected the movie industry, slowing but not stopping the Technicolor Company. By 1932, the partners introduced their three-color process and convinced Walt Disney to shoot a *Silly Symphony* cartoon, *Flowers and Trees*, with the new three-strip process. He was so impressed that he negotiated a two-year exclusive contract for the use of the process. *Flowers and Trees* was a success and won the first Academy Award for Animated Short Film. In 1934, an improved process was adopted solely for cartoon work.

The *Tech* in *Technicolor* honors the Massachusetts Institute of Technology.

Because the first Technicolor cameras required much more light than their black and white contemporaries, temperatures on the set of *The Wizard of Oz* (1939) often surpassed 100° F. Actors wearing heavy costumes, like Bert Lahr who played the Cowardly Lion, required frequent water breaks to stay hydrated. A few actors reported that they had suffered eye damage as a result of the bright lights.

All About Chess

- The game of chess sprang from a game called Chatarung, an Indian war game that was introduced to Europeans by Persian traders in AD 1000.
- In America in the mid-1700s, Benjamin Franklin wrote of the social and intellectual benefits that chess afforded in an article "The Morals of Chess." He actually enjoyed playing the game with beautiful women.
- The first man to become an American chess legend is Paul Morphy. Born in New Orleans, he won the American Chess Congress at age 20 and was invited to Europe to play the best players in England, France, and Germany.
- In 1845, the first US championship was held, and the first women's championship was held in 1937. However, women's chess has declined through the years.
- Although chess in the 18th and 19th centuries was a way for men and women to socialize, today only 3 to 5 percent of United States Chess Federation (USCF) members are women.
- The USCF awards the national master title to any player who reaches a rating of 2200. Less than one percent of rated players hold the title.

The Transformation of the Queen

In AD 1000, the Persians called the piece next to the king a *fers*, meaning a male counselor to the king. When the Europeans started playing the game, they preferred a more romantic imagery and changed the *fers* to a queen. She was the weakest piece on the board. At the end of the 15th century, she became the strongest piece.

- Grandmaster is the highest title in chess. It is an international title, and is awarded by FIDE, the Federation Internationale des Echecs, or World Chess Federation.
- A life master is a national master who has played 300 games with a rating over 2200.
- Gothic Chess, invented by Ed Trice and patented in 2000, is played on a 10-inch-by-8-inch board with two additional pawns per side and two new pieces—the chancellor and the archbishop.
- Chess960, aka Fischer Random Chess, was created by Bobby Fischer and had 960 randomized initial positions, which decreased players' abilities to memorize and analyze opening moves.
- The USCF membership doubled in 1972, when people had become fascinated with player Bobby Fischer. He had become the youngest US Champion in 1957.

Full-Time Chess

From the time the Deep Blue computer developed by IBM defeated then world champion Gary Kasparov in 1997, computers have played a major role in the popularity of chess. Deep Blue was retired after beating Kasparov, but the match inspired the creation of the game Arimaa, which is played with a chess set, but is thought to be much more difficult for computers.

Rubik's Cube

Erno Rubik, a sculptor and professor in the Department of Interior Design at the Academy of Applied Arts and Crafts in Budapest, Hungry, received a patent for his "magic cube" in 1974. Rubik often made models to illustrate the ideas and concepts that he was teaching, and the cube was a natural progression from Rubik's interest in geometry, 3D forms, and unearthing possible combinations of forms and material in theory and in practice.

- The cube won the German Game of the Year special award for Best Puzzle in 1980.
- It is said to be the world's best-selling toy, with more than 300,000,000 Rubik's Cubes and reproductions sold worldwide.

Speedcubing

Called speedcubing, competitions for solving the Rubik's Cube in the shortest amount of time occur around the world. From 2003 to 2006, there have been 72 official competitions, with 33 of them occurring in 2006 alone. The World Cube Association (WCA) sets the standards and sanctions official tournaments.

The *Guinness Book of World Records* organized the first world speedcubing championship in 1981 in Munich, Germany. The official winner, with a speed record of 38 seconds, was Jury Froeschl, a native of Munich. Thibaut Jacquinot of France holds the current world record of 9.86 seconds, set at the Spanish Open in 2007.

The 15 Puzzle

Developed by Noyes Palmer Chapman, a New York postmaster, around 1874, this sliding puzzle game is still popular today. Chapman's first puzzle of this kind had 16 numbered blocks to be put together in rows of four, with each row adding up to 34. He improved his puzzle, and in 1879, students at the American School for the Deaf started manufacturing and selling the puzzle. Chapman applied for a patent on his Block Solitaire Puzzle, but it was rejected, probably because it resembled the Puzzle-Blocks patent already granted to another inventor.

This game—aka the Gem Puzzle, Boss Puzzle, Game of Fifteen, Mystic Square, and many others—is played on a 4-inch-by-4-inch square divided into 16 squares. Sliding tiles fill in 15 of the squares, leaving one space empty so that one tile at a time can be moved. The object is to arrange the 15 tiles into numerical order.

A smaller version using a 3-inch-by-3-inch square with 8 numbered tiles is also available.

Bobby Fischer is an expert at solving the 15-Puzzle. Typically, he only needs 25 seconds to solve it.

Profile of a Thinker: Edward Jenner Father of Immunology

Born in Gloucestershire, England, Edward Jenner was the son of the local vicar. When he was 14, he began training to be a physician.

- In 1796, already a well-established doctor, he experimented on an eight-year-old boy by inserting cells from a cowpox lesion into the boy's arm.
- Jenner's experiment was successful, and he proved that a mild case of cowpox would prevent children from getting smallpox.
- The Royal Society said this was not proof enough, so Jenner experimented on other children, including his 11-month-old son.
- Finally with enough proof, Jenner's discovery was published, but the general public did not accept it. Many people, especially the clergy, thought it was repulsive and ungodly. Eventually, people understood the protection Jenner's vaccines could provide.
- Smallpox vaccinations were being used in many countries around the world before Jenner's death in 1923.

Annihilation

It was Jenner's hope that someday the smallpox virus would be annihilated. It took 180 years, but today, according to the World Health Organization, smallpox exists in only two university research laboratories.

The last case of smallpox occurred in Somali in 1977.

Scrabble

In 1931, Alfred Mosher Butts, an out-of-work architect living in New York, decided it was time for a board game that combined the anagram and the crossword puzzle. He came up with Lexiko and sold them for $1.50 each. Later on, the name changed to Criss-Cross Words, then Scrabble.

Butts studied the *New York Times, New York Herald Tribune,* the *Saturday Evening Post,* and several dictionaries. He calculated how often each letter of the alphabet was used in day-to-day communication and then assigned a numerical value to each letter. His numeric designations have remained the same for more than 75 years.

Today, Scrabble is one of the most popular games in the world, with an estimated 3 million Scrabble games in 23 languages sold each year.

Scrabble Facts

- *Official SCRABBLE Players Dictionary,* Fourth Edition (OSPD4) is the king of word sources for Scrabble players, but for words with more than 8 letters, players have to go to *Merriam Webster's Collegiate Dictionary,* Eleventh Edition (MW11).
- There are 225 squares on a Scrabble board.
- The total face-point value of Scrabble tiles is 187.
- More than a half million US children play Scrabble at school. The first National School Scrabble Championship was held in Boston in 2003.

Many popular games—Monopoly, Scrabble, Checkers, Upwords, and others—are available in versions specific for people who are vision impaired or physically challenged.

- The highest scoring English word in the game of Scrabble is *quartzy*, worth 164 points.
- More than 147,000 words can be used to score while playing Scrabble.

Two-Letter Words for a Sizable Scrabble Score

aa
ar
er
fa
hm
id
jo
mm
op
om
oy
wo

Brain Teaser

Why does a deck of playing cards have 52 cards?

Answer: They represent the 52 weeks of the year. The four suits represent the four seasons.

Crossword Puzzles

The world's first crossword puzzle debuted in the *New York World* in December 1913. The British journalist Arthur Wynne called his invention the "word-cross." It became a regular weekly feature in the New York newspaper. Ten years later Simon and Schuster published the first book of crossword puzzles. The book was an instant hit, and crossword puzzles landed on the kitchen table of almost every household in 1924.

Today, the most prestigious, and sometimes the most challenging, are the crossword puzzles found in the *New York Times.* The puzzles have run continuously in the *Times* since 1942. Will Shortz, the fourth crossword editor for the Times, founded and directs the annual American Crossword Puzzle Tournament.

A variation of the crossword, the cryptic crossword, was introduced to US puzzlers in 1968. The cryptic crosswords have appeared in a variety of publications, including *New York* and *Atlantic Monthly* magazines.

Solving timed cryptic crossword puzzles was one of the tests used to choose cryptologists for service during World War II.

Even More Cryptic

During World War II, the *Daily Telegraph* ran a series of crossword puzzles that included secret code names for military operations planned as part of Operation Overlord. *Utah,* the code name for one of the landing sites, appeared in a puzzle on May 2, 1944. Other puzzles included the landing sites *Omaha* and *Mulberry;* the secret artificial harbors. This continued for a month, until the puzzle-maker, schoolteacher Leonard Dawe, was arrested and interrogated.

The First Crossword Puzzle

By Arthur Wynne, December 21, 1913
from *The New York World*

2-3. What bargain hunters enjoy.
4-5. A written acknowledgment.
6-7. Such and nothing more.
10-11. A bird.
14-15. Opposed to less.
18-19. What this puzzle is.
22-23. An animal of prey.
26-27. The close of a day.
28-29. To elude.
30-31. The plural of is.
8-9. To cultivate.
12-13. A bar of wood or iron.
16-17. What artists learn to do.
20-21. Fastened.
24-25. Found on the seashore.
10-18. The fibre of the gomuti palm.
6-22. What we all should be.
4-26. A day dream.
2-11. A talon.
19-28. A pigeon.
F-7. Part of your head.
23-30. A river in Russia.
1-32. To govern.
33-34. An aromatic plant.
N-8. A fist.
24-31. To agree with.
3-12. Part of a ship.
20-29. One.
5-27. Exchanging.
9-25. To sink in mud.
13-21. A boy.

Solution

						R						
					F	U	N					
				S	A	L	E	S				
			R	E	C	E	I	P	T			
		M	E	R	E		F	A	R	M		
	D	O	V	E				R	A	I	L	
M	O	R	E						D	R	A	W
	H	A	R	D				T	I	E	D	
		L	I	O	N		S	A	N	D		
			E	V	E	N	I	N	G			
				E	V	A	D	E				
					A	R	E					
						D						

As the story goes, the subterfuge occurred entirely by accident. While Dawe's children played with children of military personnel, they innocently heard and repeated the military code words that Dawe then used in his puzzles.

Roger Squires

The most prolific crossword puzzle-maker is thought to be England's Roger Squires. In Spring 2007, he published his 66,666th puzzle. He also holds the record for the longest word ever used in a published crossword puzzle. Llanfairpwllgwyngyllgogerychwyrndrobwllllantysiliogogogoch is the 58-letter name of a Welsh town and was clued as an anagram.

Profile of a Thinker: Dietrich Bonhoeffer Theologian and Ethicist

Born in Breslau, Germany, in 1906, Dietrich Bonhoeffer was the son of Germany's leading empirical psychologist. He attended Tubingen University, where he received a Ph.D. in 1927. He attended Union Theological Seminary in New York City and in 1931, he was ordained as a Lutheran pastor.

Things to Know

- As head of the Confessing Church Seminary, a part of the Pastors' Emergency League in opposition of the state church controlled by the Nazis, Bonhoeffer actively called for the overthrow of the Nazi regime.
- Known for his theory of ethical behavior, Bonhoeffer drew from the teachings of Aristotle and Jesus Christ. He believed that evil could only be combated by the specific actions of responsible people, and that people have no other option than to directly oppose evil. The failure to act is to condone evil, he believed.
- He worked on his book, *Ethics*, from 1940 until he was arrested in 1943. In his book, he attempted to provide a guide for living in the reality of the world and yet follow the teachings of Christ.
- Because of his open defiance of Hitler and the Nazi regime, Bonhoeffer was executed in 1945.

A Few Other Famous Works

Sanctorum Communio (*The Communion of Saints*)
Act and Being
Letters and Papers from Prison

Profile of a Thinker: Don Miguel de Cervantes Saavedra Father of the Modern Novel

Born in Alcala de Henares, Spain, on September 29, 1547, Miguel de Cervantes was one of seven children of a barber-physician. Although his father acted as a nobleman, the family rarely had money to live the life of gentry.

Things to Know

- Cervantes joined the Spanish infantry in 1570 and served for five years. He received several serious wounds, one of which caused him to lose use of his left hand.
- A year after his marriage to Catalina de Salazar y Palacios in 1585, Cervantes published his first major work, a novel titled *La Galatea*. However, the necessity to support his family caused him to set aside his writing and begin working as a supplier for the Spanish Armada and later as a tax collector.
- Managing his own money or someone else's proved a challenge for Cervantes. He suffered a personal bankruptcy, and was jailed at least twice (1597 and 1602) because of discrepancies in his work.
- Reportedly, while in jail, Cervantes began developing what became his most important literary contribution. In 1605, he published the first part of the novel *Don Quixote*. Although it did not bring him great riches, it did establish him as a man of letters. It is considered to be the first modern novel written.

As he was returning home from military service, Cervantes was captured by pirates and held for ransom. Yes, his family did pay for his release.

All About Don Quixote

- *Don Quixote de la Mancha,* the first modern novel, is a tale of a common man who delves into a fantasy world of chivalry and valor. It is written in episodic form and is classified as a satirical work of literary humor.
- It has been translated into over 65 languages and has appeared in 700 editions.
- The work was included in *Encyclopedia Britannica*'s collection "Great Books of the Western World."

Brain Teaser

What do Cervantes and Shakespeare have in common?

Answer: They are said to have died on the same date—April 23, 1616. However, England was using the Julian calendar at the time, and Spain was using the Gregorian version. So in actuality, they did not die on the same day.

In honor of this coincidence UNESCO [United Nations Educational, Scientific and Cultural Organization] established April 23 as the World Book and Copyright Day.

A Plot to Know: Eugene Onegin

What makes this Russian novel so interesting is that it is written entirely in verse. Aleksandr Pushkin portrays the life of troubled hero, Eugene. The social scene in St. Petersburg has bored poor Eugene to tears, so he heads out to a country estate where he meets Tatyana who, like many women, falls in love with him. He passes on her charms, preferring, instead, to pick a fight with the romantic poet Lensky. They duel. Eugene wins. Lensky dies. Eugene returns to the St. Petersburg social scene, not quite as bored as before. Tatyana follows him home and comes to an important realization. Browsing through his book collection, it dawns on her what a shallow putz Eugene is. She bids him farewell, goes off and marries a prince, and becomes the toast of St. Petersburg. Of course, now Eugene is interested in her, but Tatyana, though still in love with him for some odd reason, resists his affections out of duty to her husband.

In 1977, Soviet astronomer Nikolai Stepanovich Chernykh discovered a tiny new planet, which he decided to name after his favorite Russian author, Aleksandr Pushkin. There is also a crater on Mercury that is named after the famous writer.

Profile of a Thinker: Leonardo da Vinci Painter, Sculptor, Inventor, and Genius

Born on April 15, 1452, near Vinci, Italy, Leonardo da Vinci was sent to Florence to study painting under Andrea di Cione, better known as Verrocchio, in 1466. His earliest known work is a pen-and-ink drawing of the Arno valley drawn in 1473. Between 1476 and 1478, Leonardo did several commissioned pieces including an altarpiece for the Chapel of Saint Bernard and *The Adoration of the Magi* at Scopeto, which was never completed.

Things to Know

- Leonardo had a brilliant sense of observation and perception evident in his paintings and in the pages of his notebooks. His detailed designs of machinery were 500 years ahead of his time. Along with drawings of a bicycle, airplane, helicopter, and a parachute, he also recorded observations on subjects including geology, anatomy, flight, and gravity.
- Many of the 13,000 pages of his notebooks are written in mirror image. Some scholars believe that Leonardo used this means for writing to ensure privacy, other schools of thought say that, since Leonardo was left-handed, he probably found it quicker to write from right to left.
- Leonardo's notebooks are kept in various locations including the Louvre, the national library of Spain, the British library in London, and others. There is one privately owned notebook, the *Codex Leicester*, Which was purchased by Bill Gates.

- Leonardo was a master of anatomy. He made detailed drawings of muscles and tendons as a part of his study under Verrocchio. He was so good at what he did that he was allowed to dissect human corpses at several hospitals, drawing the human skeleton, the heart, and the vascular system, as well as other organs. Several of his drawings show comparisons of human organs with the corresponding organs of birds, frogs, bears, and other animals.

A Few of Leonardo's Inventions

- Parachutes
- Flying machines
- Submarines
- Underwater rebreathing devices
- Self-flotation/ocean rescue devices
- Swimming fins
- Pumping mechanisms
- Dredging systems
- Steam calorimeters
- Water-well drill
- Swing bridges
- Canals
- Leveling/surveying instruments
- Pulley systems
- Cranes
- Street-lighting systems
- Treadle-operated lathe
- Compasses
- Contact lenses

Several people have used the specifications in Leonardo's notebooks to construct working machinery. In 2000, Katarina Ollikainen built his parachute, and skydiver Adrian Nicholas proved that it worked. Two years later, British hang-gliding champion Judy Leden successfully flew a fixed-wing glider that had been built following Leonardo's instructions.

Charles Darwin: Theory of Evolution

Born on February 12, 1809, in Shrewsbury, Shropshire, England, Charles Darwin was the grandson of china manufacturer Josiah Wedgwood. He enrolled at Edinburgh University to study medicine but developed an interest in natural history and ignored his medical studies. After two years, his father was disappointed in his lack of interest in medicine and enrolled him in Cambridge University to study theology. Again at Cambridge he slighted his studies in theology in favor of science and naturalism; however, this time he graduated, tenth in his class, with a degree in theology. He married Anne Wedgwood, a cousin, in 1839. They had ten children.

Things to Know

- Darwin began working on his theory of evolution in 1836. He first reflected on two environmental observations—geologist Charles Lyell's theory that fossils found in rocks were from animals that had lived thousands or millions of years ago; and the variety of finches found on the Galapagos Islands. Then he added in the ideas of Thomas Malthus, who expounded on man's struggle for existence, and his own concept of "survival of the fittest."
- After working for 20 years on his theory, he and naturalist Alfred Wallace, who had been working independently on the same theory, proposed a theory of evolution occurring by the process of natural selection in 1858. The next year, Darwin published *On the Origin of Species by Means of Natural Selection.*
- The theory of evolution has remained controversial from the beginning, because of the logical conclusion that

humans are simply animals. Contrary to many religious teachings, Darwin's theory intimated that humans might have evolved from apes.

- In addition to his theory of evolution, Darwin made many contributions to science, studying a variety of animals and plants. His work, along with Gregor Mendel's work in genetics, forms the basis of modern biology.

Darwin's Works

Darwin was a prolific writer. His books include:

The Voyage of the Beagle
The Origin of Species
The Descent of Man, and Selection in Relation to Sex
The Expression of Emotions in Man and Animals
The Power of Movement in Plants
The Formation of Vegetable Mould Through the Action of Worms

Darwin's Beloved Tortoise

Harriet, a Galápagos tortoise, possibly collected by Darwin, died in 2006 at an estimated age of 175. She lived at a zoo in Australia.

A Name to Drop: René Descartes

(Hint: "I think, therefore I am.")

René Descartes entered the University of Poitiers in 1614 to study law, yet became a student of philosophy, theology, and medicine to boot. In 1618, Descartes joined the military and spent four years traveling and studying what he deemed "the great book of the world."

- Descartes combined his philosophical ideas with the principles of mathematics and science. He believed that everything in nature could be explained by science and mathematics.
- One of Descartes' major undertakings was to develop a set of principles that a person could know as true without any doubt. Using methodological skepticism, rejecting any idea that could be doubted, he came up with only one principle—thought exists. From this principle comes the famous quotation, "I think, therefore I am."
- The principles of deduction and perception were of interest to Descartes. As he studied these principles, he developed the Wax Argument. He considered a piece of wax, noting its color, shape, and smell changed completely when exposed to heat, but it was still a piece of wax. From this study he asserted that only deduction—use of judgment, not perception—was reliable knowledge.
- He believed the human body was in constant motion. However, he said that the mind was a nonmaterial entity and lacked motion. In considering the relationship of the mind and body, Descartes believed in a form of dualism, saying that the mind controls the body, but that the body

also influences the mind, such as when people react to heat or cold. This theory, like many of Descartes' ideas, was not readily accepted during his time.

Three Major Works:

- *Discourse on Method,* published in 1637
- *Meditations on First Philosophy,* published in 1641
- *Principles of Philosophy,* published in 1644

Discourse on Method described the universe as a giant mathematically designed engine. "Geometry," an appendix within D*iscourse on the Method,* combined the principles of algebra and geometry into analytical geometry, known today as Cartesian geometry. His idea of using intersecting lines to identify a point is called the coordinate system. Although the system has been improved throughout the years, it is widely used today to analyze curves.

- Descartes' works were banned by the pope in 1663.
- Descartes' coordinate system ultimately enabled the development of GPS (Global Positioning System) instruments.
- Descartes is credited with inventing graph paper and exponential notation (superscripts).

Profile of a Thinker: Fyodor Dostoevsky Author of The Brothers Karamazov

Born on November 11, 1821, in Moscow, Dostoevsky enrolled in the Military Engineering Academy in St. Petersburg as a teenager. He was expected to focus his study on mathematics, but he hated the subject. Consequently, he used his spare time to write.

His first novel, *Poor Folk,* which was written while he was at the academy, was published in 1846. It was well received, making him a popular writer at age 25. He joined a literary discussion group that examined Western philosophy, a topic that was banned in Russia. His participation in the group led to imprisonment, mandatory military service, and a mock execution.

- After his release from prison in 1854, Dostoevsky spent most of his time writing and publishing his work. During this time, he wrote *The House of the Dead* (1862), *Notes from the Underground* (1864), *Crime and Punishment* (1866), *The Idiot* (1868), and *Devils* (1871).
- Considered by many people as a founder of 20th-century existentialism, Dostoevsky's novels explore human psychology in the political, social, and spiritual turmoil of 19th-century Russian society. Outside of literature, he is said to have influenced the modernist movements in philosophy and psychology.
- Fyodor Dostoevsky died on February 9, 1881.

The Major Works of Dostoevsky
Novels

- *Poor Folk*
- *Netochka Nezvanova*
- *The Village of Stepanchikovo*
- *The House of the Dead*
- *Notes from the Underground*
- *Crime and Punishment*
- *The Gambler*
- *The Idiot*
- *The Possessed*
- *The Raw Youth*
- *The Brothers Karamazov*

Short Stories

- *White Nights*
- *A Christmas Tree and a Wedding*
- *An Honest Thief*
- *The Peasant Marey*
- *The Dream of a Ridiculous Man*

The epigraph of Dostoevsky's final novel, *The Brothers Karamazov*, is also the epitaph on the author's tombstone—"Verily, Verily, I say unto you, except a corn of wheat fall into the ground and die, it abideth alone: but if it die, it bringeth forth much fruit."

A Plot to Know: Jane Eyre

From orphan to lover, young Jane makes quite a journey in this romantic novel by Charlotte Brontë. Unlike typical Victorian heroines, Jane is a bit plain but really smart. She gets shipped off to boarding school where she befriends the long-suffering Helen, who dies. From there, she becomes governess to the daughter of Edward Rochester of Thornfield Hall. She falls in love with the moody Rochester, but he has a secret. The reason he is so cold to Jane is because he has a crazy wife hidden in the attic. When Jane finds out, she flees and almost marries a clergyman. Turns out, she comes into a fortune from a long lost uncle. She leaves the odious clergyman who only wanted to marry her so she could function as a servant to him during his missionary work. In a freaky, mystic way, she hears Rochester calling to her, so she returns to Thornfield only to discover that his crazy wife burned it to the ground and jumped off the roof. Rochester is blind and crippled. Jane is wealthy and free. With the power balanced out in the relationship, they happily marry.

At age eight, Charlotte Brontë was sent along with three of her sisters to the Clergy Daughters' School at Cowan Bridge in Lancashire. The deplorable conditions there traumatized the young girl, and she was convinced that they were to blame for her poor health later in life and for the death of her two sisters, Maria and Elizabeth, from tuberculosis in 1825. That terrible experience inspired Brontë to create the Lowood School, which appears in her novel *Jane Eyre*.

A Name to Drop: Robert James "Bobby" Fischer

(Hint: Chess Grandmaster)

Born in Chicago, Illinois, during World War II, Bobby was a high-school dropout and chess prodigy. He learned how to play at age 6 from the instructions in his sister's chess set. His school records indicated that he held an IQ of 187.

- At age 13, Fischer won the United States Junior Chess Championship. The next year, he successfully defended his junior title, and then went on to win the United States Open Chess Championship, making him the youngest US champion ever.
- Fischer defeated Boris Spassky in the 1972 World Championship match—The Match of the Century. That win made him the 11th World Chess Champion and the highest-rated player in history. He appeared on the covers of *Life* and *Sports Illustrated* and on a Bob Hope television special.
- In 1992, after 20 years out of competition, Fischer challenged Boris Spassky to a "revenge match." Because of a United Nations embargo, the United States declared that it was illegal for Fischer to compete in this challenge. Following the match, a warrant was issued for his arrest.
- After denouncing his US citizenship, Fischer took refuge in Iceland. Because of contemptuous political comments that he made after the 9/11 terrorist attacks on the US, Fischer's membership in the United States Chess Federation was cancelled in 2001. In 2004, Fischer was arrested in Japan for trying to use a cancelled US passport.
- Fischer died in 2008.

Galileo Galilei: Father of Modern Physics

Born in Pisa, Italy, in 1564, Galileo became an instrumental part of the scientific revolution. The young mathematician was intrigued by the back and forth motion of a suspended lamp in the cathedral of Pisa. He found, by comparing the swinging lamp with his own pulse rate, that the swing of the pendulum always takes the same amount of time regardless of the arc of the swing.

Galileo experimented with measuring the speed of light and sound frequency. He formulated the basic principle of relativity—that the laws of physics are the same in any system that is moving at a constant speed in a straight line, regardless of its particular speed or direction—thus paving the way for Newton's laws of motion and Einstein's special theory of relativity.

Galileo created sketches for a variety of ingenious ideas, such as a candle placed in front of a mirror to reflect light throughout a building, an automatic tomato picker, a combination pocket comb and eating utensil, and what appears to be a ballpoint pen.

The Assayer (*Saggiatore*), Galileo's first book, was published in 1623. Nine years later, he published the *Dialogue Concerning the Two Chief World Systems*, which resulted in his summons to stand trial on suspicion of heresy in 1633. Found guilty, he was required to recant his heliocentric ideas and was put under house arrest. His book was banned, and he was forbidden to publish anything else.

- To measure short intervals of time, Galileo sang songs with whose timing he was familiar.
- In 1992, Pope John Paul II expressed regret for the Church's treatment of Galileo.

While under house arrest, Galileo created one of his finest works, *Two New Sciences*, a summary of the work he had done on what is now called kinematics and strength of materials. As a result of this work, Galileo is often called, the "father of modern physics."

Galileo's Inventions:

- In the late 1500s, Galileo modified earlier instruments to develop a geometric and military compass suitable for use by soldiers and surveyors. It provided a safer way to elevate cannons accurately and to quickly calculate the charge of gunpowder for cannonballs. The compass also enabled the construction of any regular polygon and allowed for a variety of calculations.
- Around 1593, Galileo used the expansion and contraction of air in a bulb to move water in an attached tube, creating a thermometer.
- In 1609, Galileo modified the existing telescope to produce a refracting telescope that would allow him to observe stars, planets, and the moon.
- In the 1620s, using elements of the telescope, Galileo developed the first known compound microscope.

Deriving It Honestly

Galileo's father, a musician, established what has been said to be the oldest known nonlinear relation in physics. He showed that when a string is stretched, the pitch varies as the square root of the tension, and that subdividing a string by a whole number produces a harmonious scale.

The Universe

Modifying telescopes, with sometimes up to 32x magnification, he made many celestial discoveries that supported the theories first put forth by the astronomer Copernicus:

- He observed Jupiter's moons, the phases of Venus, the rings of Saturn, and the lunar mountains and craters. He is also thought to be one of the first Europeans to observe sunspots.
- Galileo found that the Milky Way is a multitude of stars packed so densely that from Earth they appear to be clouds.

Tides: Galileo vs. Kepler

Galileo believed the tides were caused by the water in the ocean sloshing back and forth, speeded up and slowed down, because of the earth's rotation on its axis and its revolution around the sun. This theory only allows for one high tide per day, so Galileo claimed that the shape of the sea, its depth, and other factors, resulted in the second tide. A contemporary, Johannes Kepler, believed that the moon caused the tides, but Galileo rejected this possibility. It was later discovered that Kepler's theory was more correct.

What Goes Up...

Even before Sir Isaac Newton, Galileo performed experiments involving gravity and motion. He rolled balls down inclined planes, proving that moving objects accelerate independently of their mass. He also believed that objects maintain velocity unless a force acts upon them.

Galileo's Principle of Inertia

A body moving on a level surface will continue in the same direction at constant speed unless disturbed.

Edwin Powell Hubble: Father of Observational Cosmology

Born in 1889, Edwin Hubble taught high school, practiced law, and served a tour of duty in the military before returning to his primary interest, astronomy. After military service, he studied at the Yerkes Observatory and received a doctorate in astronomy from the University of Chicago in 1917.

A Brainy Athlete

Hubble was a star athlete in high school and college. He broke the Illinois State high jump record and excelled in basketball and boxing.

- In 1919, Hubble accepted what turned into a lifetime position at the Mount Wilson Observatory in California. One of his first tasks at the observatory was to photograph Cepheid variables, using the new reflecting Hooker telescope.
- His photographs proved that there are other galaxies similar to our own Milky Way and expanded our understanding of the vastness of the universe.
- Hubble classified the galaxies he observed, sorting them by content, distance, shape, and brightness. This led to his observation of redshifts in the emission of light from the galaxies.
- He could tell that the galaxies were moving away from each other at a rate constant to the distance between them. The formula resulting from this observation is known as Hubble's Law. Using this formula, astronomers determined the age of the universe and proved that it was expanding.

- Hubble's observations led to the thought that if the expansion was coming from a central point, something must have caused it. This idea is known as the Big Bang Theory.

Hubble Blew Einstein's Mind

Albert Einstein had developed a model of space based on his general theory of relativity, showing that space was curved by gravity and able to expand or contract. However, he could not believe his own theory and revised it, calling the universe static and immobile.

After Hubble's discovery, Einstein said that not believing his initial theory was "the biggest blunder in his life." He visited Hubble in 1931 to thank him for his discovery.

Historical Figures and Estimated IQ

In 1926, psychologist Catherine Morris Cox published a study of men and women who had lived between 1450 and 1850 to estimate what their IQs might have been. Her results were based largely on the degrees of brightness and intelligence each subject showed before age 17.

- Goethe – 210
- Emanuel Swedenborg – 205
- Gottfried Wilhelm Leibniz – 205
- John Stuart Mill – 200
- Blaise Pascal – 195
- Ludwig Wittgenstein – 190
- Bobby Fischer – 187
- Galileo Galilei – 185
- René Descartes – 180
- Madame de Staël – 180
- Immanuel Kant – 175
- Linus Carl Pauling – 170
- Sofia Kovalevskaya – 170
- Thomas Chatterton – 170
- Charles Darwin – 165
- Wolfgang Amadeus Mozart – 165
- George Eliot (Mary Ann Evans) – 160
- Nicolaus Copernicus – 160
- Olof Palme – 156

- Rembrandt van Rijn – 155
- Anna Lindh – 152
- George Sand (Aurore Dupin) – 150

Cox also determined that different fields have varying average IQs for their acknowledged leading geniuses. Her findings list:

- Philosophers – 160
- Scientists – 159
- Artists – 153
- Fiction writers – 152
- Statesmen – 150
- Musicians – 149
- Soldiers – 136

Thomas Friedman, an American journalist born in 1953, argues that in today's world, where people are virtually overwhelmed by all the information that is available, curiosity and passion are more important than intelligence alone. He sums his idea up with the equation:

CQ + PQ > IQ

In other words, Curiosity Quotient plus Passion Quotient is greater than Intelligence Quotient.

"Give me the kid with a passion to learn and a curiosity to discover," Friedman has said, "and I will take him or her over the less passionate kid with a huge IQ every day of the week."

Garry Kasparov: Chess Grandmaster

- Born in Baku, Azerbaijan, Garry Kasparov began playing chess with his father at age 5.
- In 1975, Kasparov won the Azerbaijan championship, and later that year he won the USSR junior championship. At age 15, he decided to pursue chess as a career.
- He won his first international tournament in Banja Luka, Yugoslavia, in 1979.
- Qualifying for the Candidates Tournament in 1982, after having won the Moscow Interzonal tournament, made him the youngest candidate since Bobby Fischer in 1958.

He also established a chess academy and a tournament for young players. The Kasparov Cup, for the strongest chess players under age 17, has produced several active chess professionals.

Although no longer in professional competition, Kasparov remains the strongest chess player in history. He was ranked first in the world for 20 years, from 1985 to 2005.

Deep Thought

In 1998, Kasparov introduced a new form of chess—Advanced Chess—in which a human and a computer compete. He defeated the chess computer Deep Thought in 1989, but in 1996, IBM's Deep Blue proved a more worthy competitor. The computer won the first game, with Kasparov gaining three wins and two draws to win the match.

The first computer to defeat a world champion was an updated version of Deep Blue. The 1997 competition between the computer and Kasparov was the subject of a documentary film, *Game Over: Kasparov and the Machine.*

He has also become active in politics. Even prior to his retirement, he received the Keeper of the Flame award in 1991 from the Center for Security Policy for anti-Communist resistance and the propagation of democracy. In June 1993, he helped establish the Choice of Russia, and in 1996, he took part in the election campaign of Boris Yeltsin. Kasparov is a member of the National Security Advisory Council and the International Council of the Human Rights Foundation.

Beating Kasparov

With all the hype concerning the skill with which Garry Kasparov plays chess, it has to feel great to beat him. He was defeated many times during his youth, but he became a much tougher competitor as he came of age. Here's a list of a few of the chess masters who have accomplished a win over Kasparov in a regular game since he turned sixteen:

- Vladimir Akopian, called a chess tourist by Kasparov.
- Alexander Beliavsky defeated Kasparov the year he turned 10, and he won another game in 1983.
- Krum Georgiev won the only game they played.
- Boris Gulko has a plus score against Kasparov (+3-1=4), including a win while Kasparov was world champion, making it three in a row.
- Anatoly Karpov, who won a game against Kasparov before he turned 16, has won over 20 games against him since then and has a narrow minus score, +23-29=137.
- Viktor Korchnoi is the only non-World Champion to beat both Kasparov and Fischer.
- Judit Polgar beat Kasparov in a rapid game and is the only woman on this list.
- Teimour Radjabov was 16 years old when he became the youngest player in history to defeat the world's #1 player.

He has an equal record (+1-1=1) against Kasparov at a classical time control.

- Alexander Veingold won in 1989, the year that Kasparov turned 16.

Kasparov also lost to the computer Deep Blue in 1996 and again in 1997, and lost one game of a four-game match to computer X3D Fritz in 2003.

Check your Kasparov IQ

- Garry Kasparov's real name is Garri Vaynshteyn. After his father's death, Kasparov modified his mother's maiden name, Kasparyan, to make the more Russian-sounding Kasparov.
- Kasparov has two European patents; both are for methods of playing a lottery game.
- Kasparov won the Chess Oscar a record 11 times. An annual, international award, the Chess Oscar is a coveted recognition chosen by chess experts from around the world.
- In October 2007, Kasparov announced that he would run for presidency of the Russian Federation as candidate of "The Other Russia," against incumbent Vladimir Putin.
- Kasparov appeared in an interview for Playboy in 1989.
- A fan once hit Kasparov over the head with a chessboard he had just signed, stating before the attack that he had admired Kasparov as a chess player until he gave that up for politics.
- Kasparov has appeared on several American television shows since beginning his career in politics, including *The Colbert Report*. He has also been interviewed by American television hosts Bill Maher, Wolf Blitzer, and Chris Matthews.
- Kasparov is a member of the International Council of the Human Rights Foundation, a nonprofit organization based in New York.

Sir Isaac Newton

Born on January 4, 1643, in Woolsthorpe, Lincolnshire, England, Isaac Newton was reared by his grandparents. He was a sickly child and not allowed to play with other children, so he occupied his time by making toys, including a wooden clock, sundial, and a mouse-powered mill.

He enrolled in Cambridge University in 1661, at age 19. While there he studied mathematics, optics, physics, and astronomy. He said the period when the school was closed because of the plague (1664–66) were "the prime of my age for invention." During those 18 months, he developed theories regarding gravity, light, and calculus.

His Studies

- Newton was inspired by the works of Robert Boyle and Robert Hooke on optics and light, René Descartes's work on mathematics and physics, and the works of many other great scholars.
- He observed the refraction of light by a glass prism and developed a series of elaborate experiments that led him to the conclusion that white light is made up of all the colored rays found in the rainbow. He said that light consisted of streams of minute particles.
- His unconventional ideas were strongly rejected, causing Newton to delay the publication of *Opticks* for 12 years, until 1704, although the book was already written.
- Building on his discoveries in optics, Newton constructed the first reflecting telescope in 1668, which he used to study the universe. He wondered what kept the stars from falling to Earth. This curiosity led him to develop the laws of motion and the theory of gravitation. He could then predict the locations of stars and planets around the sun.

- Newton is also credited with inventing integral calculus, and, jointly with Gottfried Wilhelm Leibniz, differential calculus.
- A great controversy surrounded the development of differential calculus, as Newton and Leibniz both claimed to have discovered the method independent of one another. Newton had developed the idea early in his studies but did not publish it until after Leibnitz published his findings. Leibniz claimed to have worked independently of knowledge of Newton's work. However, documents discovered after Leibniz's death seem to indicate that the mathematician was aware of Newton's mathematical theories.
- In the late 1680s, Newton published his greatest work, the *Philosophiae Naturalis Principia Mathematica* (*Mathematical Principles of Natural Philosophy*). This three-volume work attempts to organize scientific and mathematical principles. In these volumes we find the basics of Newton's life work.
- Several of his writings were published posthumously, including the *Observations upon the Prophecies of Daniel and the Apocalypse of St. John* in 1733.

Newton's Honors

- In 1696, he became warden of the Royal Mint, and within three years he was appointed Master of the Mint. He remained in this office until his death. He was elected a fellow of the Royal Society of London in 1671, and in 1703, he became president, being annually re-elected for the rest of his life. He was knighted in Cambridge in 1705.
- Although his theories caused controversy early on, Newton became the most highly esteemed natural philosopher in Europe. For 30 years, while carrying out his official duties at the Royal Mint, Newton spent time revising his earlier

works, studying ancient history, and defending himself against his critics.

- Isaac Newton died on March 31, 1727, and was buried in Westminster Abbey, the first scientist to be honored in such a way.

Laws of Motion:

- *Law of inertia:* Every object persists in its state of rest or uniform motion in a straight line unless it is compelled to change that state by forces impressed upon it.
- *Law of acceleration:* Force is equal to the change in momentum (mV) per change in time. For a constant mass, force equals mass times acceleration, F = ma.
- *Law of action and reaction:* For every action, there is an equal and opposite reaction.

Traces of Newton

- The Wren Library in Trinity College, Cambridge, has Newton's own copy of the first edition of *Principia*, which contains handwritten notes for the second edition.
- The Martin Bodmer Library in Switzerland has the original first edition that was owned by Gottfried Wilhelm Leibniz, the mathematician who claimed to have developed differential calculus. In it are handwritten notes by Leibniz concerning the controversy over the development of calculus.

A Name to Drop: Jean Piaget

(Hint: Theory of Cognitive Development)

Born in Neuchatel, Switzerland, on August 9, 1896, Jean Piaget published his first scientific paper about the albino sparrow at age 10. His mother had a neurotic temperament that led Piaget to study psychology, psychoanalysis, and pathological psychology. He was known as a child prodigy for his early accomplishments.

- While studying at the Sorbonne in Paris from 1919 to 1921, Piaget learned to interview mental patients while analyzing the verbal reasoning processes of children. This study led to his focus in the field of inductive and experimental psychology.
- Piaget tested his own children and made observations of their reactions. These experiments led him to propose that children up to age 12 do not believe in the constancy of material quantity, weight, and volume of a lump of modeling clay. He felt that the idea of constancy developed in stages that could be studied in concrete situations rather than by relying solely on language.
- The most critical factor in child development, according to Piaget, was interaction with peers. He said these interactions lead to cognitive conflicts that turn into arguing and debating. The conflict encourages the child to look at the other person's point of view.
- Initially trained in biology and philosophy, Piaget considered himself a "genetic epistemologist," with his main interest in how people come to know things. He believed that the ability to reason was the key to knowledge.

Piaget's Findings: Child Development

He identified four stages that all children go through in the same order, although some children go through the stages more quickly than others.

- The Sensorimotor Period – From birth to age two, children are limited to the motor reflexes.
- The Pre-Operational Period – From two to age six or seven, children start to use mental imagery and language.
- The Concrete Operational Stage – From age six or seven to age 11 or 12, children understand another person's point of view and can incorporate more than one perspective simultaneously. They can also grasp seven types of conservation: the conservation of number, liquid, length, mass, weight, area, and volume.
- The Formal Operational Stage – From age 11 or 12 through adulthood, people are capable of thinking logically and abstractly as well as theoretically. Piaget believed that not everyone reaches this stage of development.

Today many preschool and primary grades use his theory of cognitive development, encouraging children to learn through discovery. Educators support the efforts of children through positive reinforcement and challenge them to try new things just beyond the child's ability but not too far out of reach.

Piaget created the International Centre for Genetic Epistemology in Geneva in 1955 and directed it until 1980. He received 31 honorary doctorates.

Greatest Hits of Jean Piaget

- *Recherché,* a philosophic novel (1917)
- *The Language and Thought of the Child* (1924)
- *The Child's Conception of the World* (1926)
- *The Child's Conception of Causality* (1927)
- *Judgment and Reasoning in the Child* (1928)
- *The Moral Judgment of the Child* (1932)
- *The Origins of Intelligence in Children* (1936)
- *Play, Dreams, and Imitation in Children* (1951)
- *The Growth of Logical Thinking From Childhood to Adolescence* (1970)
- *Carmichael's Manual of Child Psychology* (1970)
- *Biology and Knowledge* (1971)
- *The Grasp of Consciousness* (1974)

Piaget was a prolific writer. During his lifetime, he published more than 60 books and several hundred articles. He followed a routine of rising at 4:00 a.m. and writing four publishable pages each day before going to class. He also devoted summer breaks to writing. Piaget spent nearly 75 years researching and writing. He died on September 17, 1980.

A Good Name to Know: Pablo Picasso

Born on October 25, 1881, in Malaga, Spain, Pablo Picasso learned his craft from his father, who was also an accomplished painter, instructor, and museum curator. He attended various art schools and even enrolled in college at Academia de San Fernando in Madrid but only stayed there a few months. He was married twice and had four children by three women.

Picasso lived the stereotypical "starving artist" lifestyle in Spain and France. In his early career, he sold his paintings to pay rent and burned some to stay warm. By the end of his life, his popularity was such that he was able to keep many of his paintings and had even built a substantial collection of other artists' works. At his death in 1973, Picasso had no will, so his art collection went to pay estate tax in France. These paintings are now in the Musée Picasso collection in Paris.

Cubism

- In 1901, while living in Madrid, Picasso teamed with a friend to establish the magazine *Arte Joven*. Illustrating the entire first edition himself, he began to sign his work Picasso; before he had signed Pablo Ruiz y Picasso.
- Picasso introduced analytic cubism into his painting in 1909. Using shades of brown, the artist painted pieces of objects and "analyzed" them according to their shapes.
- He developed this cubism style further when he added cut pieces of wallpaper and newspaper to his paintings, creating collages. He was the first to use collage in fine art.
- *Guernica,* his depiction of the 1936 German bombing of Guernica, Spain, is said to be his most famous work. It was commissioned for exhibit at the Spanish Pavilion in the 1937 Paris International Exposition.

Picasso During the War

Picasso stayed in Paris when the Germans occupied the city during World War II. Since the Nazis did not like his work, the artist was forbidden to display his paintings. In 1944, he joined the French Communist Party and received the Stalin Peace Prize in 1950. However, when the party criticized his portrait of Stalin, Picasso lost much of his interest in the Communist Party.

Periods of Picasso Paintings

The most commonly accepted periods for Pablo Picasso's work are:

- **The Blue Period** (1901–1904), consisting of paintings in shades of blue and green and with a recurrent theme of blindness
- **The Rose Period** (1904–1906), characterized with warm colors including oranges and pinks and many times featuring harlequins
- **The African-influenced Period** (1907–1909)
- **Analytic Cubism** (1909–1912), using brown monochrome colors
- **Synthetic Cubism** (1912–1919), which incorporates bits of paper into the paintings

Art-i-facts

Pablo Picasso's full name was Pablo Diego José Francisco de Paula Juan Nepomuceno María de los Remedios Cipriano de la Santísima Trinidad Clito Ruiz y Picasso.

Postwar Picasso

- After World War I, Picasso is said to have "returned to order" in his painting, joining the neoclassical movement that was prevalent in literature, music, and art.
- From 1968 to 1971, Picasso used a mixture of styles and more color in his paintings. During this time he worked fast and produced a number of paintings. Most of them were called incoherent scribbling. It was not until after his death that these paintings were seen for what they were—a new style named neo-expressionism. Even unto his death, Picasso seemed to be an artist before his time.
- Pablo Picasso died on April 8, 1973, in Mougins, France.

Picasso's Bestsellers

Some paintings by Picasso are considered among the most expensive paintings in the world.

- *Nude on a Black Armchair* sold for $45.1 million in 1999.
- *Les Noces de Pierrette* sold for more than $51 million in 1999.
- *Garçon à la pipe* sold for $104 million in 2004.
- *Dora Maar au chat* sold for $95.2 million in 2006.

Picasso's Firsts

- Picasso's mother said her son's first word was *piz,* Spanish slang for "pencil."
- Picasso was the first to incorporate collage techniques, using bits of paper in his paintings, in fine art.
- Along with Georges Braque, Picasso is considered the co-founder of cubism.

The Chicago Picasso

Located in Daley Plaza in the downtown Chicago Loop, the so-called Chicago Picasso definitely draws attention. The abstract metal sculpture stands 50 feet tall and weighs 162 tons. It was the first major public artwork in Chicago. Following Picasso's instructions, US Steel Corporation in Gary, Indiana, created the sculpture for $351,959.17. Picasso turned down payment of $100,000, choosing to offer the work as a gift to the people.

A Word to Know

Marquette is a prototype or scale-replica of a proposed sculpture or architectural work. Similar to a cartoonist's storyboard or a painter's pencil sketch, it shows the intricacies of an object. Visualizing a marquette allows the artist to make alterations that he could not make in the larger project itself. They are used especially for client approval of commissioned sculptures. Marquettes produced by some artists are very collectible.

Child Prodigies

A child prodigy masters a skill or art at an unusually young age. Typically a prodigy is defined as someone who masters the fundamentals and skills of a certain field by the age of 12.

- The word *Wunderkind* is sometimes used as a synonym for prodigy. It can also be used when referring to adults, such as Steven Spielberg, who achieved great success very early in their careers.
- American psychologist Michael O'Boyle recently discovered through the use of an fMRI, which measures brain activity, that the mental operations of prodigies are strikingly different than those of typical humans. His research documented that the blood flow to certain parts of the brain of a prodigy calculator was nearly seven times the amount of typical blood flow in a human doing math.
- The fMRI measures activity in certain locations of the brain to gain a better understanding of how a particular brain is functioning. They are currently being tested as possible lie detectors!

A Few Famed Child Prodigies

Kim Ung-Yong –	Earned a Ph.D. in physics before turning 15.
Zerah Colburn –	Able to multiply six-digit numbers in his head at age nine.
Blaise Pascal –	At age 11, worked out the first 23 propositions of Euclid.
Ruth Lawrence –	Youngest student to enter the University of Oxford, at age 12.

The Zodiac Killer

While the jury is still out on whether the still unnamed "Zodiac Killer" was a genius, a lunatic, or just a man who got away with an unknown amount of criminal acts, he or she certainly threw the entire West Coast for a loop.

The Zodiac is known to have murdered five victims in West Coast cities surrounding San Francisco between late 1968 and 1969, yet it remains unknown how many murders can be attributed to the faceless, nameless killer. In letters to newspapers, the Zodiac insisted that he had murdered as many as 37 people.

- Police interviewed over 2,500 suspects in the search for the Zodiac.
- There were seven confirmed victims, two of which survived their attacks.
- On August 1, 1969, a letter from the Zodiac was received at the *San Francisco Chronicle*, the *Vallejo Times-Herald*, and the *San Francisco Examiner*.
- His letters included cryptograms to be deciphered. When decoded, they contained disturbing messages which highlighted the reasons the Zodiac enjoyed killing.

Cryptograms

Cryptograms were actually used as early as the fifth century by the Spartan military in an effort to send messages that could only be decoded using a certain length of stick. The message was written on a strip of paper wrapped around a stick without overlapping. It was then unraveled and sent, only to be decoded by wrapping it around the same length stick.

Henry Lee Lucas

Widely regarded as America's most prolific serial killer, Henry Lee Lucas was thought by many to be highly intelligent and manipulative of law enforcement and the media. He claimed involvement in over 3,000 murders.

- Lucas's first murder was that of his mother in 1960. The two were involved in an ongoing argument, and Lucas lost his temper and struck his mother. He later reported that he did not know what had happened until noticing a knife in his hand. He was sentenced to 20 to 40 years of imprisonment for the crime. Lucas served less than 11 years of prison and was released in 1970.
- In 1983, Lucas had taken credit for over 213 murders. He was allowed, under close supervision, to conduct interviews and see suspects for cases he was cleared from. Lucas was able to help with the investigations, as he had memorized the details of so many murders.

In the end, Henry Lee Lucas was confirmed to have killed three victims: his mother, a woman named Kate Rich, and another named Becky Powell. The truth of the other confessions is still questionable. Lucas died in prison in March 2001, ending one of the most famous studies of criminal psychology in history.

Family Ties

Lucas's distant cousin, Bobby Joe Long, was convicted in the state of Florida for ten murders in the 1990s. He admitted to raping over 50 women, whom he had selected from newspaper classified ads.

Fascinating Details About Mark Twain

Named by William Faulkner as "the Father of American literature," novelist Mark Twain can be found on the bookshelves of many southern homes. Most good ol' boys and southern belles are familiar with *The Adventures of Huckleberry Finn*, but how much do they really know about Twain? Several biographies, such as *Mark Twain: A Life*, by Ron Powers, illustrate the man behind the genius.

- Twain was a vegetarian and was radically opposed to the dissection of living animals for scientific research.
- Twain, born Samuel Clemens, had several pen names. These include Thomas Jefferson Snodgrass, Rambler, Sergeant Fathom, and W. Epaminondas Adrastus Blab.
- In 1849, at age 14, Twain dropped out of John Dawson's school to concentrate on working for the *Hannibal Gazette* and later the *Hannibal Journal*.
- Twain held three patents for inventions he funded: an automatically self-adjusting vest strap, a memory-improving history game, and a self-pasting scrapbook.
- Twain despised organized religion, and wrote posthumously published books on the matter. Among these are *Letters from the Earth* and *The Mysterious Stranger*.
- While living briefly in New Hampshire, Twain rented housecats to keep him company.
- Before publishing his first book, Twain held many jobs, including that of a steamboat pilot and a gold prospector.
- Although he briefly volunteered in the Confederate Calvary, Twain later became a staunch abolitionist.

The Nibelungenlied

This famous German epic poem was written around 1200 and inspired much of Wagner's opera *Der Ring Des Nibelungen*. In a nutshell, the hero, Siegfried, travels to Worms to win the hand of the lovely Kriemhild. Her three brothers get the skinny on Siegfried—turns out he is a war hero, he owns a cape of darkness which makes him invisible, and he is thick-skinned, literally, because when he killed a dragon, its blood washed over him, making him a bit scaly and horny. Not the prettiest complexion, perhaps, but a darn useful one in battle. They approve of him as a spouse for their sister, but first one of them needs a favor.

Brother Gunther is in love with Queen Brunhild of Iceland, but he needs help in winning her love. Siegfried agrees to help him in exchange for his sister, Kriemhild. Brunhild will be no easy catch for Gunther, however. She has sworn that she will only marry a man who can throw a spear farther than her. Siegfried, in his invisible cape, helps Gunther pull off the stunt. Gunther marries Brunhild; Siegfried married Kriemhild. However, Brunhild suspects that her darling Gunther really isn't as strong as she is. So, like so many brides, on their wedding night she ties little Gunther into a knot and hangs him on a wall like a picture. This was not Gunther's idea of fun. In a kinky display of heroism, Siegfried arrives in his invisible cloak and wrestles Brunhild into submission. He steals her girdle and ring and gives them to Kriemhild. Later, in a catfight between the two brides, Kriemhild shows Brunhild that she now has her girdle and ring, thus proving that Siegfried fooled the hefty Brunhild.

From this bizarre episode, the plot takes numerous turns. Kriemhild betrays Siegfried and he gets killed by her brothers. She remarries and kills her brothers, but then gets killed herself proving a story that is truly the stuff of opera.

Solipsism

A widely explored philosophical idea, solipsism is the metaphysical position that denies proof of anything outside the mind. Solipsism is thought to have been introduced by the Greek sophist Gorgias, who stated, in his own words, the following principles:

- Nothing exists.
- Even if something exists, nothing can be absolutely known about it.
- Even if something could be known about an existing thing, that knowledge could not be communicated to others.

Supporting Arguments

- One of the strongest arguments for solipsism is the question of the effect of "existing" objects. If something can never affect a person in any way, can it be said to exist, and if so, in what sense?
- Some use the example of the moon: If the moon never affects a person, can it be said to exist? The light from the moon has an effect, as does the gravitational pull of the moon, but the moon itself seems to have no effect. A solipsist would argue that the existence of the light and the gravitational pull do not "prove the moon."
- Within the field of neuroscience, studies of the brain suggest that humans are subject to many strong misperceptions of the generally held notion of the objective material world. Thus, the "world" of each human is that of the human, not necessarily one absolute material world shared and perceived by many.

Critiques

- Other people die, yet the solipsist is still alive, so the question of existence is somewhat irrelevant, as to a solipsist the person who dies is only a phantom of the mind. Also, it is safe to assume that throughout history, solipsists have died. Yet, solipsism still exists, suggesting that the idea exists outside the mind of the solipsist.
- Many people have special skills, such as mathematical ability and writing talent. If these things are created in the mind of the solipsist, why does the solipsist herself not possess them?
- Solipsism suggests that the solipsist creates the world in her mind. One argument suggests that if this were so, there would be no imperfections, such as pain, suffering, injury, and misfortune. The fact that these imperfections exist suggest that the world is actually transcendent of the brain.

Useless Trivia

- The poet Lord Tennyson loved "tavern food" including steak, cheese, and new potatoes.
- Best known for his Church of Scientology self-help books, L. Ron Hubbard is an Eagle Scout.
- Belgian writer Georges Joseph Christian Simenon was able to write 60 to 80 pages a day and published 450 novels and short stories during his career.
- Geoffrey Chaucer's father was kidnapped in 1324 by one of his aunts, who hoped he would force his son to marry her daughter. She was arrested and fined £250.

What's in a Phrase?

Diamond in the Rough

Meaning:
Someone who has good intentions and qualities but is associated with being deviant of the law or mainstream society.

Origin:
The first recorded usage of the phrase was in John Fletcher's *A Wife for a Month* in 1624. The phrase was used to describe a "rough" woman with the potential for becoming as valuable and cherished as a diamond.

Upper Crust

Meaning:
The more desirable or valuable part of something.

Origin:
During the 1500s, bread was divided according to social class and status. Workers were allotted the burnt bottom of the loaf, a family was given the middle, and guests were offered the top of the loaf, or the upper crust.

Under the Weather

Meaning:
Feeling ill or sickly.

Origin:
During rough seas and bad weather, passengers on seaborne ships often became seasick. Passengers would head below deck (or underneath the weather), both to escape the weather and toward a more stable part of the ship, near the keel.

Read Between the Lines

Meaning:
To understand what is implied, not literally stated.

Origin:
Long ago, in the days of hand-delivered messages, writers would write in substances that could only be revealed using a re-agent. For example, lemon juice is typically transparent but becomes discolored when heated. The author of a message would write a message in ink and then write the real message "between the lines" using an invisible substance.

To Do the Bush Thing

In 1992, President George H. W. Bush visited Japan for a state dinner with dignitaries including Japanese Prime Minister Kiichi Miyazawa. After turning white as a sheet and nearly sliding out of his seat in pain, he threw up in Miyazawa's lap. Ever since, the Japanese have honored Bush with the word *bushusuru*, which literally means "to do the Bush thing," or to vomit.

Bernoulli's Principle

Bernoulli's Principle is one that can help illustrate how pressure affects velocity of liquids. The principle, in part, explains the way water moves through a pipe, the way an airplane's wings rely on pressure, and the way airflow and pressure systems relate to one another. In simple terms, the principle states that when velocity of a fluid is increased, the pressure the fluid releases is decreased.

The principle comes from Bernoulli's equation, which shows that the sum of energy of fluid flowing on an enclosed path, or streamline, is the same at any point on the path. Consider water moving through a pipe: If the diameter of the pipe decreases, the speed of the water flow must increase, and vice versa.

Bernoulli's Principle only applies to incompressible flow, such as liquids, which have constant densities and are unaffected by pressure. This is untrue of gases. Bernoulli used liquids in all of his experiments, and therefore his equation can only be applied to incompressible flow with constant density.

Bernoulli's Equation

$$p + \frac{1}{2} pV2 + pgh = \text{constant}$$

where p is the pressure, p is the density, V is the velocity, h is elevation, and g is the gravitational acceleration

Many textbooks falsely attribute the cause of an airplane's lift to Bernoulli's Principle. While the principle does lay the groundwork to understanding pressure and velocity, it does not explain the airflow above and below the wings of a plane. Newton's Third Law of Motion is actually a better explanation of airplane lift, since Bernoulli's Principle is only an explanation of liquids. Newton's Third Law of Motion holds that in order for an airplane to lift, the wing must push air down.

Sociopolitical Systems

Marxism

Marxism is the ideology born from following the theories of Karl Marx and Friedrich Engels, two political scientists of the 19th century. The main ideas of Marxism involve the production of society and the class systems. Marxism argues that the labor force drives the means of production and ought to control it.

Communism

The final stage of Marxism, communism seeks to create a classless society based on common ownership of a state's means of production. It is said to date back to hunter-gatherer times, when food was gathered and divided among a society and when work was distributed according to ability and efficiency.

Socialism

Socialism, a transitional system between communism and capitalism, encompasses all doctrines or political movements that argue for a socioeconomic system in which all wealth and property is controlled by the community in an equal distribution. Socialists strive to increase equality and community cooperation and raise the welfare of the state as a whole.

Capitalism

Capitalism refers to the common economic system of private ownership and a competitive market economy. Common practice in capitalism is for individuals and groups to act as corporations or legal entities that produce, sell, and trade goods. Corporations and persons abide by a system of pricing that is dictated by the market, instead of the state or central government. Since the disappearance of feudalism, capitalism has been prevalent in Western society, and the free market system has continued to shape politics and economics.

A Name to Drop: Dmitri Mendeleev

(Hint: Periodic Table Inventor)

Born in Tobolsk, Siberia, on February 8, 1834, Dmitri Mendeleev entered the Main Pedagogical Institute in St. Petersburg in 1850. Although he was sick for the last year of his undergraduate study, he received his diploma, still ranking number one in his class, in 1854. He then moved for a short time to the Crimean Peninsula to improve his health. He returned to St. Petersburg and received his master's degree in 1856 and a Ph.D. in 1866. He married twice and had six children.

- Between 1859 and 1861, he spent time studying in other countries. He observed the density of gases in Paris, and the workings of the spectroscope in Heidelberg.
- Mendeleev was considered one of the greatest teachers of his time. He became professor of chemistry at the St. Petersburg Technological Institute in 1863, and in 1867, he was named Professor of Chemistry at the University of St. Petersburg. In 1868, he wrote what was called the definitive two-volume textbook of the time—Principles of Chemistry.
- He often spent time with people of the working class, drinking tea and discussing his research as it related to agriculture or other areas of interest to them. His dedication to chemistry, and his popularity with colleagues, students, and the general public, transformed St. Petersburg into an internationally recognized center for chemistry research.

Mendeleev is most remembered for classifying chemical elements into the Periodic Table, which he called the Periodic System. Unknown to him at the time, John Newlands, Lothar Meyer, and other scientists were attempting to do the same thing. In the end, Mendeleev's table included more elements and was more practical to use.

- As the story goes, Mendeleev wrote the properties of the 63 known elements on pieces of paper and tried organizing them in various ways. He suddenly realized that, by arranging the elements in order of increasing atomic weight, certain types of elements regularly occurred. He left space for new elements, three yet-to-be-discovered elements, and pointed out accepted atomic weights that were in error.
- The original table has been modified and corrected several times through the years. There are now more than 100 known elements.

Things to Know

- In 1893, as director of the Bureau of Weights and Measures, Mendeleev used his knowledge of molecular weights to conclude that, to be in perfect molecular balance, vodka should have one molecule of ethyl alcohol diluted with two molecules of water, or approximately 38 percent alcohol to 62 percent water. He established by Russian law that all vodka had to be produced at 40 percent alcohol by volume.
- Mendeleev investigated the composition of oil fields and helped establish the first oil refinery in Russia.
- A lunar crater and element 101, radioactive mendeleevium, are named in honor of Mendeleev.
- Dmitri Mendeleev died from influenza in 1907 in St. Petersburg, Russia.

Michelangelo di Lodovico Buonarroti Simoni

Michelangelo was born into an upper-class family in 15th-century Tuscany; however, because of his mother's ill health, he spent his first few years in a stonecutter's home. Although Michelangelo wanted to pursue art, his father sent him to study Latin with Francesco Galeota from Urbino. While at the school, Michelangelo befriended a student who was studying painting, and soon, he too was studying for his own artistic vocation.

- At age 13, Michelangelo moved to Florence and began an apprenticeship in the workshop of the painter Domenico Ghirlandaio. He then, in 1489, went on to study at the sculpture school in the Medici gardens, where he stayed for about three years. While there, Michelangelo studied human anatomy, with special permission to examine corpses.
- By age 16, Michelangelo had produced at least two relief sculptures—*The Battle of the Centaurs* and *The Madonna of the Steps*.
- Michelangelo traveled to Venice, Bologna, and then to Rome where he studied classical statues and ruins. He soon produced his first large-scale sculpture, *Bacchus*, one of his few non-Christian works.
- In 1497, Michelangelo was commissioned to sculpt the *Pieta*, which was to become one of his most famous works of art. Completed in 1500, the masterpiece is still in its original place in St. Peter's Basilica. After it was placed in St. Peter's, Michelangelo overheard an admirer say the sculpture was the work of another artist. That night, in a fit of anger, Michelangelo inscribed Mary's

sash, saying in Italian, *Michelangelo Buonarroti, Florentine, made this*. This is the only work that Michelangelo ever signed.

- The great statue of David was Michelangelo's next project. He worked on the sculpture from 1501 to 1504. He believed David to be a model of heroic courage, what he wanted to instill in his countrymen. He insisted that the statue be placed before Florence's Palazzo Vecchio to serve as a warning that "whoever governed Florence should govern justly and defend it bravely."
- In April 1508, Michelangelo was in Rome working on Pope Julius II's tomb when the pope requested that the artist turn his attention to painting the ceiling of the Sistine Chapel. Michelangelo tried to turn down the commission, but he accepted the challenge and was given freedom to choose which subjects he would paint. By the end of October 1512, he had painted over 300 figures on the ceiling of the Sistine Chapel.
- More than 20 years later, Michelangelo painted the fresco of the Last Judgment in the Sistine Chapel. He worked seven years on this massive project, which spans the entire wall behind the altar. It was completed to the sound of public outcry, as many people believed that the nude characters that made up the fresco were inappropriate for a church. The pope fended off the critics; however, after Michelangelo's death, he did agree to have the paintings touched up.

- Michelangelo said after a day's work painting the ceiling of the Sistine Chapel, he could not read a piece of paper without tilting his head back and holding it close to his eyes.
- Michelangelo was once described as *inventor delle porcherie* (inventor of obscenities).

Know Your Michelangelo

- When Florence was under siege, Michelangelo hid for a time in a small room underneath the church of San Lorenzo. Today, tourists can still see some of Michelangelo's sketches on the wall there.
- In addition to painting and sculpting, Michelangelo served as architect for many projects in Florence and Rome, including St. Peter's Basilica, the Palazzo Farnese, and the Sforza chapel.
- When he wasn't painting, sculpting, or designing, Michelangelo was writing poetry. He is considered one of the great Italian lyric poets of his time. In the mid-1530s, Michelangelo met poet Vittoria Colonna. He and the widow wrote sonnets to each other for many years.

Brain Teaser

How tall is Michelangelo's sculpture *David*?

Answer: 14.24 feet

Diamonds and Zircon (Are Forever)

Diamond is the hardest substance in nature. It is four times harder than corundum, the next hardest material. However, it will split to a jeweler's tap because it has four directions of cleavage.

Even experienced jewelers can be fooled by zircon. When clear, this naturally occurring mineral has similar luster and fire as a diamond. Zircons may also be brown or green. These are often heat treated to make beautiful blue and golden colors. Zircon makes a very attractive and affordable gemstone.

- Zircon is the birthstone for December.
- Zircon and cubic zirconia are not the same things. Cubic zirconia is a manmade gem.
- Zircon is a naturally occurring mineral found in Norway, Pakistan, Russia, Canada, and the United States.

The World's Largest Diamonds

The world's largest cut diamond weighs 545.67 carats. The Golden Jubilee was given to the king of Thailand in 1997 to mark the 50th anniversary of the King's coronation.

The world's largest uncut diamond, weighing 3,106 carats, was discovered in 1905. The stone was split into 11 gems, including the 530.2-carat Great Star of Africa.

Diamonds & Pencils – Common Ties

Diamond and graphite (pencil lead) share the same chemical composition. However, a diamond is transparent. Graphite is opaque.

Aluminum

The most abundant metal on the earth's crust, aluminum eluded scientists for decades. In 1825, Hans Christian Oersted was the first person to isolate aluminum. He heated aluminum chloride and an alloy of potassium. Oersted produced small amounts of aluminum, but it was more than 60 years before Charles Martin Hall patented an inexpensive way to produce the metal.

Hall passed an electric current through a nonmetallic conductor to separate the very conductive aluminum from aluminum oxide. He went on to establish, along with Alfred E. Hunt, the Pittsburgh Reduction Company, now known as ALCOA (Aluminum Company of America).

Modern Uses for Aluminum

Today aluminum is used for everything from beverage cans to beams for bridges. Here's just a brief list of specific objects made from aluminum:

- The Hayden Sphere in New York City's American Museum of Natural History
- The State Capitol Dome in Austin, Texas
- Jaguar XJ
- Cadillac Escalade
- Ford Expedition
- Range Rover
- Lincoln Town Car
- Hang gliders
- Bicycles
- Mopeds
- Canoes
- Golf carts

Aluminum or Aluminium: What's the Difference?

The mineral alum was used centuries ago as a medicine, as an astringent, and to facilitate dyeing fabric. In the 1700s, the name *alumine* was coined for the base element in alum. In the 1800s, the name alumium was coined for the metal and was later changed to aluminum. The term *aluminium* was adopted by the International Union of Pure and Applied Chemistry to match the "ium" endings of most elements. In 1925, the American Chemical Society reverted back to aluminum, which remains the accepted spelling in the United States today.

Building with Aluminum

In 1953, the first all-aluminum building was built in Pittsburgh, Pennsylvania. Constructed to house the ALCOA headquarters, the building is 30 stories tall and has exterior walls made of thin stamped aluminum panels.

ALCOA moved its corporate headquarters to Pittsburgh's North Shore in 1998, but the building still stands. Today it is home to 90 businesses and nonprofit organizations.

Aluminum Time Line

- 1808—Sir Humphry Davy (Britain) proved the existence of aluminum and named it.
- 1821—P. Berthier (France) discovered a material containing 52 percent aluminum oxide near the village of Les Baux in southern France. He called it bauxite, now known as the most common source of aluminum.
- 1825—Hans Christian Oersted of Denmark successfully produced minute quantities of aluminum.

- 1827—Friedrich Wöhler of Germany discovered a process for producing aluminum as a powder by reacting potassium with anhydrous aluminum chloride.
- 1854—Henri Sainte-Claire Deville (France) improved Wöhler's method to create the first commercial process. Although this process help to decrease the price of the metal, which was once more costly than gold and platinum, the price remained too high for widespread use.
- 1886—Paul Louis Toussaint Héroult of France and Charles Martin Hall of the US, simultaneously invented a process (now called the Hall-Héroult Process) that today is the basis for all aluminum production. They discovered that if they dissolved aluminum oxide (alumina) in a bath of molten cryolite and passed a powerful electric current through it, then molten aluminum would be deposited at the bottom of the bath.
- 1889—Karl Josef Bayer of Austria, the son of the founder of the Bayer chemical company, invented the Bayer Process for large-scale production of alumina from bauxite.

Brass Facts

Brass, made with a combination of zinc and copper, dates back to biblical days and even further. Archaeologists believe the early brass objects were likely made using a technique that roasted the zinc ore with the copper and the resultant zinc fumes absorbed into the melting copper.

According to the Bible, Tubal-cain, a seventh-generation descendant of Adam, was an instructor in brass and iron.

Sapphires

Rubies and sapphires are the same rock, except rubies have the trace amounts of chromium that make them red. All other colors of this mineral (corundum) are called sapphires. In the jewelry industry, sapphires other than blue are called fancies.

Kashmir sapphires are some of the most valuable sapphires available. They were discovered in 1880 after a landslide. Their velvety blue color with violet undertones is often referred to as Kashmir blue.

- Burmese sapphires, royal blue to deep cornflower blue, are also highly valued.
- The oldest sapphires are from Sri Lanka. These sapphires have a light to mid-blue color.
- Most blue sapphires come from Australia or Thailand.
- New seams of sapphires have been found in Madagascar, Tanzania, and Brazil.

The Largest Sapphire

The largest carved sapphire weighs 80,500 carats. The multicolored (blue, gold, gray) polished rock was displayed during the annual Unifour Parade of Gems at the Hickory Metro Convention, North Carolina, in 2005.

Friedrich Nietzsche

(It's pronounced Neech-uh, by the way...)

Born on October 15, 1844, near Leipzig, Prussia, Friedrich Nietzsche attended a prestigious boarding school, Schulpforta, near Naumburg from 1858 to 1864, where he worked on poems and musical compositions. From there he went on to study philology at the universities of Bonn and then Leipzig. At age 24, he became a professor of classical philology at the University of Basel, where he taught for ten years.

He spent only a few months serving as an orderly in the Franco-Prussian War, but while witnessing the horrific effects of battle, he contracted diphtheria and dysentery, possibly damaging his health permanently.

- As a philosopher, Nietzsche challenged the foundations of traditional morality and Christianity. He introduced the idea that "God is dead" and identified the difference between *master* and *slave* moralities—the former celebrating life, the latter resenting those who celebrate. This distinction is in essence "good and bad" vs. "good and evil."
- A frequently recurring theme in Nietzsche's work is the "will to power," which links to his concept of *Übermensch* (superman or superhuman). Nietzsche claimed the *Übermensch* as a goal that humanity can achieve for itself or that an individual can set for himself.

Nietzsche's Bestseller List

- In 1872, Nietzsche published his first book, *The Birth of Tragedy, Out of the Spirit of Music.* When his colleagues expressed little enthusiasm over the work, he said he felt isolated within the philological community.
- Beginning with *Human, All Too Human* in 1878, Nietzsche published one book (or major section of a book) each year for ten years. In 1888, he actually completed five books.
- *The Gay Science* was published in 1882, followed by *Thus Spoke Zarathustra,* which he wrote in only ten days. His writing and philosophy became even more unusual and less accepted. In 1885, he printed only 40 copies of the fourth part of *Zarathustra,* and gave a few out to close friends.
- He self-published *Beyond Good and Evil* and revised some of his earlier works. *Twilight of the Idols* and *The Antichrist* were both written in 1888. On his 44th birthday, he began the autobiography *Ecce Homo.*

The Downfall of Nietzsche

Until 1887 or 1888, Nietzsche had been a close friend with German composer Richard Wagner, but their friendship ended abruptly. It was also around this time when Nietzsche experienced a public breakdown, followed by his sending short letters, called "madness letters," to several of his friends. Realizing that he was in need of help, his friends took him to a psychiatric clinic in Basel. He remained in the care of his mother and then his sister, until his death.

Table Tennis

Table tennis began as an impromptu game. In the 1880s, British army officers in India and South Africa used cigar box lids to hit rounded corks back and forth across a stack of books set up in the middle of a table. However, it wasn't until 1900 that it was given a proper name—Ping Pong.

James Gibb, after visiting the US, returned home to England with a few hollow celluloid balls in his pocket. He and his friends in the UK started playing table tennis and someone commented on the neat sound the hollow balls made. Gibb, in his own eureka moment, said "ping ... pong." However, John Jacques registered the term Ping Pong as a trade name in 1901, before Gibb had the chance. He turned right around and sold the American rights to Parker Brothers, who started selling tons of the "new" Ping Pong game.

A year or so after Parker Brothers came out with their version of Ping Pong, E. C. Goode tried covering his paddle with textured rubber. The rubber caused the ball to spin when hit.

The first world championship Ping Pong tournament was held in London in 1927. Table tennis became an Olympic sport in 1988, with singles and doubles competition for both men and women.

Dinner Table Tennis

Maxwell Woosnam, an Olympic champion and Wimbledon winner who once captained the New England football team, once beat famous film director Charlie Chaplain in a notable game of table tennis. Woosman defeated Chaplain in the game using a butter knife instead of a racket.

Now Defunct Game Shows That Test Smarts

- *Weakest Link* – a game show that ran from 2001 to 2002. Based on a British show, it features a team of contestants who take turns answering general trivia questions. After a series of questions, the contenders vote off the "weakest link" from their team. This continues until two are left, resulting in a head-to-head competition.
- *Win Ben Stein's Money* – a game show that ran from 1997 to 2003. It features three contestants who compete in general trivia to win the grand prize of $5,000 from the show's host, Ben Stein. After defeating the first opposing contestant, contender's play against show host Ben Stein. The winner of this round advances to the final stage of the show: a face-off with Ben Stein himself.
- *Press Your Luck* – a game show broadcast from 1983 to 1986. Contestants collect "spins" by answering trivia questions and then used the spins on a game board full of cash and prizes. The person who builds the most in cash and prizes at the end of the game wins. With *Whammy! The All-New Press Your Luck,* the Game Show Network recreated the show from 2002 to 2003 with minor differences in play.
- *Beat the Geeks* – a comedy game show that aired from 2001 to 2002. Contestants face off in trivia matches against "geeks" who are well versed in music, movies, and television. There is also a fourth geek whose area of proficiency differs with each show but generally covers other "geeky" subjects, such as video games and super heroes. The object of the competition is to outsmart the geeks at their subjects of expertise.

A Name to Drop: Blaise Pascal

(Hint: Mathematician, Physicist, and Philosopher)

Before age 13, Blaise Pascal proved the 32nd proposition of Euclid and discovered an error in Descartes' "Geometry," which Descartes dismissed since the argument came from a child's mind. Pascal is noted as a child prodigy for this feat.

- Pascal invented one of the first mechanical calculators. It is called the Pascaline. When he was 16, his father asked him to total long lists of numbers. Thinking there had to be a better way, he began designing a calculating machine. He finally perfected the Pascaline in 1653, but people did not like it. Since it could do the work of six accountants, they believed it would create unemployment.
- In 1650, Pascal began focusing on religion instead of mathematics; however, in 1653 he did several experiments involving the pressure exerted by gases and liquids. Also, during this time, he invented the arithmetical triangle and created the calculus of probabilities.
- The *Pensées* [*Thoughts*] are considered Pascal's most influential religious writings. Found as numerous scraps of paper grouped in a tentative order after his death, the full, authentic text was not published until the 19th century.
- Pascal invented the barometer, the hydraulic press, and the syringe.

Reportedly, Pascal injured his health by incessant study, and at the time of his death he was physically worn out. (Today, scholars speculate that he suffered stomach cancer or tuberculosis.) Blaise Pascal died in Paris on August 19, 1662, at age 39.

A Name to Drop: Linus Carl Pauling

(Hint: Molecular Biologist)

Born in Portland, Oregon, on February 28, 1901, Linus Carl Pauling is known as the father of molecular biology. He taught quantitative analysis at State College before becoming a fellow at the California Institute of Technology (CalTech), where he received his Ph.D. in chemistry in 1925.

- He used theoretical physics—quantum theory and quantum mechanics—when studying chemical bonding. Teaming with other scientists, Pauling published the structures of hundreds of inorganic substances, including topaz and mica.
- He went on to make significant discoveries in genetic diseases, hematology, immunology, brain function and psychiatry, molecular evolution, nutritional therapy, diagnostic technology, statistical epidemiology, and biomedicine.
- In the mid-1930s, Pauling studied the molecular structure of biological compounds known as proteins. This interest expanded to the magnetic properties of hemoglobin and the roles of antigens and antibodies in the immune response. He began experimenting with the orientation of iron atoms and the structure of crystals, developing what is called the "Pauling Rules" that govern ionic or covalent bonding.
- In 1945, a physician describing sickle cell anemia sent Pauling to the drawing board—or lab bench. After three years of study, he identified the disease as molecular in origin, caused by a genetically transmitted abnormality

in the hemoglobin molecule. This new concept of molecular disease launched a search for similar disorders and has become the main focus of human genome research.

- Working with proteins, Pauling discovered that the polypeptide chain, formed from sequences of amino acids, would coil into a particular helical structure. He called this the alpha helix.

A Genius of All Trades

Pauling was also an inventor. During World War II, he invented a meter to monitor oxygen levels in submarines and airplanes. The device has proved invaluable in maintaining safe levels of oxygen for infants in incubators and for surgery patients under anesthesia.

The Nature of the Chemical Bond, called the most influential scientific book of the 20th century, was first published by Pauling in 1939. The book, in its third edition, is still in publication today. It has been translated into many languages.

Pauling was gifted in explaining the most complex scientific principles in understandable language. This endeared him to the general public. He wrote a variety of articles and books for the mainstream audience, including *Vitamin C and the Common Cold, Cancer and Vitamin C* (with Ewan Cameron, M.D.), and *How to Live Longer and Feel Better.* He was also a popular speaker for conferences.

Wise Words of Linus Pauling

- I have always liked working in some scientific direction that nobody else is working in.
- When an old and distinguished person speaks to you, listen to him carefully and with respect—but do not believe him. Never put your trust in anything but your own intellect.

Pauling's Awards

Pauling is the only person to receive two unshared Nobel Prizes. He was awarded the Nobel Prize for Chemistry in 1954, and in 1963, he received the Nobel Peace Prize for his role in the signing of the Partial Test Ban Treaty, calling for the reduction of aboveground nuclear testing, which was proven to cause risk to public health.

Among his other numerous awards is the American Chemical Society Award in Pure Chemistry; he became the first recipient of the award in 1931. President Harry Truman presented the Presidential Medal for Merit to Pauling in 1948, acknowledging the scientist's contributions in support of the military during World War II. He was named one of the 20 greatest scientists of all time by the British magazine New Scientist.

The Electric Car

Linus Pauling was instrumental in developing the first speed-controlled electric car. In the 1950s, Pauling proved that smog was a product of automobile emissions instead of chemical plant emissions, as was generally thought. He then teamed with engineers at Eureka Williams Company to build a battery-powered car. Unfortunately, battery power was not strong enough to compete with gasoline power.

Brain Teaser

What was the first speed-controlled electric car called?

Answer: Henney Kilowatt

William Shakespeare

Born in the 16th century in Stratford-on-Avon, William Shakespeare has been called the greatest playwright who ever lived. Although few specifics are known about William Shakespeare's early life, the use of language and depiction of human nature in his writings indicate that he was well educated. And there are records that show that his father was a leather craftsman, an alderman, and bailiff. We also know that he married Anne Hathaway and had three children.

He was around age 30 when he began acting and writing for this troupe. After only a couple of years in this position, he received a coat of arms and was able to buy a home in Stratford that he used in his retirement years.

Although written in the 16th century, Shakespeare's works are considered timeless, since the elements of his plays have the intrigue, humor, and complex characters that have resonated with readers even into the 21st century. Shakespeare's plays are almost continually performed in countries throughout the world.

- Shakespeare is reportedly the most quoted author of all time.
- Arguably, Shakespeare's works are the most criticized and critiqued works by any single author. Because his works do not maintain a consistency of philosophy, religion, or ideology, many critics have proposed that Shakespeare's works were a collaborative effort.
- Many writers are thought to have written under Shakespeare's name including Francis Bacon, John Donne, his wife, Anne Hathaway, James I, Ben Johnson, Christopher Marlow, Sir Walter Raleigh, Edmund Spenser, and Queen Elizabeth I.

Scholars have objected to Shakespeare's mix of comedy and tragedy. Some, John Dryden and Samuel Johnson in particular, accused Shakespeare of corrupting the language with false wit, puns, and ambiguity—the very properties that appeal to contemporary readers.

Shakespeare's Poetry

It is widely believed that Shakespeare wrote poetry before plays. He used several poems within his plays.

- *Love's Labour's Lost* contains three of his sonnets.
- *The Passionate Pilgrim*, a collection of 20 poems published in 1599, was attributed entirely to Shakespeare; however, after much scholarly study, only five of the poems are now said to have been written by Shakespeare.
- Shakespeare's sonnets were first published in 1609, and were probably written during the 1590s. The first 126 of the 154 sonnets speak to a man whose identity continues to intrigue scholars. And sonnets 127 to 152 hold an equal mystery as to the identity of the Dark Lady.

Shakespeare's Comedies

All's Well That Ends Well
As You Like It
The Comedy of Errors
Cymbeline
Love's Labour's Lost
Measure for Measure
The Merchant of Venice
The Merry Wives of Windsor
A Midsummer Night's Dream
Much Ado About Nothing
Pericles, Prince of Tyre
The Taming of the Shrew
The Tempest
Twelfth Night; or What You Will

The Two Gentlemen of Verona
The Two Novel Kinsmen
The Winter's Tale

Shakespeare's Tragedies
The Life of Timon of Athens
The Tragedy of Antony and Cleopatra
The Tragedy of Coriolanus
The Tragedy of Hamlet, Prince of Denmark
The Tragedy of Julius Caesar
The Tragedy of King Lear
The Tragedy of Macbeth
The Tragedy of Othello, the Moor of Venice
The Tragedy of Romeo and Juliet
The Tragedy of Titus Andronicus
The Tragedy of Troilus and Cressida

Know the Bard

- Shakespeare was part-owner of two theaters—the Globe and the Blackfriars.
- *The First Folio*, published in 1623, includes all the Shakespeare plays except *Pericles* and *The Two Noble Kinsmen*. In 1709, Nicholas Rowe produced the first edition of Shakespeare's works that included divisions for acts and scenes and notes for exits and entrances.
- John Fletcher is thought to be Shakespeare's coauthor for *The Two Nobel Kinsmen* and *King Henry VIII*.
- Thomas Thorpe published the first edition of Shakespeare's sonnets.

Shakespeare's Histories

The First part of King Henry IV
The Second part of King Henry IV
The Life of King Henry V
The First Part of King Henry VI
The Second Part of King Henry VI
The Third part of King Henry VI
The Famous History of the Life of King Henry VIII
The Life and Death of King John
The Tragedy of King Richard II
The Tragedy of King Richard III

Shakespeare's Poems

"A Lover's Complaint"
"Phoenix and the Turtle"
"The Rape of Lucrece"
"Venus and Adonis"
154 untitled sonnets

Brain Teaser

In which of Shakespeare's plays will you find the following quotations?

- "A horse! A horse! My kingdom for a horse!"
- "All the world's a stage and all the men and women merely players…"
- "If music be the food of love, play on."
- "How sharper than a serpent's tooth it is to have a thankless child."

Answer: *King Richard III*; *As You Like It*; *Twelfth Night*; *King Lear*

A Plot to Know: Paradise Lost

Almost everyone is familiar with the story of Adam and Eve, but John Milton tells the tale of the fall from paradise in such a unique way that the old story gains a fresh, if not slightly devilish, perspective. Milton wrote his 1667 epic poem in twelve books, giving the reader a panoramic sweep of heaven, hell, and the brief paradise in between. Surprisingly, some argue that the real hero of the book is the rebel with a (flawed) cause, Satan. Poet William Blake once said that Milton was "of the Devil's party without knowing it." Satan comes off as a Promethean hero battling against an unfair god, at least for the first half of the story where he begins as a fallen angel curious about God's latest creation. He calls a council of fellow fallen angels and they agree to send him on a fact finding mission. As we all know, he eventually tempts Eve to eat the forbidden fruit, but again, Milton takes a slightly radical approach. He portrays Eve as the more intelligent of the two humans. She deliberates and reasons and poor Adam just follows along. After the couple's expulsion from the garden, the angel, Michael, ends the story on a happy note as he assures the pair that the Son of God has already offered himself as a ransom to pay for their misdeeds.

Tourette Syndrome

There are many common misperceptions about Tourette syndrome, but the condition is far less rare than many people think. As is the case with many brain disorders, scientists have not pinpointed an exact cause of Tourette syndrome or located a specific Tourette's gene.

- It is estimated that 1 in 100 people has a mild form of Tourette syndrome.
- Scientists have found that the tics and symptoms of Tourette syndrome come from abnormalities in the thalamus, frontal cortex, and basal ganglia of the brain. Symptoms also come from neurotransmitter dysfunction between the nerve cells inside the brain.
- Tourette syndrome has a specific genetic origin and begins to occur around the age of six. Patients will display symptoms by age 18 if the condition is present. Boys are three or four times more likely to get Tourette syndrome than girls.

Famous People with Tourette Syndrome
Dan Aykroyd, actor
Mozart, composer
Samuel Johnson, 18th-century author
Mahmoud Abdul-Rauf, former basketball player
Jim Eisenreich, former baseball player

Tics can also be classified as simple or complex. A simple tic involves a sudden contraction of a very small number of muscles. A simple motor tic could be eye-blinking, and a simple verbal tic might be a repetitive clearing of the throat.

A complex tic is defined by coordinated patterns of many different muscle groups, such as a combination of shoulder jumping, twirling, and fist clenching. A complex verbal tic would involve a sudden expression of a group of words out of context, or inappropriate swearing.

Over time, a person with Tourette syndrome can experience a movement of tics downward through the body. Tics may begin around the face and neck but can often spread down to the legs and feet.

The Real Tourette's

Most people think of Tourette syndrome as a condition where a person repeatedly and uncontrollably blurts out profanities. In actuality, this symptom comes from the rarest form of Tourette's. The most common symptoms are known as tics. Some common tics include:

- eye blinking
- muscle contraction
- verbal tics
- shoulder shrugging
- clenching of fists

Tics are classified as motor or verbal. Motor tics are involuntary muscle movements, and vocal tics are involuntary verbal utterances.

Theory of Evolution

The theory of evolution, emphasized by Charles Darwin in his book *Origin of Species,* seeks to explain the biology of man by linking humans to a timeline of evolving primates. The theory describes the evolution of man as follows:

- 70 million years ago – First primates (micelike shrews)
- 40 million years ago – Monkeys
- 20 million years ago – Apes
- 8 million years ago – Gorillas
- 5 million years ago – Chimpanzees
- 4 million years ago – Hominids (bipeds that walked on two feet)
- 300,000 years ago – Homo erectus
- 100,000 years ago – Homo sapiens

Darwin explained that once humans evolved into hominids and walked upright on two feet, they began developing neurologically and became increasingly intelligent. He described the process as a system of natural selection, where the inherited traits of a population modify from one generation to the next based on survival and reproduction efficiency. Since before Darwin's *Origin of Species* was ever written, the idea of evolution as it relates to humans has been highly controversial, due to the scientific evidence behind it, as well as the theory's inherent conflict with religious beliefs.

Theory of Relativity

The theory of relativity, proposed by Albert Einstein, explains that the speed of light is constant and an absolute boundary of motion. It states that for any objects moving near the speed of light, movement will be slower and shorter in length from the point of view of an observer on Earth. For instance, an object moving at light speed in space would appear to be moving much slower from Earth.

What is the Space-Time Continuum?

From the theory of relativity, Einstein derived the "curved space-time continuum," which shows space and time as a two-dimensional surface into which massive objects can create impressions. This explained the idea of light bending around the sun, helped predict black holes, and allowed new discoveries to be made in the Big Bang Theory.

The concept of relativity was actually not introduced by Einstein, but his major contributions to the study earned him a Nobel Prize in 1921.

Atomic Theory

Atomic theory states that all matter is composed of units called atoms, and it explains why matter cannot be divided infinitely. The theory was born from studies in the field of stoichiometry, where chemists studied the particles of nature and named them atoms. At the turn of the 20th century, physicists determined that the atom was actually made up of various subatomic particles which could be separated.

The Atomic Bomb

The atomic bomb involves an explosion caused by nuclear reactions. The fusion or fission of atoms produces enough force to cause an explosion large enough for the demolition of an entire city, even in a small atomic bomb. In the history of the world, only two nuclear bombs have been detonated, both by the United States military. The first was dropped on the Japanese city Hiroshima, on August 6, 1945. The second came three days later and demolished the city of Nagasaki.

The Major Subatomic Parts of an Atom

- Protons – positively charged
- Neutrons – neutral charge
- Electrons – negative charge

Mind-Blowing Facts

- There are more atoms in one full bucket of water than there are full buckets of water in the entire Atlantic Ocean.
- Nearly 3,000 earthquakes shake the earth every single day.
- If Mt. Everest, the world's highest mountain, was moved to the bottom of the deepest part of the ocean floor, its peak would still be submerged more than a mile beneath the surface.
- Carbon monoxide, a well-known poison, is used in the chemical industry to purify many types of metals.
- About 70 percent of the earth's surface is water. By coincidence, 70 percent of the human body is also water.
- The star Sirius B has such a high density that a sugar cube of its size would weigh several hundred tons.
- A quantum computer, in a few days, could find the two prime numbers that create a 300-digit prime product. The same search would take the world's fastest supercomputer nearly 7,000 trillion years to complete.
- The speed of light, at 670 million mph, sounds very fast. But at this speed, a light ray would take about 26 billion years to cross the visible universe.
- The most common element in the universe is hydrogen, which makes up more than 90 percent of the universe and 70.68 percent of the solar system.
- Oxygen is thought to be the most common element in the earth's crust.
- The most common element in the earth's atmosphere is nitrogen.
- The least common element in the earth's atmosphere is the radioactive gas radon.

Walt Disney: American Screenwriter and Entrepreneur

Almost everyone knows the name Walt Disney from cartoons, movies, or the popular amusement parks around the world. Born in Chicago in 1901, Disney spent much of his youth in Missouri, where he learned to draw. While attending high school in the daytime, he took night classes at the Chicago Art Institute to perfect his drawing skills.

- In his early 20s, Disney struck out for California. He teamed with his brother, Roy, to form Disney Brothers Studio, later called Walt Disney Enterprises. Their first animation project was a silent cartoon called "The Alice Comedies," based on Alice in Wonderland.
- He debuted his most famous cartoon character—Mickey Mouse—in the silent cartoon *Plane Crazy* and then in the 1928 cartoon *Steamboat Willie*. This animated film was the first ever to combine sound with motion.
- When the Mickey Mouse Club organized in 1929, children got together every Saturday afternoon to watch cartoons and play games in local theaters across the nation. There were several million members who knew a secret handshake, special greeting, code of behavior, and club song.
- In the 1930s, Mickey's animated friends came along, including Minnie Mouse, Clarabelle Cow, Horace Horsecollar, Goofy, Pluto, Donald Duck, Peg-Leg Pete, and others.

> I only hope that we don't lose sight of one thing—that it was all started by a mouse.
> —Walt Disney

- Disney invented the multiplane camera in 1937 and changed the world of animation. This special camera increased the quality of cartoons and made full-length animated film possible. *Snow White and the Seven Dwarfs* was the first full-length animated film shot with the camera.
- Walt Disney was a decidedly patriotic man, and with the advent of World War II, he stopped nearly all commercial productions and concentrated on aiding the war effort by issuing training films, doing goodwill tours, and designing posters and armed forces insignia.
- For all of the cartoons through World War II, Disney himself served as the voice of Mickey. From 1946 to 1974, Jim Macdonald was Mickey's voice. Today, Mickey's voice is that of Wayne Allwine.

The Wonderful World of Disney

When Disney died in 1966, 240 million people had seen at least one Disney movie, 80 million had read a Disney book, 50 million had listened to a Disney record, 100 million had watched a weekly Disney television program, and 80 million children had watched a Disney educational film.

A Walt Disney Rap Sheet

- Disney first called his famous mouse Mortimer, but with encouragement from his wife the mouse's name was changed to Mickey.
- Disneyland opened in Anaheim, California, in 1955.
- Walt Disney World opened near Orlando, Florida, in 1971.
- Other Disney amusement parks are in Paris, Tokyo, and Hong Kong.

- Disney earned 22 Academy Awards, 8 Emmy Awards, an honorary degree from Harvard, and the Medal of Freedom, the United States' highest civilian award.
- Disney's Fantasia, starring Mickey as the sorcerer's apprentice, debuted in 1940. It used animation techniques and stereophonic sound that other studios could not match for a decade.
- In 1955, *The Mickey Mouse Club* became the most successful children's television show ever.

Disney Around the World

Disney comic books have been distributed in Australia, Austria, Belgium, Brazil, Bulgaria, the People's Republic of China, Colombia, Czech Republic, Denmark, Egypt, Estonia, Finland, France, Germany, Greece, Guyana, Hungary, Iceland, India, Indonesia, Israel, Italy, Latvia, Lithuania, Mexico, the Netherlands, Norway, Poland, Portugal, Romania, Russia, Saudi Arabia, Slovenia, Spain, Sweden, Thailand, Turkey, the United Kingdom, USA, and the former Yugoslavia.

All About Earth's Moon

- The moon was born shortly after the solar system began its formation, over 4.5 billion years ago, according to the most prominent astronomical theory. The moon is said to have been created when a rock as big as Mars hit Earth.
- The same side of the moon is always facing Earth. As Earth orbits the sun, the moon revolves around Earth always facing the planet. A long time ago, Earth's gravity slowed the rotation of the moon to the point that it became locked in orbit with Earth. Thus, we have never seen the "dark side of the moon."
- The cratered surface of the moon is the result of the constant bombardment by space rocks on the lunar surface. These craters have not eroded because there is not much geological activity on the moon, such as earthquakes or mountain formation.
- The moon is actually not round, but egg shaped. One of the small ends points directly toward Earth. The center of the moon's mass is not at the geometric center of the moon's body, causing its "eccentric" shape.
- Earth's moon is actually larger than the former planet Pluto. Some scientists actually argue that the moon is more like a planet and refer to it as a "double-planet." Pluto and its moon were also once referred to as a "double-planet."

MRI Machine

July 3, 1977, marked a monumental day in medical history. The first human being was placed inside an MRI machine and photographed. Five hours later, one fuzzy image was produced. The machine, labeled *Indomitable,* is now inside the Smithsonian Institute.

Today, an MRI machine can produce detailed pictures of the body in just seconds. The technology involved is complicated but is a giant breakthrough in the field of medicine.

How It Works

MRI stands for magnetic resonance imaging. The heart of the MRI system is a large magnet. A horizontal tube, called a bore, runs through the magnet and allows a patient to slide inside. The magnet is so large it is rated with a unit called a tesla. The magnet works by imposing a tremendous magnetic force while a patient is inside the bore. The magnet causes the nuclei of hydrogen atoms within the cells of the body to react in certain ways specific to their atomic properties. For example, the protons of hydrogen atoms have a spin of ½, and will align in a certain way to the magnetic field. Images are then captured of the cell activity, and the MRI is able to detect many things, including tumors, infections, torn ligaments, tendonitis, cysts, and strokes.

A Giant Magnet

Any metal objects in the room during the MRI can potentially be sucked inside the machine with great force, a great danger to the patient inside. The force of the magnet increases exponentially as objects move closer to the machine. Patients with metal inside their bodies cannot undergo an MRI, one of the downfalls of the technology, as many people are ineligible for testing.

The Functional MRI

An fMRI, or functional magnetic resonance imaging, involves using an MRI to measure haemodynamic (blood flow) response in the brain and spinal cord. The blood flow directly corresponds to neural activity and can give doctors and scientists a plethora of information about the way a brain is functioning.

Advantages

- The fMRI can noninvasively measure the neural activity of the brain without any risk of radiation damage.
- Measuring the blood flow inside the brain can potentially tell scientists more about cognitive activity.

Disadvantages

- The fMRI only measures neural activity but does not account for the influence of outside nonneural activity on the brain.
- Some theoretical models suggest that the signals given by the fMRI are too vague and unspecified to be considered scientific.

The New Lie Detector

The fMRI could possibly be used as lie-detecting technology that would be far more advanced than the long controversial polygraph. Since the fMRI can measure blood flow and neural activity in the brain, the testing can aid in the detection of lying, as researchers have pinpointed the areas of the brain that are used for recognition and creation. When patients are placed in the fMRI machine and asked certain questions, the imaging can detail which areas of the brain are called upon during the answering of questions, allowing researchers to determine whether the answers are being recalled or created.

What Is the Internet?

For starters, when most people think of the Internet, they think of the World Wide Web. It is important to note that while this is the newest and most popular part, it is not the extent of the Internet.

The Internet is based on many protocols, standards that control the way communication is held between two endpoints. Protocols allow computers all over the world to access common files and one another. The TCP/IP protocol allows computers to describe data to one another through a network.

- **TCP** stands for transmission control protocol. TCP takes information and breaks it down into tiny pieces to be sent in packets to another point or computer.
- **IP** stands for Internet protocol. The IP takes the packets sent by the TCP and directs them through computers to get to their appropriate destinations.
- In a sense, the TCP is the packager, and the IP the shipper.

Other Common Terms

- SMTP: simple mail transfer protocol – works with e-mail
- FTP: file transfer protocol – guides the uploading and downloading of file between computers
- ISP: an Internet service provider – allows the computer to connect with a server

A Name to Drop: William Gilbert

(Hint: Magnetic Theory)

Born in 16th-century England, William Gilbert received his M.D. from Cambridge University in 1569. He set up his medical practice in London and, in 1600, became president of the Royal College of Physicians. He served as physician to Queen Elizabeth I in the last few years of her reign and then to the succeeding monarch, King James I.

- Gilbert studied magnetism and the amber effect (what we call static). He based his theories of magnetism on the magnet's polarity in relationship to the polarity of Earth.
- He believed magnetism was the soul of Earth and that a perfectly spherical lodestone, when aligned with Earth's poles, would spin on its axis, just as Earth spins on its axis.
- This theory went against traditional belief that the earth was fixed at the center of the universe. Much of Galileo's claim for the earth revolving around the sun came from his study of Gilbert's theories.

Published in 1600, Gilbert's De Magnate, "On the Magnet," presented the time's leading theories on magnetism and electricity and was widely accepted throughout Europe.

A Name to Drop: Abu Musa Jabir ibn Hayyan

(Hint: The Father of Chemistry)

Born in AD 721 in Iran, Abu Musa Jabir iban Hayyan grew up in Yemen. As an adult he lived in Iran and practiced alchemy, as his father had.

- He is also known as Geber, the Latin version of his name.
- Many of the chemical elements, processes, and laboratory equipment used today were discovered or invented by Geber. He developed chemicals such as hydrochloric acid and aqua regia (one of the few substances that can dissolve gold). He is also credited with the discovery of citric acid, acetic acid, and tartaric acid.
- Geber applied his chemical knowledge to improving the way steel and other metals were made, preventing rust, and engraving gold. He developed the use of manganese dioxide in glassmaking, to counteract the green tinge produced by iron, a process that is still used today.
- In *Book of Stones,* he wrote intentionally to "baffle and lead into error everyone except those whom God loves and provides for." Because his works rarely made sense, the term gibberish is believed to have originally referred to his writings.
- As Iran was under political turmoil, in 803, Jabir was placed under house arrest where he remained for several years before his death.

A crater on the moon is named for Geber. The lunar impact crater is located in the rugged south-central highlands of the moon.

Déjà Vu Explained All Over Again

Studies show that 60 to 70 percent of humans admit to experiencing what they know to be déjà vu at least once in their life. With over 40 different theories of what déjà vu actually is, there is certainly no definitive answer at this time. Still, there is much to learn about this perplexing phenomenon.

What Is Déjà Vu?

Déjà vu is a French term meaning "already seen." In psychology, the term describes the feeling of thinking one has already experienced a new situation at some point in the past.

Often, references are made to déjà vu which actually *aren't* déjà vu. For instance, often people misuse the term to describe precognitive experiences, or a feeling that one knows what will happen next.

There are several types of déjà vu, as defined by researchers in the field of psychology:

Biological déjà vu: This classification describes patients who suffer from temporal lobe epilepsy and report a high frequency of déjà vu. Patients report strong feelings of déjà vu directly before having a seizure. Researchers suggest that this type of déjà vu could be significantly different from others, as patients seem to truly believe they've experienced the exact same situation before instead of having a short feeling that quickly disappears.

Associative déjà vu: The most common type, associative déjà vu, affects a large amount of normal, healthy people. It involves seeing, hearing, smelling, or experiencing in some way a thing that causes an association with the sensation of something experienced before. Researchers believe that this type of déjà vu could be based in the memory centers of the brain.

Chronic déjà vu: There are known cases of individuals who report enduring a chronic state of déjà vu. Within four specific cases in the United Kingdom, patients complained that they could not watch the news because they were already certain of what would be said. Others said they would not see a doctor because they felt they had already been and didn't see the benefit of repeating the experience. Researchers believe that this type of déjà vu could be a result of failure in the temporal lobe of the brain. They suggest that the activation of memory has actually, in essence, gotten "stuck," causing a person to create memories that are nonexistent.

There are many ways in which a déjà vu experience can manifest in the brain. Below are some examples and their literal meanings:

- **Déjà entendu**: already heard
- **Déjà éprouvé**: already experienced
- **Déjà pensé**: already thought
- **Déjà fait**: already done
- **Déjà connue**: already known
- **Déjà vécu**: already lived
- **Déjà trouvé**: already found

Nanotechnology: Smaller Is Better?

Nanotechnology is a broad term that encompasses the study of matter on the atomic and molecular level. The limits of nanotechnology are unknown, as it is a relatively new science.

The main principle of nanotechnology is that atoms are the building blocks of matter, and atoms can be rearranged to transform the substance and function of matter. For instance, the atoms in sand can be rearranged to create computer chips, and the atoms in coal can be rearranged to produce diamonds. All matter is a result of a particular formulation of atoms. There are two major approaches to nanotechnology:

- Bottom-up approach: materials are built from molecular components that are chemically assembled
- Top-down approach: objects are built from larger entities with no atomic control (in essence, substances come from a large entity of matter)

Nano-Fundamentals

- A nanometer is one billionth of a meter. For reference, a DNA double-helix has a diameter of 2nm.
- Using the bottom-up approach, scientists hope to use small components of matter to construct complex assemblies. The sand-to-computer-chips assembly is an example.
- Using the top-down approach, researchers seek to create small devices from large bodies of matter to direct the construction. For example, scientists have used solid-state silicon methods to create features from microprocessors smaller than 100 nm.

Fencing

Evidence indicates that fencing has been around for at least 3,000 years. It began as a way for soldiers to practice for war and has developed into an organized sport, with lightweight rapiers being used instead of heavy swords.

The rapier was created during the 16th century. Not only were they lighter in weight, but they were also longer than the swords that had been used. With a rapier, opponents had to fight at a distance with quick, controlled lunges. They used shields in their other hands to defend their opponent's thrusts.

During the reign of Louis XIV in France, the shorter sword, called the court sword, came into use. It was lighter, stronger, and shorter than the rapier.

There are three kinds of modern fencing weapons. The foil is a special kind of court sword used for practice. The colichemarde, made for dueling, evolved into the modern épée. The third weapon, a saber, is an adaptation of the Turkish scimitar. Originally, the saber was made of very heavy, curved metal. The modern weapon is lightweight and straight and has one sharp edge.

Fencing came to America with the colonists. They were skilled at fencing in England and continued the sport in the New World. After the Civil War, many colleges and athletic clubs included fencing as a part of their sports programs. The Amateur Fencers League of America, now called the US Fencing Association, was established in 1891.

> An Egyptian temple that was built around 1190 BC has an illustration of a fencing match on its walls.

Golf

The origin of golf is often a subject for debate. The Chinese, Dutch, and Scots all claim to have invented it, but most people think it began in Scotland sometime around the 12th century.

Since its early beginnings, golf has been a favorite sport for players, but not always for people in authority.

- In 1452, King James II banned golf in Scotland because it kept his subjects from their archery practice. And in 1659, golf was banned from the streets of Albany, New York. There are several recorded incidents of clerics criticizing parishioners for playing golf on Sunday.
- There are almost 32,000 golf courses in the world. Half of them are in the US.
- The first golf course in the People's Republic of China opened in the mid-1980s, and by 2005, there were 200 courses there.

22 Holes

Golf didn't start out as 18 holes. In fact, all early golf courses had varying numbers of holes. At some courses, a player could sink 5 holes. At the Musselburgh Old Course, you could play 7 holes, and in 1832, you could play an extra 8th hole. Montose Links had 25 holes in 1866, and in 1764, at St. Andrews Old Course a player could get in a quick 22 holes. The course had 12 holes and 10 were played twice. St. Andrews, in 1857, was the first to have a complete 18-hole course, where a player could play 18 holes without having to go back to some of the holes twice.

Two Scottish Links

St. Andrews Links

The golf course at St. Andrews Links in Scotland is said to be one of the oldest golf courses in the world. Records show that the game was played there in the 15th century. Early golfers established a course at the links following the terrain of a narrow strip of land on the sea's edge. Today there are six public golf courses there.

Musselburgh Links

Musselburgh Links was common land granted to the Scots of Musselburgh in the 1700s for recreation and leisure purposes. Among other things, they played football and golf and practiced archery there. In 1816, a racetrack was built around the golf course, and people began racing horses here also.

- Built up near the same time period as the St. Andrews Links, Musselburgh Links is said to have been a favorite of Mary Queen of Scots.
- Today, one of the popular features of Musselburgh Links is the John Muir Way, named for the father of the conservation movement. He was born in Dunbar, East Lothian, in 1838. The route along the coastal edge of the links is said to be an excellent area for bird watching. Each year, tourists and citizens alike enjoy golfing, horse racing, and nature walks along this historic meadowland.

The First Female Golfer

Mary Queen of Scots was the first known female golfer. Nearly 300 years after she swung her first golf club, the first recorded competition for women golfers was held at the Links in 1811.

Feathery, Gutta, and Pneu-matic: Golf Balls with Funny Names

The very first golf ball was a round of goose or chicken feathers sewn in a leather pocket and was called a Feathery. Several pieces of leather were tightly stitched, then turned inside out. Feathers that had been boiled and softened were stuffed tightly into the leather casing, forming a hard ball. For the finishing touches, the ball was hammered into roundness and coated with several layers of a paintlike coating.

Guttas were invented in 1848 by Adam Paterson. He used gutta-percha, the evaporated milky juice from a tree found in Malaysia, to make a smooth round ball somewhat like plastic. When dry, the plant secretion is hard and not easily broken, but Paterson discovered that when heated, it becomes pliable enough to form into golf balls.

One of the problems golfers had with the Gutta balls wasn't really a problem after all. If used in warm weather, the guttas would become misshapen and nicked by the clubs. Golfers could and would boil the balls and smooth them out after a game, but some golfers played with nicked balls. And these players are the ones who discovered that the nicks caused the balls to have greater and more accurate distance. Soon players began hammering their Guttas to give them an even pattern and improve their play. Later, Gutta balls were pressed in iron molds that created patterns or markings on the ball. At this point, a variety of surface patterns were used.

The rubber ball came along in 1898. It was invented in the US by Coburn Haskell, a golfer, and Bertram Work, an employee of the B. F. Goodrich Company. The first rubber golf ball had thin rubber bands wound around a solid rubber core. Seven years later, in 1905, William Taylor of England gave us the first dimple-pattern for golf balls.

In the early 1900s, players tried using the Pneu-matic golf ball. This was a rubber ball filled with compressed air. The new ball increased the player's distance, but if the weather was warm, the balls exploded—sometimes in the player's pocket.

In 1921, standards for golf balls' weight and size came from the R&A and the USGA. Today's golf balls are made from space-age plastics, silicone, and improved rubber.

Golf Has Come a Long Way, Baby!

Now, somewhere around 500 years after the first golf game was played, dedicated players can find a lost ball by using radio frequency identification technology (RFID), similar to the technology department stores use to take inventory. The US company Radar Golf has made a golf ball that contains a radio frequency ID tag. Using what the developers call Ball Positioning System (BPS) technology, golfers can point a handheld device in the direction of the lost ball, and when the ball is detected, the device will emit a beep. Indeed, golf has come a long way since the Feathery.

A Name to Drop: Ivan Petrovich Pavlov

(Hint: Russian Physiologist)

Born on September 14, 1849, in Ryazan, Russia, Ivan Petrovich Pavlov attended the church school and later seminary school there. He soon realized his interest in science, and in 1875, Pavlov entered the Academy of Medical Surgery.

- Pavlov studied the physiology of the pancreatic nerves and then the nervous system of the heart. He won gold medals for his work in both studies.
- He married Seraphima (Sara) Vasilievna Karchevskaya in 1881; they had five children.
- In 1890, Pavlov accepted the position of director of the Department of Physiology at the Institute of Experimental Medicine, a position he would hold for 45 years. Under his direction, the institute became one of the most important centers of physiological research.
- He also served as professor of pharmacology at the Military Medical Academy.

Pavlov's Theory of Conditioning

Pavlov spent much of his career studying the digestive system in mammals. However, his study of conditioned reflexes and behavior is what he is most remembered for. Noting the reflex regulation of the digestive system compelled him to study conditioned reflexes more closely. The discovery of the phenomenon that he called "psychic secretion" enabled researchers to study all psychic activity objectively, instead of resorting to the customary subjective methods.

Pavlov's work with salivating dogs came about simply by observation. He noticed when dogs in the lab encountered food, they began to salivate, but they also drooled when no food was in sight. Being a good scientist, Pavlov had to know why. After a few experiments and a little observation, he realized that the dogs were reacting to lab coats. The person who fed the dogs always wore a lab coat. The dogs reacted to the lab coat just as they did to food.

This observation led to a series of experiments in conditioned reflex. He discovered that animals typically associate stimuli relevant to survival. What is now called Pavlovian training has been used to treat people with phobias and to encourage consumers to purchase particular brand-name items.

Charles J. Pedersen

DuPont chemist Charles Pedersen was conducting experiments with complexes of vanadyl ion (VO) and multidentate phenolic ethers. As he looked at the crystals that resulted in the "brownish goo," he discovered a new class of chemical compounds that he called "crown" ethers.

Pedersen retired from DuPont in 1969, but his initial discovery led the way to establishing the field of research that enables the building of structures at the molecular level, or nanotechnology.

The Nobel Prize for chemistry was awarded to Pederson in 1987.

The America's Cup: Yachting

Perhaps the most fought-after sports title afloat today, the America's Cup had its beginnings in 1851 when Captain W. H. Brown accepted the challenge put forth by Queen Victoria three years earlier. In 1848, she had created the One Hundred Guinea Cup yacht race open to all nations. The trophy was 134 ounces of solid silver and 27 inches tall.

Brown and the *America* made history and deemed US yachters as serious competitors. The wooden schooner, which had been commissioned by John Cox Stevens and several other members of the New York Yacht Club at the time, went bow to stern with 16 British ships to bring home the silver cup.

As the story goes, when Brown passed the Royal Yacht, putting the *America* in first place, Queen Victoria asked who was in second place. The infamous reply, "Your Majesty, there is no second," has since served as a symbol of the New World's significance as a separate and independent country.

Stephens and the other men who owned the *America* donated the silver cup to the New York Yacht Club, stating that the trophy was to be "a perpetual challenge cup for friendly competition between nations." The trophy was named America's Cup in honor of the sailboat *America*.

The US kept the cup for 132 years, defeating every opponent until 1983, when the season was right for Australia to seize the cup. This record remains the longest continuous winning streak in sports history. Since then, the cup has been awarded to New Zealand and Europe.

The first distress call, the one used by the *Titanic*, was CQD. CQ means "a message is coming," and D means "distress" or "danger."

What happened to the *America*?

From its proudest moment in 1851 until 1860, the *America* had several owners. Both the Confederate States of America and the Union Army used it as a blockade-runner in the Civil War. After the war, the ship was used for training at the US Naval Academy and was again entered in the America's Cup race (by the Navy) in 1870. This time, she finished fourth. In 1873, the *America* went into private ownership. It was used for casual sailing and occasionally for racing, until it fell into disrepair and ultimately was destroyed in 1945.

Six Degrees of Presidential Separation

- George Washington was James Madison's half cousin twice removed, Queen Elizabeth II's second cousin seven times removed, Robert E. Lee's third cousin twice removed, and Winston Churchill's very distant cousin.
- James K. Polk was a great-grandnephew of John Knox, the founder of the Scottish Presbyterian Church.
- Theodore Roosevelt was Martin Van Buren's third cousin twice removed.
- Grover Cleveland was Ulysses S. Grant's sixth cousin once removed.
- Franklin D. Roosevelt was related to Winston Churchill and to his own wife, Eleanor (a second cousin). He was also related by either blood or marriage to eleven other presidents: John Adams, John Quincy Adams, Ulysses S. Grant, William Henry Harrison, Benjamin Harrison, James Madison, Theodore Roosevelt, William Taft, Zachary Taylor, Martin Van Buren, and George Washington.
- George W. Bush is distantly related to Benedict Arnold and Marilyn Monroe. He is also Franklin Pierce's fifth cousin four times removed, Theodore Roosevelt's seventh cousin three times removed, and Abraham Lincoln's seventh cousin four times removed.

Antibiotics

An antibiotic is a selective poison that targets bacteria, fungi, and protozoans in the body. As a chemotherapeutic agent, it works to block functions of particular cells of microorganisms to inhibit growth.

- Antibiotics from microbes have few side effects on mammals and are able to target and kill microorganisms without harming other parts of the body.
- The first recorded use of antibiotics was in ancient China more than 2,500 years ago.
- Antibiotics work to destroy bacteria but do not affect viruses. Viruses are not living, and therefore antibiotics cannot impede their spread.
- A virus is simply a piece of DNA that reproduces in the body, therefore spreading. It is not alive and cannot be combated using an antibiotic.
- Modern antibiotic therapy began with the development of Salvarsan in 1909. Invented by Paul Ehrlich, the drug provided the first hope for the treatment of syphilis. The drug, no longer in use, introduced antibiotics as potential cures for many other diseases.
- With the reintroduction of penicillin in 1929, antibiotic research began to take off. Today, many once-fatal bacterial infections can be treated quickly and easily with antibiotics.

All About Drugs

- In 1899 German chemist Felix Hoffman created aspirin by modifying salicylic acid from the bark of a willow tree.
- The first drug ever to be marketed in tablet form was Bayer aspirin in the year 1900.
- Federal spending on the war on drugs increased from $1.65 billion in 1982 to $17.7 billion in 1999. Regardlessly, a 1999 study showed that more than half of all students in the United States had tried an illegal drug before graduating from high school.
- In 1998, an American Medical Association study showed that adverse reactions to drugs are estimated to cause over 100,000 deaths per year in the United States.
- According to the National Institute of Mental Health, three to five percent of the general population of the United States suffers from ADHD. Methylphenidate, the drug commonly known as Ritalin, treats the disorder by stimulating the central nervous system and producing a calming effect.
- "Soldier's disease" is a term used for morphine addiction. It is estimated that the American Civil War produced over 400,000 morphine addicts.
- The drug quinine, used to treat malaria, is created from the bark of the Andean cinchona tree.
- The first heart medicine ever discovered came from an English garden in 1799. Physician John Ferrier discovered the positive effects of dried leaves of the foxglove plant on the heart. The plant is known as digitalis and is still used to slow the pulse and increase blood flow.
- Found in Madagascar, the rosy periwinkle plant is used as a treatment for leukemia.

Mind-Blowing Approximations

- An average penguin swims at approximately 15 mph.
- A dog can make approximately 100 different facial expressions.
- A baby cannot produce tears until it is approximately six to eight weeks of age.
- When a human reaches the age of 35, he or she begins to lose approximately 7,000 brain cells per day. The brain cells cannot be regenerated.
- Approximately 2,000 workers died building the Panama Canal, and close to 20,000 contracted yellow fever and malaria.
- The human eyeball weighs approximately 28 grams.
- There are approximately 2,700 species of mosquitoes in the world.
- Approximately 45 billion fat cells exist in the average human body.
- The Empire State Building, located in New York City, weighs an estimated 365,000 tons.
- There are close to 250,000 sweat glands in average human feet.
- Nearly 125 people in the United States die each year from anaphylaxis to foods every year.
- There are approximately 250 billion stars in our galaxy.
- Approximately 65 percent of students have tried cigarettes by the time they are in 12th grade.
- An average cup of coffee contains over 1,000 chemical components, none of which can be distinguished from one another by taste.

Uncommon Facts About the Human Body

- A human sneeze can exceed the speed of 100 mph.
- An average human being loses between 40 and 100 strands of hair every day.
- Human babies are born with 300 bones, yet by adulthood humans have only 206 bones in their bodies.
- By the age of 60, most humans have lost one half of their taste buds.
- Every human being once spent nearly one half-hour as a single cell.
- The small intestine, if removed from the body, would stretch out to a length of 22 feet.
- The average human sheds 600,000 particles of skin every hour. This adds up to nearly one and a half pounds per year. At that rate, by the age of 70, most humans will have lost 105 pounds of skin.
- The average woman speaks approximately 7,000 words per day, while the average man speaks just over 2,000.
- The ashes of an average cremated human body weigh approximately nine pounds.
- An average human pregnancy lasts about 270 days, counting from conception to birth.
- The left human lung is smaller than the right, in order to make room for the heart.
- The largest cell inside the human body is the ovum, the female reproductive cell. The smallest is the male sperm.
- A human body comprises over 600 muscles, which make up for 40 percent of body weight.

- The average human life expectancy is 77.8 years, or 2,455,128,440 seconds.
- In the year 1900, the average age of death was 47.
- Approximately 10 percent of the world's population is left-handed.
- Accounting for all uses of water, including drinking and washing, humans use an average of 176 gallons of water per day.

In the average human makeup, there is:

- Enough iron to construct a three-inch nail
- Enough sulfur to kill every flea on the average dog
- Enough carbon to create 900 pencils
- Enough fat to construct seven bars of soap
- Enough water to fill a ten-gallon tank

Useless Trivia

While in college in 1940, Ronald Reagan was voted "Most Nearly Perfect Male Figure" by his classmates at the University of California. His prize? The opportunity to pose nude for university art students learning how to sculpt the human body.

What Is Schizophrenia?

Schizophrenia is a brain disorder that affects about one percent of the world population over the age of 18. Symptoms usually develop in the late teens and early 20s, and can include disordered thinking, disordered movement, hallucinations, delusions, cognitive deficits, and social withdrawal.

Despite popular belief, schizophrenia is not a condition classified by split personalities or the Jekyll-and-Hyde effect. It simply means that all human attributes that contribute to a personality, such as expression, feelings, perception, and logic, have become separated.

The word *schizophrenia* was coined by Swedish psychiatrist Eugene Bleaker in 1911 to describe a condition where mental processes were disconnected. The term translates literally to "a split mind."

Famous Schizophrenics:

- John Nash: Nobel Prize-winning mathematician
- Lionel Aldridge: Football player and Super Bowl champion
- Peter Green: Guitarist for Fleetwood Mac
- Tom Harrell: Notable jazz musician
- Mary Todd Lincoln: Wife of Abraham Lincoln

Factitious Disorders

Factitious Disorders encompass a group of mental disorders defined by a patient's behavior of deliberately creating or exaggerating symptoms of a physical or mental illness. Some patients with factitious disorders will go as far as to undergo risky operations or tests in the search for the sympathy and attention that an ill person might receive. There are two classifications of factitious disorders.

Factitious Disorder with Mostly Psychological Symptoms

Consistent with the name, sufferers of this condition mostly manifest the disorder through mimicking a mental illness such as schizophrenia. They may make sudden absurd statements, appear confused or incoherent, report hallucinations and voices, or impersonate other actions of a true mentally ill patient. One example, Ganser syndrome, was first detected in prisoners and is often referred to as "prison psychosis." It is defined by short episodes of bizarre behavior shown by people with serious mental deficits.

Factitious Disorder with Mostly Physical Symptoms

People suffering from this disorder mimic the symptoms of physical illnesses such as stomach pain, fever, and chest pain. The disorder is also referred to as Munchausen syndrome, which is named after an 18th-century German officer whose fame came from his embellished stories of his life experiences.

Some Symptoms of Factitious Disorders

- Inconsistent and dramatic medical history
- Unclear symptoms that change once treatment is commenced
- Extensive knowledge of medical terminology
- Eagerness to undergo medical tests or observations
- Appearance of new symptoms after negative test results

Obtaining statistics on factitious disorders is difficult because of the inherent dishonesty associated with the condition. It is unknown how many people suffer from the illness, and treatment is often difficult. Psychiatrists attempt to modify patients' behaviors by limiting misuse of and access to medical resources. Although there are no medications to treat the disorder, behavioral therapy and family therapy have been found to assist in the treatment of factitious disorders.

Ludwig van Beethoven: The Unkempt Genius

During its brief reign over the pop charts in the 1990s, grunge rock celebrated the dirty hair and thrift-store dress of its major contributors. Critics of the time likened the style of the era to that of '70s rocker Neil Young, christening him the father of grunge. Musically he may have had more in common with the stars of the period, but the careless appearance of the musician dates back much farther to the time of German composer Ludwig van Beethoven. The composer of nine symphonies, Beethoven was singularly concentrating on music; cleanliness and clothes were of little importance:

- After becoming famous, he was arrested by a policeman who refused to believe that the "great Beethoven" would have such wild, sloppy hair and filthy clothes.
- Friends regularly replaced Beethoven's old rags with new clothes, and, according to legend, Beethoven never noticed.
- Beethoven regularly had to move, sometimes multiple times a year. Upon visiting him, Beethoven's landlords would find their property to be a complete mess, filled with rotting food and dirty laundry.

Beethoven also shared a rude moodiness with the grunge rockers, making it difficult to be around him:

- If people whispered during a performance, Beethoven would stop and leave abruptly.
- While eating in a restaurant, Beethoven became angry with the waiter and dumped a plate of food on the man's head.
- Beethoven once wrote a piece called "Praise to the Fat One," for an obese violinist.

Aphorisms

An aphorism expresses a general truth in a succinct sentence and is often sarcastic in nature. These often become overused, resulting in their becoming clichés, as is the case with Benjamin Franklin's aphorism, "A penny saved is a penny earned." The first writer to employ the term aphorism was the father of medicine, Hippocrates, in his *Aphorisms of Hippocrates*. In the text, Hippocrates provides a series of suggestions concerning the symptoms and diagnosis of disease and the art of medicine. Here are several illustrations of such wisdom:

- "Old men support fasting well: people of a ripe age less well: Young folk badly, and children less well than all the rest, particularly those of them who are very lively."
- "Those who are very fat by nature are more exposed to die suddenly than those who are thin."
- "When two illnesses arrive at the same time, the stronger silences the weaker."
- "Life is short, art is long, opportunity fugitive, experimenting dangerous, reasoning difficult: it is necessary not only to do oneself what is right, but also to be seconded by the patient, by those who attend him, by external circumstances."
- "Persons who are difficult to vomit, and are moderately fat, should be purged downward, avoiding the summer season."
- "Those things which require to be evacuated should be evacuated, wherever they most tend, by the proper outlets."
- "When the brain is attacked with sphacelus, the patients die in three days; or if they escape these, they recover."

Unusual Literary Terms

Anaphora (n) – the deliberate repetition of a word or phrase at the beginning of several successive verses, clauses, or paragraphs

Anthropomorphism (n) – the act of attributing human forms or qualities to entities that are not human

Bibliomancy (n) – a prediction based on a Bible verse or literary passage chosen at random

Cacophony (n) – harsh, discordant sounds

Ekphrastic (adj) – art where there are initially two imaginations at work, that of the original artist, and that of the respondent through his/her medium

Denotation (n) – the literal meaning of a word, the dictionary meaning

Euphony (n) – soothing pleasant sounds

Kenning (n) – a magic poetic phrase, a figure of speech, substituted for the usual name of a person or thing. Kennings work in much the same way as epithets and verbal formulae and were commonly inserted into Old English poetic lines.

Metonymy (n) – the substitution of a word for another word closely associated with it

Onomatopoeia (n) – a word that imitates the sound it represents

Portmanteau (n) – the combination of two or more words to create a new word

Stanza (n) – a unified group of lines in poetry

Synecdoche (n) – when one uses a part to represent the whole

Verisimilitude (n) – the appearance of truth; the quality of seeming to be true

A Plot to Know: Remembrance of Things Past

Writer Alain De Botton published a book called *How Proust Can Change Your Life,* which gives you some indication of the respect with which the author of *Remembrance of Things Past* is treated. This seven-volume meganovel is difficult to describe because so much of it is "in search of lost time." Proust relies heavily on memory and flashbacks to show how consciousness changes over the course of a lifetime. Volume 1, *Swann's Way,* recalls the narrator's childhood and his love for Swann's daughter, Gilberte, and for Odette. In *Within a Budding Grove* the narrator falls out of love with Gilberte and in love with Albertine. Volume 3, *The Guermantes Way,* finds the narrator climbing the social ladder. In *Cities of the Plain* he discovers that one of the upper crust, Baron Charlus, is gay. The homosexual theme doesn't stop there, however. As it turns out, the narrator learns that Albertine may be a lesbian. He was about to break up with her, but this discovery makes her suddenly cool again. By volume 5, *The Captive,* Albertine is living with the narrator, but she runs away amid various scandals. As one can tell from the title of the next volume, *The Sweet Cheat Gone,* Albertine dies. Gilberte has risen in the social ranks to become Mlle de Forcheville. In the final volume, *The Past Recaptured,* World War I wages as the narrator realizes that his fellow socialites are much less interesting than his own personal memories.

A Name to Drop: Plato

(Hint: Greek Philosopher)

The birth date of Plato is estimated at around 428 or 427 BC, and he was likely born in Athens, Greece. Plato was probably educated in grammar, music, and gymnastics by the best teachers of his time. At age 40, Plato established in Athens one of the earliest known organized schools in western civilization. The Academy was closed in 529, when Justinian I of Byzantium saw it as a threat to Christianity. Many intellectuals studied at the Academy, including Aristotle.

Although philosophers existed before Plato, some scholars call philosophy his invention because of the way in which he approached issues and influenced the world. As a matter of fact, his writing has influenced every era forward, even today. Few thinkers have come close to his understanding and ability. Aristotle, his student Aquinas, and Immanuel Kant are counted among those few.

Plato's works have influenced many contemporary thinkers, including Albert Einstein, Friedrich Nietzsche, Karl Popper, and Leo Strauss. Some agree with Plato's assertions, while others use his philosophy as a point of argument.

Although some scholars have tried to classify Plato as a historian, the time frame of his depictions are not consistent with known historical events. Therefore, he was probably not intending his dialogues to be used as historical accounts.

The trial of Socrates, the central, unifying event of Plato's dialogues, is an example. Historically, the charges against him were not crimes in fifth century Athens. Plato's dialogues present Socrates with a distinctive personality who has friends and enemies that appear with him from dialogue to dialogue. However, the Socrates character does not always have the same ideas from one dialogue to another.

Many scholars are intrigued with Plato's analogies in the

dialogues. He compares the philosopher to the medical doctor, the body to a prison for the soul, and the brain to a birdcage with pieces of knowledge fluttering about in it, in the manner of doves and pigeons.

Plato was not the only author to write about Socrates. Aristophanes employed him as one of the principal characters in the comedy *Clouds*, and Xenophon, a historian and military leader, wrote an account of Socrates' trial and other works in which Socrates appears as a principal speaker.

Plato's writing is often compared with the work of his most famous student, Aristotle; however, the student overshadowed the teacher and Aristotle became "the Philosopher."

The Three Periods of Dialogues

Scholars have attempted for years to determine the order in which Plato wrote his dialogues. Currently, the dialogues are grouped into three periods with a few considered transitional works.

Early dialogues

Called the Socratic dialogues, each of these dialogues is considered indirect teachings. Most of them employ Socrates' discussing a subject, such as friendship, piety, and so forth, with another person. Through a series of questions he explains the topic to his opponent. This period also includes several dialogues related to the trial and execution of Socrates.

Apology
Crito
Charmides
Laches
Lysis
Euthyphro
Menexenus
Hippias Major

Hippias Minor
Ion

Transitional dialogues

Gorgias
Protagoras
Meno

Middle dialogues

In the middle dialogues,Plato's own views appear and he allows Socrates to answer some of his own questions. Some of the topics in this period include immortality, justice, truth, and beauty.

Euthydemus
Cratylus
Phaedo
Phaedrus
Symposium
Republic
Theaetetus
Parmenides

Late dialogues

The late dialogues reveal Plato's mature thought on most of the issues that he dealt with in his earlier writing. Although these later works are difficult and challenging, they are more logical than his earlier works.

Sophist
Statesman
Philebus
Timaeus
Critias
Laws

Famous Firsts, Part II

- Colin Pitchfork of Narborough, Leicestershire, England, became the first person to be convicted because of evidence provided by DNA fingerprinting.
- Marie Curie became the only person to ever win two Nobel Prizes when she received a prize for chemistry in 1911. Her first prize was won in 1903 for physics.
- The first black hole thought to be discovered was reported in 1970. Cygnus X-1, is about 7,000 light-years from Earth.
- The first female Pulitzer prize winners came in the 20th century:
- 1921 – Edith Wharton – Fiction (*The Age of Innocence*)
- 1923 – Edna St. Vincent Millay – Poetry (*The Ballad of the Harp-Weaver*)
- 1983 – Ellen Taaffe Zwilich – Music
- In 1951, Florence Chadwick became the first woman to swim across the English Channel in each direction.
- George Jorgenson was the first person in the world to receive a sex-change operation in 1952.
- In 1953, Elizabeth II was the first monarch to have her coronation televised.
- In 1957, a dog named Laika aboard the Soviet satellite Sputnik 2 became the first living creature to ever orbit Earth.
- In 1998, Carlos Santana became the first Latino inducted into the Rock and Roll Hall of Fame.
- Eileen Collins went to space in 1999, becoming the first woman astronaut ever to command a space shuttle mission.
- On October 20, 1999, Abdurrahman Wahid became the first elected president of Indonesia.

- When she was elected to the Senate in the year 2000, Hillary Rodham Clinton became the first First Lady to be elected to a national office.
- Steve Fossett became the first balloonist to make a solo flight around the world, landing in Australia on July 4, 2002.
- Established in 1751 by Benjamin Franklin and Dr. Thomas Bond, the first hospital in the United States was Pennsylvania Hospital.
- Charles Curtis was the first American Indian to become a United States senator in 1907. He represented Kansas until resigning in 1929 to serve as Herbert Hoover's vice president.
- The first handheld electronic calculator was invented in 1967 by Jack Kilby.

Useless Trivia

Infatuation may be one form of flattery, but when it comes to obsessed readers, this tale of super-literate enthusiasts takes the cake. Giddy about their chance to see their names in print, 19 lucky readers paid to become part of a permanent piece of literary history. The bidding was a fundraiser for the First Amendment Project, a nonprofit group that protects freedom of information and self-expression. Participants pulled out their checkbooks in hopes of being named after a person or place in upcoming works by authors Stephen King, John Grisham, and Lemony Snicket. Super-fan Pam Anderson of Fort Lauderdale, Florida, shelled out a whopping $25,100 so her brother, Ray Huizenga, could find his name in Stephen King's *Cell*. However, the "honor" was not guaranteed to be flattering—*Cell* is about a trouble-making mob of zombies. Only John Grisham promised his winning bidder would be cast as a "good guy."

A Name to Drop: Sir Karl Popper

(Hint: Critical Rationalism)

Born in Vienna in 1902, Karl Popper attended the University of Vienna, where he received a Ph.D. in philosophy in 1928 and later taught secondary school. His first book, *Logik der Forschung,* was published in 1934 and was translated into English in 1959. Here he questioned some of the popular thought of the day and introduced his theory of falsifiability.

In 1937, Popper left Vienna to escape political oppression. He accepted a teaching position at Canterbury University College, New Zealand, lecturing in philosophy. He moved on to England in 1946 to become reader in logic and scientific method at the London School of Economics.

Popper was among the most influential philosophers of science in the 20th century. He called his philosophy *critical rationalism.* He believed that positive outcomes that result from experimental testing couldn't confirm a scientific theory. His insistence that a theory should be considered scientific only if it is falsifiable led him to question psychoanalysis, quantum mechanics, and other popular theories. However, he was a proponent of Albert Einstein's theories about the universe.

Popper received many honors, including being chosen as president of the Aristotelian Society, knighted in 1965, and elected as a fellow of the Royal Society in 1976. He also received a variety of awards, including the Lippincott Award from the American Political Science Association, the Sonning Prize, and the Grand Decoration of Honour in Gold from Austria.

Karl Popper died in 1994 at the age of 92.

Open Society

An idea first presented by Henri Bergson, an open society is based on political freedom and human rights. Karl Popper further defined this idea, saying an open society ensures that political leaders can be overthrown without the need for bloodshed; a closed society would call a bloody revolution or coup d'état to change the leaders. He believed that the ideas of individuality, criticism, and humanitarianism would be impossible to suppress in an open society once the people were aware of them. According to Popper, after experiencing an open society, it would be impossible to return to a closed society.

Alcohol, Tobacco, and Presidential Campaigns

Before smoking and drinking became today's health taboo, many candidates chose to win voters' hearts with tobacco and alcohol. Some passed out whiskey bottles. After Prohibition was repealed, FDR passed out shot glasses that read, "Happy Days Are Here Again." Tobacco-related campaign giveaways originated with free snuffboxes during early nineteenth-century elections. In the 1950s, Ike passed around cigarettes by the dozen, and in the 1960s, candidate Adlai Stevenson actually pasted his own face on a pack of cigarettes. In 1972, Nixon campaigned with bubblegum cigars.

Jane Addams

Born in Cedarville, Illinois, in 1860, Laura Jane Addams was the first female to win a Nobel Peace Prize. She grew up with the town's library in her home, and thus she was well read before attending Rockford Female Seminary.

While at the seminary, Addams developed her leadership skills and was named valedictorian of her class. After graduation, she traveled to Europe, where she became familiar with the idea of socialized housing, which eventually led her to found the US Settlement House Movement.

- In 1889, she and friend Ellen Gates Starr opened a social settlement, Hull House, in Chicago. Women, and a few men, came from across the nation to live and work at Hull House.
- Addams's efforts led to garbage collection, a kindergarten, and the first playground in Chicago. Hull House grew to include an art gallery, a public kitchen, a gym and swimming pool, a bookbindery and library, an employment bureau, and much more.
- In 1905 Addams was appointed to Chicago's Board of Education and subsequently became chairman of the School Management Committee.

Addams became a respected public philosopher and social leader. She drew the attention of the leading philosophers of the day, John Dewey, William James and George Herbert Mead. Throughout her lifetime, Addams authored or coauthored a dozen books and more than 500 articles for both scholarly and popular periodicals. A dynamic speaker, she traveled nationally and internationally to make presentations that supported her progressive values.

- She became the first woman president of the National Conference of Charities and Corrections in 1909.
- She led investigations on midwifery, narcotics consumption, milk supplies, and sanitary conditions.
- In 1910, she received the first honorary degree ever awarded to a woman by Yale University.
- She lectured at the University of Wisconsin and later published a book of her lectures, *Newer Ideals of Peace*.
- She spoke in 1913 at a ceremony commemorating the building of the Peace Palace at The Hague and, for the next two years, spoke out against America's involvement in World War I.
- In January 1915, she became chairman of the American Women's Peace Party and then president of the International Congress of Women.
- She later served as president of the Women's International League for Peace and Freedom until 1929, when she was named honorary president for the remainder of her life.
- After experiencing a heart attack in 1926, Addams's health continued to decline. She was admitted to a Baltimore hospital on the day, December 10, 1931, that the Nobel Peace Prize was being awarded to her. She died of cancer in 1935.

Addams' outspoken opposition to war caused her to be expelled from the Daughters of the American Revolution, which may have only served to increase her campaign. She began providing food to the women and children of the enemy nations.

One of the most recognized and admired figures in the United States, Addams was instrumental in the establishment of the National Association for the Advancement of Colored People, the American Civil Liberties Union, and the Women's International League for Peace and Freedom.

Begging the Question

In the field of logic, the term begging the question is used to describe a logical fallacy.

- It occurs when the conclusion of a particular argument is assumed within a premise of the argument. In other words, the argument relies on itself or portions of itself to, in essence, *prove* itself.
- The argument must rely on what it argues to be fact in order to be true.
- Closely related to the fallacy of *circular argument* or *circular reasoning,* the concept is thought to have been created by Aristotle in 350 BC, in his work *Prior Analytics.*

The term *begs the question* is quite often used incorrectly, typically when a person actually means to use the term *raises the question,* a similarly sounding but contextually different phrase.

An Example of Begging the Question

Jack: God must exist.
Jill: Why must God exist?
Jack: Because it says so in the Bible.
Jill: Why should the Bible be absolutely believed?
Jack: Because it was written by God.

In the above dialogue, Jack uses the assumption that God exists to validate his *proof* for God's existence: because God wrote the Bible. The proof of the argument relies on the original assumption made in the argument, making it fallacious.

Paradox

A paradox is a group of true statements that lead to a contradictory conclusion, or one that defies reason or intuition.

Mathematical Paradoxes

- Apportionment Paradox: Because of rounding, results of a particular representation might seem unreasonable or unintuitive.
- Population Paradox: A quick-growing state can lose votes to a slower-growing state.
- Arithmetic Paradox: Obviously false expressions can be "proved" by writing a large expression and dividing by another expression that equals to zero.
- Statistical Paradox: Due to correlation, a conclusion can be drawn between two occurrences, when in fact the two occurrences have little effect on one another. For instance, there is a strong positive correlation between eating ice cream and drowning. However, this is simply due to the fact that both eating ice cream and swimming are done during the warmer months of the year. The two actions actually have very little effect on one another.

Physical Paradoxes:

- Archimedes Paradox: It is possible for a large battleship to float in just a few liters of water.
- Mpemba Paradox: Hot water, under certain conditions, freezes faster than cold water even though it must pass through a lower temperature before freezing.
- Twin Paradox: If an identical twin travels to space, he or she will have aged less than the twin who remained on Earth.

A Name to Drop: Pythagoras

(Hint: Pythagorean Theorem)

It is generally believed that Pythagoras was born sometime around 580 BC, on the Greek Island of Samos. He is thought to have traveled extensively in his youth, perhaps visiting Egypt and Persia. As an adult, he settled in the city of Crotone in southern Italy and began teaching mathematics and other disciplines. His students were known as the Pythagoreans. They were mostly upper-middle class and politically active.

- Pythagoras was the first man to call himself a philosopher. He drew heavily on the theories of Plato, yet none of his writings ever survived, so little is known about his life.
- It is suggested that the Pythagorean Theorem contains more known proofs than any other theorem. The book *Pythagorean Proposition,* written by mathematician Elisha Scott Loomis, contains 367 proofs of just the one theorem.

Pythagorean Theorem

The square of the length of the hypotenuse of a right triangle equals the sum of the squares of the lengths of the other two sides

The equation can be expressed in many ways. One popular one is:

$a^2 + b^2 = c^2$

The theory states that if any two sides of a right triangle are known, the other side can be determined.

Fact: The number system we use today was invented in India. The scientist Aryabhatta invented the digit zero.

A Good Name to Know: Archimedes

Born in Sicily, in 287 BC, Archimedes studied in Egypt and Alexandria. In some of his writings, he tells about sharing his theories with friends in Alexandria. When he caught on that his friends were claiming his theories as their own, he sent them two false theories.

- Perhaps best known for his principle of the lever—"Give me where to stand, and I will move the earth"—Archimedes invented many things that were used as weapons of war for his government. He invented the compound pulley and hydraulic screw and gave mathematics numerous theorems.
- As the story goes, Archimedes began thinking about hydrostatics when he stepped into a bathtub and noted the displacement of the water. At this point, he is said to have exclaimed, "Eureka!"
- Archimedes' "Eureka" moment came with his discovery that a body immersed in fluid loses weight equal to the weight of the amount of fluid it displaces. Today, this is known as the Archimedes' principle and is found in his book titled *On Floating Bodies*. This work also contains his notes on other principles of hydrostatics relating to floating bodies of different shapes and different specific gravities.
- With his country involved in war and taken over by the enemy, Archimedes met his death when confronted by a Roman soldier. It is said that he was working on calculations and angered the soldier by not telling his name. His only words to the soldier—"Don't disturb my circles"—were for naught as the soldier slashed the famous mathematician with his sword, and the work of Archimedes was destroyed.

The Archimedes Screw

Archimedes is best known for his principle of the lever and for inventing the compound pulley. However, he also invented the hydraulic screw for raising water from a lower to higher level. First used to pump bilge water out of the holds of ships, today this tool continues to prove invaluable in many areas.

- A tiny Archimedes screw facilitates a pump system used to maintain a patient's blood circulation during coronary bypass surgery and other surgical procedures.
- Archimedes screws are used at Sea World in San Diego, California, to lift water for the Shipwreck Rapids water ride.
- Farmers use Archimedes screws to irrigate their fields.
- A wastewater treatment plant in Memphis, Tennessee, uses seven Archimedes screws to pump water from one area to another.

"Give me a lever long enough and a fulcrum on which to place it, and I shall move the world."
—Archimedes

A Name to Drop: Daniel Bernoulli

(Hint: The Fluid Equation)

Born in 1700 in the Netherlands, Daniel Bernoulli spent much of his youth in Switzerland. He learned about calculus from his father, who was a professor of mathematics first at Groningen University in the Netherlands and then at Basel University. Although his father pushed him to study medicine, Bernoulli was always more interested in mathematics.

English physician William Harvey's book *On the Movement of Heat and Blood in Animals* showed Bernoulli how the study of medicine and mathematics could be combined. After receiving his medical degree, Bernoulli sought a position in academics so that he could continue to study the way fluids move.

- At age 23, he won first prize in a competition at the French Academy of Sciences for his design of a ship's hourglass that would produce a reliable trickle of sand even in stormy weather.
- When he was 25, he was invited to become professor of mathematics at the Imperial Academy in St. Petersburg, Russia. There he took on assistant Leohnard Euler (who had been a student of Bernoulli's father), and together they developed a way to measure blood pressure by puncturing a patient's artery (it was another 170 years before the blood pressure cuff was invented).

Family Competition

In 1734, the French Academy of Sciences awarded Bernoulli and his father a joint prize. This led to his father's banning Bernoulli from his house because he could not admit that his son was an equal. Bernoulli published his work on fluids in *Hydrodynamica,* which reportedly his father heavily plagiarized for a work of his own. Saddened by his father's competition, Bernoulli spent the rest of his life working only in medicine and physiology. Daniel Bernoulli died in 1782, in Basel, Switzerland.

The Lincoln-Kennedy Coincidences

While some think the strange-but-true links between Abraham Lincoln and John F. Kennedy are incredible, others are skeptical. Freaky but historically true, is this timeline a twilight-zone trick or simply a coincidence? You be the judge.

- Lincoln was elected to Congress in 1846.
- Kennedy was elected to Congress in 1946.
- Lincoln was elected president in 1860.
- Kennedy was elected president in 1960.
- The names Lincoln and Kennedy both contain seven letters.
- Both lost their children while living in the White House.
- Both were shot with one bullet, in the head, on a Friday.
- Lincoln was shot in Ford Theatre.
- Kennedy was shot in a Ford Lincoln vehicle.
- Lincoln's secretary was named Kennedy.
- Kennedy's secretary was named Lincoln.
- Both men's successors were named Johnson. Andrew Johnson was born in 1808. Lyndon Johnson was born in 1908.
- John Wilkes Booth, who assassinated Lincoln, was born in 1839.
- Lee Harvey Oswald, who assassinated Kennedy, was born in 1939.
- Booth ran from the theater and was caught in a warehouse. Oswald ran from a warehouse and was caught in a theater.
- Both assassins were assassinated before their trials.

Profile of a Thinker: Viktor Schauberger Father of Implosion Technology

The forest was a fascination for young Viktor Schauberger. Born in Austria in 1885, Schauberger's family were foresters, so he grew up studying water flow and other natural phenomena related to cultivating trees.

In 1929, Schauberger began patenting inventions related to water engineering. He built a water turbine to produce hydroelectricity. His water ram pump had a spiral flow that he attributed to having learned about when visiting an Egyptian pyramid.

During World War II, the German government forced Schauberger to continue his research into vortex (implosion) technology in order to develop a better cooling system for German airplanes. His work during this time led to a flying saucer that he called the Repulsine in 1944.

Implosion

Implosion is the process of destroying objects by causing them to collapse on themselves. In fluid dynamics, Schauberger's area of expertise, implosion is used to describe the process when matter flows inward rather than outward, such as it does during explosion. When matter moves inward, it moves in a spiraling path known as a vortex. Schauberger's theories are highly controversial among scientists. Today, it is classified as a pseudoscience.

A Name to Drop: Enrico Fermi

(Hint: Nuclear Physicist)

Born in 1901 in Rome, Italy, Enrico Fermi was very close to his brother Giulio, so when his brother died at a young age, Enrico found solace in studying physics and mathematics. He made gyroscopes, measured the magnetic field of the earth, and studied science and mathematic books given to him by a friend of the family.

At age 17, he enrolled in Scuola Normale Superiore in Pisa. There he earned bachelor and doctoral degrees. In 1925, he began teaching at the Institute of Physics in Rome and there formed a notable team of scientists to help with his research. This team made important contributions to practical and theoretical aspects of physics, including Fermi-Dirac statistics, the theory of beta decay, and the discovery of slow neutrons.

Although Fermi was certainly able to complete the most complicated mathematical equations, he often opted for the simpler route in order to receive quicker results. He also kept meticulous notes on his research and referred to his earlier findings to help him solve new problems.

Fun Fermi Facts:

- Fermi's lecture notes, especially those for quantum mechanics, nuclear physics, and thermodynamics, were transcribed into books that are still in print.
- *Time* magazine listed Fermi among the top 20 scientists of the 20th century.
- The Fermilab particle accelerator and physics lab in Batavia, Illinois, is named after him.
- Fermi 1 & Fermi 2 nuclear power plants in Newport, Michigan, are named after him.

Fermi's Large Feats

Fermi won the Nobel Prize in physics in 1938, the same year he moved his family to the US and began working at New York's Columbia University. He then moved to the University of Chicago where he began research that led to the construction of the first nuclear reactor—Chicago Pile-1. This massive pile of graphite bricks and uranium fuel was constructed under the football stadium at the University of Chicago.

After World War II, Fermi served on the General Advisory Committee of the Atomic Energy Commission, which advised the commission on nuclear matters and policy. It was during this time that he wrote opposition to the development of a hydrogen bomb, stating moral and technical rationales.

In his later years, Fermi experimented with particle physics and concentrated on teaching at the University of Chicago. He died in 1954, at age 53.

Fermi's son Giulio worked with Nobel laureate Max Perutz on the structure of hemoglobin.

A Name to Drop: Louis Pasteur

(Hint: Germ Theory)

Louis Pasteur lived during a time when typhoid fever threatened the lives of many people. He actually lost three children to the illness, and many believe this was a motivator for his study of infectious disease and his work with vaccines.

His early research focused on the fermentation process of grapes and developing a way to kill the germs (microorganisms) that facilitate fermentation. Today, this method of processing fruit juices and milk is called pasteurization.

Throughout his career, Pasteur studied the diseases that affected silk worms, chickens, and cows, all of which centered on combating microorganisms.

One of Pasteur's most famous experiments was with soup. He used a variety of containers—some with filters, some without filters, and one with a long tube to inhibit dust particles—to prove that germs would not grow in the heated broth. Therefore, the living organisms that grew in such broths came from outside, as spores on dust, rather than spontaneously generating within the broth—the popular theory of the day.

Pasteur proved that the introduction of a weak form of bacteria could produce immunity to those bacteria. He called these diluted diseases vaccines. He produced the first effective vaccine for rabies.

He is also credited with discovering anaerobiosis, the fact that some microorganisms can develop and live without air or oxygen.

Because of his research and tenacity, doctors began to see the need for sterilizing instruments and providing a clean environment for treating patients.

Profile of a Thinker: George Washington Carver

George Washington Carver, the son of slaves, revolutionized the farming industry with his theory of crop rotation. He recommended that southern cotton farmers plant peanuts or peas every other year to replenish the nitrate that cotton depleted from the soil.

- When this innovative plan caused a surplus of peanuts, Carver began experimenting to discover practical uses for the legume. During his career, he developed 325 uses for the peanut, including cooking oil and printer's ink.
- He went on to discover that sweet potatoes and pecans also enriched depleted soils. From those crops, he developed synthetic rubber, material for paving highways, and several other uses.
- After earning bachelor's and master's degrees from Iowa Agricultural College (now Iowa State University), Carver moved to Tuskegee, Alabama, to work at Tuskegee Institute. He spent his career and life savings to establish a research institute at Tuskegee.

"Since new developments are the products of a creative mind, we must therefore stimulate and encourage that type of mind in every way possible."
—George Washington Carver

Sir Richard Arkwright Father of the Modern Industrial Factory System

Born in Great Britain in 1732, Richard Arkwright was largely self-taught. At an early age he became an apprentice barber and learned to make wigs. Armed with a secret method for dyeing hair, Arkwright traveled around the country purchasing human hair for use in the manufacture of wigs.

He soon left wig making and focused his attention on making a machine to spin yarn. By 1767, a machine was used for carding cotton, and the spinning jenny spun the carded cotton into yarn. Arkwright teamed with a clockmaker, John Kay, who had been working on a mechanical spinning machine of his own. Arkwright made improvements to Kay's spinner and was able to produce a stronger yarn and use less physical labor than the spinning jenny. His new water-powered carding machine, known as a water-frame, was patented in 1775.

Arkwright established factories in Derbyshire, Staffordshire, and Lancashire and in Scotland. He was knighted in 1786.

In 1792, Sir Richard Arkwright died in Great Britain.

Arkwright constructed a horse-driven spinning mill at Preston and eventually developed mills in which the whole process of yarn manufacture was accomplished by only one machine. He often hired whole families, with the women and children working in the factory to make yarn and the men working at home to weave the yarn into cloth. This division of labor greatly improved efficiency and increased profits. Arkwright was also the first to use James Watts's steam engine to power textile machinery. With this steam engine and the water-frame, he eventually developed the power loom.

Louis Braille

At age three, French-born Louis Braille lost his sight due to an accident. When he was ten, he went to study at the Paris school for the blind. While there he developed a desire to read and became determined to find a way for people like himself to have access to the written word.

- In 1821, Charles Barbier showed Braille night writing, a series of dots and spaces. Barbier invented the code to help soldiers communicate with each other in the dark. This prompted Braille to came up with a system of raised dots that could be read by touch. The Braille system has been adapted to almost every known language, from Albanian to Zulu.
- The Braille Institute was founded in 1919 as the Universal Braille Press to provide services to the blind. The institute produces more than 5 million Braille pages each year.

In 1945, the National Braille Association was established to provide continuing education for people who prepare Braille and to provide Braille materials to persons who are visually impaired.

Wilde's Wit

Oscar Wilde was both loved and hated during his years as an Irish novelist and playwright. He was also well known for his venomous wit. Many can be found in *Michael Moncur's (Cynical) Quotations*.

- "Fashion is a form of ugliness so intolerable that we have to alter it every six months."
- "A man cannot be too careful in the choice of his enemies." – from *The Picture of Dorian Gray*
- "I suppose that I shall have to die beyond my means." – upon being told the cost of an operation
- "I think that God in creating Man somewhat overestimated his ability."
- "It is a very sad thing that nowadays there is so little useless information."
- "Seriousness is the only refuge of the shallow."
- "Most people are other people. Their thoughts are someone else's opinions, their lives a mimicry, their passions a quotation." – from *De Profundis*
- "The secret of life is to appreciate the pleasure of being terribly, terribly deceived." – from *A Woman of No Importance*
- "Whenever people agree with me I always feel I must be wrong."
- "Why was I born with such contemporaries?"
- "The public is wonderfully tolerant. It forgives everything except genius." – from *The Critic as Artist*
- "One can survive everything, nowadays, except death, and live down everything except a good reputation."

Modern Classics

Generally, when the term *classic* is applied to literature, visions of dusty bookshelves, outdated language, and orphans named Pip come to mind. Readers assume that classic means aged and often relate it to tedious, and often neglected, reading assignments from their school days. Fortunately, writing remains a craft assumed by bright minds of our era, many of which continue to produce books that are becoming instant classics. Here are four examples of recent contributions that are destined to be remembered.

- *Beloved* by Toni Morrison (1987) – The novel recounts the story of two slaves, adhering to the slave narrative tradition and also tackling subjects like sexual abuse, previously ignored in similar texts.
- *Kafka on the Shore* by Haruki Murakami (2002) – Comprised of two interrelated but independent plots, the novel intermingles popular culture and Shintoism while relating the convergence of a young man fleeing from an Oedipal curse and another with a mysterious ability to locate cats.
- *Middlesex* by Jeffrey Eugenides (2002) – The novel spans eight decades of a family and deals with the subject of intersexuality, as well as the themes of growing up as a first-generation American.
- *A Confederacy of Dunces* by John Kennedy Toole (1980) – A brilliant criticism of human folly, the novel follows the experiences of an unemployed and obese protagonist who finds himself forced to comply with modern life. Published 11 years after the author's suicide, it provides readers with one of America's most memorable characters.

A Good Name to Know: Charles Babbage Computer Pioneer

Born in 1791, Englishman Charles Babbage was a gifted mathematician. After graduating from Cambridge University, he taught calculus at the Royal Institution. He helped establish the Astronomical Society in 1820, the first organization to challenge the dominance of the Royal Society.

Babbage worked on a project that he called the "difference engine," a machine that could perform mathematical calculations. He actually built a six-wheeled model and took it around with him to show to audiences.

Another of his projects, the analytical engine, was a larger, more complex device that secured his reputation as a computer pioneer. Babbage planned for the machine to use punch cards and perform unlimited mathematical calculations. The analytical engine was to contain a memory unit to store numbers and many other fundamental components that are found on today's computers. Ada Byron Lovelace worked with him on this project; however, a working prototype was never completed in Babbage's lifetime.

Fast Facts from History

- The world's first travel agency, Thomas Cook, was developed in 1848. Thomas Cook, the founder, began planning group excursions through Europe, focusing on holiday travel. The company still exists, though it has merged with My Travel to form Thomas Cook Group PLC.
- Findings from the excavations of Egyptian tombs that date as far back as 5000 BC show that ancient Egyptian kids played with toy hedgehogs.
- The first account of a sighting of the Loch Ness Monster was recorded in AD 565.
- Only one of the Seven Wonders of the World still survives today, the Great Pyramid of Giza.
- The first product ever trademarked was actually beer. Bass Pale Ale, a British beer, was trademarked in 1876.
- During the 1500s and 1600s in Spain and Holland, urine was commonly used as a dental cleaning agent.
- The first person to ever encode communications was Julius Caesar. His method became known as the Caesar Cipher. In the simplistic method, a letter is replaced with a letter of a constant number of letters away. For instance, if C is replaced with E, then H is replaced with J, as the distance used is two letters.
- The use of soap was first documented on Sumerian clay tablets around 2500 BC The soap was formed from water, alkali, and cassia oil.

Ada Byron Lovelace

With a poet for a father and a mother who was terrified that her daughter would grow up to be just like her father, Ada Byron was brought up to be a mathematician and scientist. She waned to be what she called "an analyst and a metaphysician." She wanted to find a way to incorporate poetry with science. Her mathematical approach was filled with imagination and described in metaphors.

- When she was 17, Ada met Mary Somerville, a writer and educator. Through Somerville, Ada met Charles Babbage who was planning a new calculating engine, the analytical engine. He conjectured: what if a calculating engine could not only foresee but could act on that foresight.
- Ada herself saw foresight in Babbage's description and later suggested that Babbage write a plan for how the engine might calculate Bernoulli numbers. This plan is now regarded as the first computer program.
- Babbage worked on plans for this new engine and reported on the developments at a seminar in Turin, Italy, in the autumn of 1841. Subsequently, a summary of Babbage's talk was published in an article in French.
- Ada, married to the Earl of Lovelace and the mother of three children, translated the article and showed it to Babbage. He encouraged her to add her own notes to the translation. Her translation of the article was published in 1843 with her notes containing predictions that such a machine might be used to compose complex music and to produce graphics and might be used for both practical and scientific use.

In 1979, the US Department of Defense developed a software language named "Ada," in honor of Lady Ada Byron Lovelace.

King vs. Steel: The Bestseller Competition

Between them, fiction writers Stephen King and Danielle Steel have written over 50 books featured on the *New York Times* Bestseller List, making them the two most-sold novelists of today. King currently has 29 bestsellers. Steel trails close behind with 27. Here's a list of the bestsellers from each:

Stephen King

Title	Date First Reached #1
The Dead Zone	October 14, 1979
Firestarters	September 28, 1980
Cujo	August 23, 1981
Different Seasons	August 15, 1982
Pet Sematary	November 13, 1983
The Talisman (with Peter Straub)	October 28, 1984
Thinner (as Richard Bachman)	April 28, 1985
Skeleton Crew	June 23, 1985
It	September 14, 1986
The Eyes of the Dragon	February 1, 1987
Misery	June 7, 1987
The Tommyknockers	November 29, 1987
The Dark Half	November 5, 1989
The Stand	May 13, 1990
Four Past Midnight	September 16, 1990
Gerald's Game	July 19, 1992
Dolores Claiborne	December 6, 1992
Insomnia	October 23, 1994
Desperation	October 13, 1996
Bag of Bones	October 11, 1998
The Girl Who Loved Tom Gordon	May 2, 1999
Dreamcatcher	April 8, 2001
Black House (with Peter Straub)	September 30, 2001

Everything's Eventual	April 7, 2002
From a Buick 8	October 13, 2002
Song of Susannah	June 27, 2004
The Dark Tower	October 10, 2004
Cell	February 12, 2006
Lisey's Story	November 12, 2006

Danielle Steel

Title	Date First Reached #1
Full Circle	June 3, 1984
Family Album	March 31, 1985
Wanderlust	July 20, 1986
Fine Things	March 29, 1987
Kaleidoscope	October 25, 1987
Zoya	May 15, 1988
Star	February 26, 1989
Daddy	November 19, 1989
Heartbeat	February 24, 1991
Jewels	May 17, 1992
Mixed Blessings	November 22, 1992
Accident	February 27, 1994
The Gift	August 7, 1994
Five Days in Paris	December 3, 1995
Silent Honor	December 1, 1996
Special Delivery	July 20, 1997
The Ghost	November 30, 1997
The Long Road Home	April 26, 1998
The Klone and I	July 12, 1998
Bittersweet	April 25, 1999
The Wedding	April 23, 2000
The House on Hope Street	July 16, 2000
Leap of Faith	July 15, 2001
The Kiss	November 11, 2001
Answered Prayers	November 17, 2002
Johnny Angel	July 20, 2003
The House	May 19, 2006

al-Razi

Born in Iran in AD 865, al-Razi studied alchemy, medicine, and spiritual philosophy. He is said to be one of the greatest thinkers of the Islamic world. He composed 33 treatises on natural science, mathematics, and astronomy.

As chief physician and director of a hospital in Baghdad, he is said to have given patients full treatment without charging any fee, nor demanding any payment. When he was not occupied with pupils or patients, he was writing and studying.

Many medical firsts are attributed to al-Razi. He gave the first scientific description of smallpox and was the first to distinguish between smallpox and measles. He also discovered allergic asthma (also known as hay fever) and wrote articles about allergy and immunology, becoming the first physician to do so. In his study of allergies, he became the first to realize that fever is a natural defense mechanism of the body.

He is the one who developed pharmaceutical mortars, phials, flasks, and spatulas to aid in the concoction of ointments and other treatments for his patients. He also developed methods of distillation and extraction, leading to his discovery of sulfuric acid and ethanol.

In his later years, al-Razi went blind, reportedly from cataracts. He died in 925.

Today al-Razi is honored by the Al-Razi Institute in Tehran and Razi University. The annual Razi Day (meaning Pharmacy Day) is observed in Iran on August 27.

Robert Boyle
Inventor of the Air Pump

Born in 1627 in Ireland, Robert Boyle began studying at Eton College at age eight. After only two years, he then traveled extensively in Europe with a tutor.

Before the 1650s, scientists typically discussed their research among themselves. They rarely recorded their findings in systematic reports for publication. Boyle became the first prominent scientist to use controlled experiments and then publish the details of his work, including the procedures, equipment used, and observations.

He used this method of conducting experiments and publishing his results in all areas of his study for the rest of his life. He studied chemistry, philosophy, medicine, and religion with the same dedication.

Boyle is perhaps best known for his theory that says, as the volume of a gas is decreased, pressure increases proportionally. Today, this is known as Boyle's law. He also worked on a universal "corpuscular theory" of chemistry, defined the modern idea of an element, and introduced the litmus test to tell acids from bases.

Robert Boyle died in 1691 in London.

In 1660, Boyle and 11 other natural philosophers formed the Royal Society in London. They met to share information on the current work being done and to demonstrate experiments. In 1680, he refused to be named president of the society because the required oath violated his religious principles.

Alexander Graham Bell
Speech Specialist

Born in 1847, in Edinburgh, Scotland, Alexander Graham Bell became interested in language at an early age. Encouraged by his father and grandfather, he began researching the mechanics of speech at age 16.

Bell accepted a teaching position in the US and moved in 1870. His father had been working on a system that he called visible speech to teach deaf-mute children. Bell continued that work and, in 1872, opened a school in Boston to train teachers of the deaf. A year later the school became part of Boston University, where Bell was appointed professor of vocal physiology.

Bell, fascinated with transmitting speech, developed a simple receiver that could turn electricity into sound. Several other people were working on this idea also; however, Bell received a patent for the telephone in 1876. A year later, the first telephone exchange was built in Connecticut, and Bell Telephone Company was created.

In 1880, Bell received the French Volta Prize for his invention and used the money to open the Volta Laboratory in Washington. There he conducted experiments in communication, medical research, and techniques for teaching the deaf.

Bell was also interested in aviation and experimented with several ideas for improving flight. In 1888, he became one of the founding members of the National Geographic Society and served as its president from 1896 to 1904, also helping to establish its journal.

Bell died on August 2, 1922, at age 75.

Cornelius Drebbel Inventor of the Submarine

Born in Alkmaar, Netherlands, in 1572, Cornelius Drebbel first worked as an apprentice to painter and engraver Hendrick Goltzius; however, he also worked on his own, inventing, among other things, a perpetual motion machine that told the time, date, and season.

In 1604, King James I invited Drebbel to England to demonstrate a number of his inventions. He was also invited to Prague in 1610 and again in 1619. Unfortunately, he was arrested both times that he was in Prague, but his being an inventor got him pardoned.

- Drebbel's most famous invention was the submarine. He raised the sides on a rowboat, covered it in greased leather, put a watertight hatch in the middle, and gave it a rudder and four oars. Under the seats were large pigskin bladders with pipes connecting them to the outside. At launch the bladders were tied off with rope, and then when the shipped dived, the ropes were untied and the bladders filled with water. To surface, the crew squeezed the bladder to expel the water.
- Drebbel built several submarines, the largest of which had six oars and could carry 16 passengers. It could stay submerged for three hours at a depth of 15 feet.

When Charles I became king of England, he hired Drebbel to make secret weapons, including an unsuccessful floating petard (bomb).

Drebbel died in London in 1633.

Robert Hooke
Scientist

Micrographia, published in 1665, is one of several collections of scientific observations by Robert Hooke. Here he recorded details of using magnifying lenses to look at fleas, cork, and lunar craters, among other things. The book includes Hooke's use of the word *cell* in a biological context, referring to cork.

- Hooke's Law, which says a spring is proportional to the weight hanging from it, came about as he studied flight and the elasticity of air.
- Hooke worked with Robert Boyle to perfect the air pump. For one experiment Hooke was submerged in a sealed vessel while the air was gradually pumped out. He emerged from this experiment with damage to his ears and nose.
- Throughout his career, Hooke served as a land surveyor, architect, inventor, and scientist.

In *Attempt to Prove the Motion of the Earth,* written in 1674, Hooke proposed a theory of planetary motion based on inertia and a balance between an outward centrifugal force and an inward gravitational attraction to the sun.

Fascinated with the heavens, Hooke built the first reflecting telescope, observed the rotation of Mars, and noted one of the earliest examples of a double star.

The universal joint on a car is also known as a Hooke's joint.

Robert Hooke invented the spring control of the balance wheel for watches and a wheel barometer.

Eli Whitney
Cotton Gin

Born in Westboro, Massachusetts, Eli Whitney graduated from Yale University in 1792. He began work at Mulberry Grove, a plantation owned by Mrs. Nathaniel Greene. She appealed to Whitney's creative nature and asked him to come up with a way to separate the seed from cotton that was grown on the plantation.

It only took Whitney ten days to fashion a machine from wood and a few metal parts. He made a few improvements and had the world's first cotton gin ready for processing the 1793 season's cotton crop. The cotton gin was a fantastic success, and demand was great.

- Whitney and plantation manager, Phineas Miller, formed a partnership and began manufacturing the machines. Although they received a patent in 1794, other people started making the cotton gins without authorization.
- In 1807, Whitney and Miller won a legal battle to protect their patent but were denied a renewal five years later.

Whitney also owned a firearms factory, where workers used mass-production techniques to make muskets with standardized, interchangeable parts.

Michael Faraday Electromagnetism and Electrochemistry

Born in 1791 in south London, Michael Faraday worked as an apprentice to a local bookbinder and spent his free time reading books on science. In 1812, at age 21, Faraday attended several lectures given by the chemist Humphry Davy at the Royal Institution. This prompted him to write to Davy asking for a job as his assistant. Although Davy initially turned him down, the next year he appointed Faraday to the job of chemical assistant at the Royal Institution.

While at the Institute, Faraday published his work on electromagnetic rotation (the principle behind the electric motor), helped other researchers with their projects, and began giving lectures of his own. He also founded the Royal Institution's Friday Evening Discourses and the Christmas Lectures, both of which continue today.

In 1831, Faraday discovered electromagnetic induction, opening the door for the development of the electric transformer and generator. He coined several words including *electrode*, *cathode*, and *ion*.

In 1830, Faraday became professor of chemistry at the Royal Military Academy in Woolwich, where he served until 1851. In addition, he served as scientific adviser to Trinity House from 1836 to 1865.

Michael Faraday died in 1867 in England.

Novel, Novella, Novelette

Novella vs. Novel

Just like novel, the word novella is derived from the Italian novella, which means tale. The word novella typically refers to a work of fictional prose that is longer than a short story but shorter than what might be considered a novel. The exact definition or length is typically determined within a specific book genre. For instance, in science fiction writing, a novella is a fictional work that reaches a word count between 17,000 and 40,000 words, with anything over that being classified as a novel. In mainstream adult fiction, a full length novel manuscript is generally considered to be at least 80,000 words or more, further blurring the lines. Most genres hold that a work that falls between 20,000 and 40,000 words is, indeed, a novella.

A Few Famous Novellas

- *A River Runs Through It*, Norman Maclean
- *Breakfast at Tiffany's*, Truman Capote
- *Anthem*, Ayn Rand
- *The Bicentennial Man*, Isaac Asimov
- *Animal Farm*, George Orwell
- *Heart of Darkness*, Joseph Conrad
- *Mrs. Dalloway*, Virginia Woolf
- *Of Mice and Men*, John Steinbeck
- *The Old Man and the Sea*, Ernest Hemingway
- *The Turn of the Screw*, Henry James
- *The Stranger*, Albert Camus

Novella vs. Novelette

A novelette is, much like a novella, a short piece of prose fiction that is longer than a short story, but shorter than a novella. A novelette can fall anywhere between 7,500 words and 20,000 words. The term can also be used in a negative way, to speak of novels or novellas that "fall short" of standards, seeming trite or contrived. Novelettes tend to appear in the genre of science fiction more than in any other genre.

Famous Novelettes

- *The Birds*, Daphne du Maurier
- *Flat Diane*, Daniel Abraham
- *A Colder War*, Charles Stross

Lee de Forest
The Father of Radio

Born in 1873 in Council Bluffs, Iowa, Lee de Forest grew up in Alabama. His father, a minister, was president of Talladega College (Talladega, Alabama). De Forest received his Ph.D. from Yale University in 1899.

During his lifetime, de Forest received hundreds of patents. However, he may be most often remembered for his development of the vacuum tube.

In 1907, he added a grid to the Fleming valve, an element found in the lightbulb. His device, what he called the audion and today we call a triode, was in essence a three-electrode vacuum tube. It could detect radio waves and convert them into audio frequency that could be heard using headphones or amplified for a loudspeaker. He was making the first steps to creating what he called a radiotelephone.

De Forest formed his own radiotelephone company in 1907, and he eventually sent audio broadcasts of opera singers, patriotic music, and even reports of the 1916 presidential election returns.

Three years later, in 1919, he came up with the Phonofilm process, enabling synchronized sound for movie film. Phonofilm was used to record stage performances, speeches, and musical acts. He premiered 18 short films on Phonofilm in 1923. This invention eventually earned de Forest an Academy Award and a star on the Hollywood Walk of Fame.

In reflecting on his accomplishments, de Forest said, "Why should anyone want to buy a radio … nine tenths of what one can hear is the continual drivel of second-rate jazz, sickening crooning by degenerate sax players, interrupted by blatant sales talks?"

De Forest died in Hollywood, California, in 1961.

Urushiol: A Poison Humans Know Well

Urushiol is not just a strange-sounding word. It's also a poisonous substance in poison ivy and poison oak that can give a person a very uncomfortable rash. That's because urushiol is the main ingredient of poison ivy and poison oak, two plants that are highly poisonous to most humans.

Nearly one in five human beings are immune to the urushiol in poison ivy and poison oak and suffer no symptoms from coming in contact with the pesky plants.

How Does Poison Ivy Work?

In the immune system, a person must have enough T-cells to recognize urushiol as an antigen. White blood cells called microphages are released through the body to attack the antigen. The blistering, itchy rash that occurs on most people is caused by the tissue damage of the macrophages as they attempt to eat the poison.

- Many animals actually ingest poison ivy with no adverse effects. Some scientists believe that animals that eat urishiol-carrying plants become immune to the chemical.
- Humans can become infected with urishiol from touching a plant, an article of clothing, an animal, or brushing up against anything that has contacted the poison. The urishiol can hang on to material for quite some time. For example, a human can become infected by petting a dog that has been romping in the woods through poison ivy or poison oak.

From the Mouths of Classical Composers

- "I pay no attention whatever to anybody's praise or blame. I simply follow my own feelings." – Wolfgang Amadeus Mozart
- "Neither a lofty degree of intelligence nor imagination both together go to the making of genius. Love, love, love, that is the soul of genius." – Wolfgang Amadeus Mozart
- "The world is a king, and, like a king, desires flattery in return for favor; but true art is selfish and perverse—it will not submit to the mold of flattery." – Ludwig van Beethoven
- "What you are, you are by accident of birth; what I am, I am by myself. There are and will be a thousand princes; there is only one Beethoven." – Ludwig van Beethoven
- "Friends applaud, the comedy is over." – Ludwig van Beethoven's last words
- "There's nothing remarkable about it. All one has to do is hit the right keys at the right time and the instrument plays itself." – Johann Sebastian Bach
- "Simplicity is the final achievement. After one has played a vast quantity of notes and more notes, it is simplicity that emerges as the crowning reward of art." – Frédéric Chopin
- "Truly there would be reason to go mad were it not for music." – Peter Ilyich Tchaikovsky
- "I sit down to the piano regularly at nine o'clock in the morning and Mesdames les Muses have learned to be on time for that rendezvous." – Peter Ilyich Tchaikovsky
- "My music is best understood by children and animals." – Igor Stravinsky

How Does a Gourmet Kitchen Work?

Executive Chef

In an upscale restaurant or hotel, the executive chef is at the top of the totem pole. Most of the duties of the executive chef are administrative and supervisional. He or she usually has a degree from a culinary school, has more experience and skill than anyone in the restaurant, and is responsible for planning the menu.

Sous Chef

The sous chef is second in the restaurant hierarchy, is a first assistant to the executive chef, and helps with planning of menus and supplies. The sous chef supervises the kitchen staff and inspects the cooking process. It is the responsibility of the sous chef to make sure that food is properly prepared and that the schedule is maintained.

Line Chef

The line chef, otherwise known as a station chef, is in charge of a certain region of the kitchen, such as the ovens or stoves. The line chef, in a larger kitchen, would supervise all of a particular cooking section of the kitchen. In a smaller restaurant, he or she might actually be in charge of the actual roasting, baking, or sautéing.

Cook

Last but not least, the cook is actually in charge of preparing a variety of foods. A cook must create large portions of food in a small amount of time. The cook gives very little thought to the presentation of the food, since that is taken care of by other kitchen staff further up the line. All executive chefs begin as cooks and work their way up the culinary ladder.

Arthritis

Of the many topics of the world, arthritis is perhaps one of the most mysterious, full of myths and old wives tales. There are many causes associated with arthritis, and some are just plain untrue. Arthritis can be broken into two categories.

Rheumatoid Arthritis

Rheumatoid arthritis is an autoimmune disease where the body attacks itself due to an immune system malfunction. Joints begin to ache, and a patient will experience fever and fatigue.

Osteoarthritis

Osteoarthritis is caused by the gradual deterioration of cartilage around a joint. Common in elderly people, it is most prevalent in weight-bearing joints such as the knees and hips.

- Overworking joints does not cause osteoarthritis. Scientists claim that if this myth were true, all right-handed individuals would suffer from the disease in the wrist and elbow by age 30.
- Cracking the knuckles does not cause arthritis.
- Cold weather does not *cause* arthritis but can *aggravate* the joints if arthritis is already present.
- Similarly, poor posture cannot cause arthritis, though osteoarthritis can lead to the degeneration of the spine and cause a "stooped" look.
- Not all elderly people suffer from joint pain and arthritis. There is a large percentage of elderly individuals who show no signs whatsoever of arthritis.

Abstract Expressionism

A post–World War II movement in the United States, abstract expressionism came out of surrealism and emphasized subconscious creativity and spontaneous art. In the postwar era of the 1940s, there were very few galleries and critics who were willing to accept and follow the work of the New York expressionists.

From abstract expressionism grew lyrical abstraction, pop art, minimalism, and neo-expressionism in the '60s and '70s. A wave of hard-edge painting in the later decades served as a rebellion against abstract expressionism, with painters such as Frank Stella and Robert Indiana. Popular artists who stemmed from the decades after abstract expressionism include Andy Warhol, Claes Oldenberg, and Roy Lichtenstein, all of whom achieved fame and prominence in the United States and Britain.

The term is now used to refer to a group of artists who focused on nonobjective artwork, such as Jackson Pollock, Jane Frank, and Mark Rothko.

Major Abstract Expressionists

- Sam Francis
- Ad Reinhardt
- Hedda Sterne
- Cy Twombly
- Herbert Ferber
- Jack Bush
- Adolph Gottlieb
- Philip Guston
- Franz Kline
- Joan Mitchell

- Robert De Niro Sr.
- Albert Kotin
- Lee Krasner
- Seymour Lipton

Major Works of Abstract Expressionism

- *Woman V*, Willem De Kooning
- *Man Looking at Woman*, Adolph Gottlieb
- *Black and Red*, Sam Francis
- *Leda and the Swan*, Cy Twombly
- *Cronos*, Isamu Noguchi
- *Aurora*, Mark di Suvero
- *Elegy to the Spanish Republic No. 110*, Robert Motherwell

Collage

Adhering extraneous items to oil painting became popular in the 20th century. Pablo Picasso began the fad with his 1912 painting *Still Life with Chair Caning*. He added a patch of oilcloth with a chair-cane design to the painting. Artists, including Georges Braque, followed suit, adding newspaper and bits of colored paper to their artwork.

Chinese artists began adding paper to their artwork as soon as paper was invented around 200 BC Japanese artists used the technique during the 10th century, and Europeans added paper to their art during the 13th century.

Today, surrealists often use collage techniques, cutting an image into squares and reassembling them on a canvas, cutting parts away from an existing image to reveal another image, and so forth.

A Name to Drop: Tim Burton

(Hint: American Film Director, Writer, and Designer)

Known for his quirky, gothic masterpieces of film, Tim Burton is an Academy Award-nominated film director from Burbank, California. A highly imaginative childhood full of isolated creativity led Burton to begin creative projects in an offbeat, horror genre.

- It is rumored that at an early age, he staged an axe murder so realistic that neighbors called the police. He repeated the incident several times afterward, and spent his school days absorbed in horror films.
- Burton won a Disney scholarship after graduating high school and attended the California Institute of the Arts in Valencia, California, where he studied art and animation.
- He worked as a cel painter on the animated version of *The Lord of the Rings* and was later hired by Walt Disney Studios as an animator's apprentice. During this time at Disney, Burton wrote the poem and created the drawings that later became one of his most famous works, *The Nightmare Before Christmas*.

Burton's Major Works

- *Pee Wee's Big Adventure* (1985)
- *Beetle Juice* (1988)
- *Batman* (1989)
- *Edward Scissorhands* (1990)
- *Batman Returns* (1992)
- *The Nightmare Before Christmas* (1993)

- *Ed Wood* (1994)
- *Mars Attacks!* (1996)
- *The Melancholy Death of Oyster Boy: and Other Stories* (children's book, 1996)
- *Sleepy Hollow* (1999)
- *Planet of the Apes* (2001)
- *Big Fish* (2003)
- *Charlie and the Chocolate Factory* (2005)
- *Corpse Bride* (2005)
- *Sweeney Todd* (2007)

Tim Burton – Up Close

- Burton frequently has dinner table scenes in films he directs, notably in *Beetlejuice*, *Edward Scissorhands*, and *Charlie and the Chocolate Factory*.
- Often his films have gothic subtexts.
- Burton always personalizes the production logo at the beginning of each of his films.
- He is known for featuring clowns, snow, dead pets, black and white floors, butterflies, redheads, and scarecrows in his films.
- Most of his films are released close to the holiday season.
- His stop-motion films most often feature characters with long, stringy legs and small feet.

A Name to Drop: Roman Polanski

(Hint: Film Director, Writer, Actor, and Producer)

Roman Polanski was born as Rajmund Roman Liebling in Paris in the early 1930s. Known for a dramatic and tumultuous life, he is one of the most celebrated arthouse filmmakers of Hollywood history.

- In 1969, Polanski's wife, Sharon Tate, was murdered by the Manson Family in the famous Charles Manson mass murder.
- In 1979, he was arrested and pleaded guilty to having unlawful sexual intercourse with a 13-year-old and fled back to France to escape sentencing. He is still looked upon as a fugitive by the United States.
- Polanski refuses to return to the United States for fear of arrest but continues to produce films in Europe, his most recent being *Oliver Twist* in 2005.

Famous Works

- *Knife in the Water* (1962)
- *Rosemary's Baby* (1968)
- *Macbeth* (1971)
- *Chinatown* (1974)
- *Tess* (1979)
- *Pirates* (1986)
- *Bitter Moon* (1992)
- *The Ninth Gate* (1999)

- *The Pianist* (2002)
- *Oliver Twist* (2005)

Awards

- BAFTA Award for Best Direction, 1974, *Chinatown*
- Golden Globe Award for Best Director-Motion Picture, 1975, *Chinatown*
- César Award for Best Director, 1980, *Tess*
- Academy Award for Best Director, 2002, *The Pianist*
- BAFTA Award for Best Direction, 2002, *The Pianist*
- César Award for Best Director, 2002, *The Pianist*

Useless Trivia

MGM Studios often turns to secondhand clothes at garage sales around Hollywood, so while preparing for the 1939 film *The Wizard of Oz*, based on the book by L. Frank Baum, they hit the sales for some costumes. Ironically, when *Wizard* actor Frank Morgan put on his wardrobe for filming one day, he noticed a label on his overcoat that read "Property of L. Frank Baum." Morgan got a laugh out of it, but after the filming, Baum's wife looked at the costume and confirmed that it had been the author's. They had donated the jacket to charity several months before.

The Sundance Film Festival

Many DVD cases feature the recognizable symbol for a Sundance nomination or selection, but many people do not know what the Sundance Film Festival really is. Held in Park City, Utah, the festival is the largest independent cinema celebration in the United States and hosts films and filmmakers from all over the world in January every year.

The festival began in1978, originally called the Utah/US Film Festival, in an effort to attract more filmmakers to the state of Utah. It contained a small program of films made outside of the mainstream Hollywood production system, which became known as independent films.

In 1981, Robert Redford founded the Sundance Institute, and, in 1985, became the inaugural chairman of the festival. He renamed the event the Sundance Film Festival in 1991. Originally, the festival was held in September but was moved to January under the advice of director Sydney Pollack, who thought the festival would be more attractive during ski season.

Over the years to follow, big-name actors and directors became involved in the festival, gaining widespread popularity and interest for the January gathering.

Robert Redford named the Sundance Film Festival after his character from the western *Butch Cassidy and the Sundance Kid.*

A Name to Drop: Akira Kurosawa

(Hint: Japanese Film Director, Producer, and Screenwriter)

Born in Tokyo at the turn of the 20th century, Akira Kurosawa was the youngest of seven children in a well-to-do family. His parents embraced Western culture and took the family to see many films that were only just beginning to appear around Japan. Even when Japanese culture began to shun Western films, Kurosawa's father continued to present films as an educational experience.

In 1923, the Great Kanto Earthquake shook Japan and demolished the city of Tokyo, killing close to 100,000 people. Kurosawa and his brother made a walking tour of the city and examined the devastation. According to him, the experience taught him to look fear in the face to defeat it. Kurosawa died of a stroke at the age of 88.

- In 1930, Kurosawa was hired as a film director's apprentice, beginning his career in films.
- He directed his first film, *Sanshiro Sugata,* and gained the attention and skepticism of the Japanese government, who heavily censored material and encouraged wartime propaganda.
- His first postwar film was quite different, however. *No Regrets for Our Youth* was highly critical of the former Japanese regime and followed the life of a political dissident's wife.
- Later, his film *Rashomon* gained Kurosawa international fame and won the Golden Lion at the Venice Film Festival and won an Academy Award for Best Foreign Film.

Akira Kurosawa: Rap Sheet

The films of Kurosawa have a unique look, as he experimented with telephoto lenses and multiple camera angles. He was known as a perfectionist and spent large amounts of time on particular scenes in order to achieve the effects he desired.

Major Works

- *Rashomon* (1950)
- *The Seven Samurai* (1954)
- *Throne of Blood* (1957)
- *Hidden Fortress* (1958)
- *Yojimbo* (1961)
- *Red Beard* (1965)
- *Ran* (1985)
- *Dreams* (1990)

Where Credit Is Due

Kurosawa's film *Yojimbo* is the basis for several western films, including *A Fistful of Dollars, Last Man Standing*, and *Lucky Number Slevin.*

His film *The Seven Samurai* has been remade into many versions, all of which share Kurosawa's original plot structure:

The Magnificent Seven, 1960
Beach of the War Gods, 1973
Sholay, 1975
Battle Beyond the Stars, 1980
World Gone Wild, 1988

Kurosawa's Awards

- Venice Film Festival Golden Lion, 1951, *Rashomon*
- Honorary Academy Award: Best Foreign Language Film, 1951, *Rashomon*
- Venice Film Festival Silver Lion, 1955, *The Seven Samurai*
- Academy Award: Best Foreign Language Film, 1975, *Dersu Uzala*
- Cannes Film Festival Golden Palm, 1980, *Kegemusha*
- Légion d'honneur, 1984
- Fukuoka Asian Culture Prize, 1990
- Academy Award for Lifetime Achievement, 1989
- Iran Cinema Celebration, special honor, 2006

Useless Trivia

When industrial rock group Nine Inch Nails was brainstorming for cool effects to put in their new music video for the song "Down With It," they thought it would be pretty awesome if lead vocalist and keyboarder Trent Reznor were portrayed as dead. After a heavy dose of pale makeup, Reznor lay on the ground while his band mates tied the camera to a helium balloon for a cool angle shot from above. However, the balloon-cam drifted away and landed in a nearby field. NIN never recovered the video, but the farmer who found it was so freaked out that he gave the tape to the Federal Bureau of Investigation.

A Name to Drop: Noam Chomsky

(Hint: American Linguist, Philosopher, Writer, and Lecturer)

Born in 1928 in Philadelphia, Avram Noam Chomsky was raised in a Jewish neighborhood that was divided into a Yiddish side and a Hebrew side. Yiddish was forbidden in Chomsky's household, and Catholicism was heavily discouraged.

- According to Chomsky, he identified with the politics of anarchism by age 13. Later, at the University of Pennsylvania, he began to study philosophy and linguistics.
- His particular interests settled in the mathematics of language structure. His political views were shaped heavily by the views of linguist and professor Zellig Harris.
- Chomsky married Carol Shatz in 1949 and received his Ph.D. in linguistics in 1955.

Chomsky has since become an instrumental figure in American leftist politics and linguistics theory, publishing many titles in both foreign policy and language theory.

Besides contributing heavily to the shaping of western linguistic theory, Chomsky was one of the leading opponents of the Vietnam War and gained both wide criticism and popularity during the late 1960s for his essays expressing American dissent.

Though he is frequently sought after for opinions and critiques of political ideas, Chomsky is also highly controversial and received many death threats because of his critique of United States foreign policy.

Some Major Works: Linguistics

- *Logical Structure and Linguistic Theory*, 1955
- *Syntactic Structures*, 1957
- *The Sound Pattern of English*, 1968
- *Language and Thought*, 1993
- *On Nature and Language*, 2001

Some Major Works: Politics

- *The Responsibility of Intellectuals*, 1967
- *American Power and the New Mandarins*, 1969
- *Human Rights and American Foreign Policy*, 1978
- *The Race to Destruction: Its Rational Basis*, 1986
- *Necessary Illusions*, 1989
- *Deterring Democracy*, 1992
- *The Common Good*, 1998
- *Propaganda and the Public Mind*, 2001
- *Failed States: The Abuse of Power and the Assualt on Democracy*, 2006

Chomsky in Film

- *Manufacturing Consent: Noam Chomsky and the Media*, 1992
- *Last Party 2000*, 2001
- *Power and Terror: Noam Chomsky in Our Times*, 2002
- *Distorted Morality—America's War On Terror?*, 2003
- *Noam Chomsky: Rebel Without a Pause*, 2003
- *The Corporation*, 2004
- *Peace, Propaganda & the Promised Land*, 2004

A Name to Drop: Stanley Kubrick

(Hint: American Film Director and Producer)

Born in 1928 in Manhattan as the first of two children, Stanley Kubrick grew up in the Bronx as the son of a doctor. He had a great interest in jazz music, photography, and chess.

Kubrick attended William Howard Taft High School and was a D-average student. His failures in school eliminated his chance at a college education, as soldiers returning from World War II were flooding colleges.

- After high school, Kubrick worked as a freelance photographer selling photographs to New York magazines. He registered for night school and eventually became a full-time staff photographer for *Look* magazine. He was married to his first wife, Toba Metz, in 1948 and lived with her in Greenwich Village.
- In the early 1950s, Kubrick began making his first short films. He sold his first film, *Day of the Fight,* for $100 to a distributor. His career in narrative films began in 1953 with *Fear and Desire,* a movie about a team of soldiers in a fictional war. During the making of the film, Kubrick divorced Toba and married his second wife, an Australian dancer and designer.
- In 1964, he produced the film *Dr. Strangelove, or: How I Learned to Stop Worrying and Love the Bomb,* which became a cult classic and gained a large following. It is known today as a masterpiece of dark humor. The film was based on the novel *Red Alert* but was rewritten as a satire by Kubrick, Peter George, and satirist Terry Southern.
- Five years later, Kubrick finished his next film, *2001: A*

Space Odyssey. Kubrick wrote the screenplay with Sir Arthur C. Clarke, a science fiction writer. The screenplay was based on Clarke's short story *The Sentinel*. The film had an enormous cultural impact, and both it and *Dr. Strangelove* brought Kubrick to the front burner in dark film.

- Later, two of Kubrick's most famous films were produced: *A Clockwork Orange* and *Full Metal Jacket*. Both films have since become cult classics.
- He also made *The Shining*, adapted from Stephen King's famous novel, and *Eyes Wide Shut*, from Arthur Schnitzler's novella *Traumnovelle.*
- Kubrick has won countless awards for his groundbreaking films.
- He is considered one of the greatest filmmakers of the 20th century. He died on March 7, 1999. His work on the film *A.I.: Artificial Intelligence* was completed posthumously by director Stephen Spielberg.

Kubrick's early film *Fear and Desire* was an embarrassment to him later in life, as it did so poorly commercially. It is rumored that Kubrick eventually bought up every copy of the film that he could find to keep others from watching it. At least one copy of the film was kept by a private collector, and eventually the movie was bootlegged on both VHS and DVD.

Kubrick's Major Works

- *Paths of Glory* (1967)
- *Spartacus* (1960)
- *Lolita* (1962)
- *Dr. Strangelove: Or How I Learned to Stop Worrying and Love the Bomb* (1964)
- *2001: A Space Odyssey* (1968)

- *A Clockwork Orange* (1971)
- *Barry Lyndon* (1975)
- *The Shining* (1980)
- *Full Metal Jacket* (1987)
- *Eyes Wide Shut* (1999)

Spartacus

Stanley Kubrick's Academy Award–winning film *Spartacus*, based on the social condition of Rome before the birth of Christ, explores a historical slave as he fights as a gladiator for the amusement of the upper class. As Spartacus studies how to be a fighter and an entertainer, he leads an uprising among his fellow slaves and they fight for their rights as men, husbands and fathers.

Before the film was even released, some movie critics were in an uproar because *Spartacus* vaguely suggested that protagonist Marcus Crassus was a little light on his feet (he was bisexual). The Production Code Administration had the story line changed and warned that the loincloth costumes better not show too much skin.

A Name to Drop: Wes Anderson

(Hint: American Writer, Producer, and Director)

Hailing from Houston, Texas, Wes Anderson grew up the son of an advertiser and an archaeologist. He attended St. John's School, a private Houston school that he later used in his second film, *Rushmore*. He met actor Owen Wilson at the University of Texas. Together they produced a short-film version of the later hit *Bottle Rocket* and attracted the notable producer James Brooks.

- Anderson is known as an auteur, as he is involved in almost all aspects of the production of his films, including writing, designing, music selection, cinematography, and direction.
- He notes French directors Francois Truffaut and Louis Malle as major influences in his work and approach to film.
- Often, Wes Anderson features the same actors and collaborators in his movies. Some of his most prominent collaborators are Owen Wilson, Luke Wilson, Bill Murray, Anjelica Huston, Noah Baumbach, Robert Yeoman, Jason Schwartzman, and Eric Chase Anderson, his brother.

Criticism and Acclaim

- After the release of *Bottle Rocket*, many thought Anderson would become a major voice in American cinema.
- Filmmaker Martin Scorsese wrote raving reviews and praise about Anderson's films in an *Esquire* article.
- *The Royal Tenenbaums* garnered an Academy Award nomination and heavy praise for Anderson.

- Anderson has been criticized for his allegedly shallow and stereotypical portrayals of minority characters in his films.

Wes Anderson's Major Films

Bottle Rocket (1996)
Rushmore (1998)
The Royal Tenenbaums (2001)
The Life Aquatic with Steve Zissou (2004)
The Darjeeling Limited (2007)

Short Films

Bottle Rocket (1994)
Hotel Chevalier (2007)

"I want to try not to repeat myself. But then I seem to do it continuously in my films. It's not something I make any effort to do. I just want to make films that are personal, but interesting to an audience. I feel I get criticized for style over substance, and for details that get in the way of the characters. But every decision I make is how to bring those characters forward."
—Wes Anderson

A Name to Drop: Darren Aronofsky

(Hint: Film Director, Screenwriter, and Film Producer)

Born in Brooklyn in 1969, Darren Aronofsky was the son of two schoolteachers. He attended Harvard University after backpacking through Europe and the Middle East for several months following his high school graduation.

- At Harvard, he studied anthropology and animation, and for a senior thesis he produced the film *Supermarket Sweep*. The film was a finalist in the 1991 Student Academy Awards.
- Aronofsky began developing his first feature film, Pi, in 1996. The script received positive reactions, and he was encouraged to produce the psychological thriller.
- Realizing he didn't have the funds to complete the film, Aronofsky and associate producer Scott Franklin asked every person they knew for $100.
- Eventually contributors forked over enough cash to complete the film, and the movie was made for a total production cost of around $60,000.

The Snorricam

The movie Pi featured the use of the Snorricam, a camera device that is attached to the body of an actor to portray the character's visual point of view. The Snorricam is somewhat of a trademark of Aronofsky, as few of his films get by without including it somewhere in the cinematography.

Requiem for a Dream was Aronofsky's next major motion picture, based on a novel by Hubert Selby Jr. The film and shows the harsh realities of its consequences in a raw, unforgiving way. The film received a 13-minute standing ovation at the Cannes Film Festival in 2000. Actress Ellen Burstyn garnered an Academy Award nomination for her groundbreaking performance as Sara Goldfarb, a main character in the film.

In 2002, Aronofsky began producing *The Fountain*. It was released on DVD in late 2006, as production was halted and casting was changed due to differences in vision of the actors and producers.

Aronofsky's Personal Life

Aronofsky is currently engaged to actress Rachel Weisz, whom he began dating in 2004 during the filming of *The Fountain.* Weisz played the main female character in the film, replacing the original actress, Cate Blanchett, in the role.

Aronofsky's Major Works

- *Pi* (1998)
- *Requiem for a Dream* (2000)
- *The Fountain* (2006)

The Brain's Neurons

To understand the brain, it is important to note first that the brain is comprised of neurons. These are the hundreds of billions of nerve cells that transmit electrochemical signals to one another, much like the wiring in a computer.

- Neurons can pass messages over long distances, even as far as several meters, in order to communicate throughout the body.
- They contain three basic parts:
  - The cell body contains all the cell components and DNA.
  - The axon is a cablelike part that carries electrochemical messages through the cell. It is covered with a substance called myelin, made of fat, which helps increase the speed of the transmission through the cell.
  - The dendrites—branchlike attachments to the cell—make connections with other cells and give the neuron awareness of its environment.

- Neurons have different shapes and sizes depending upon their specific function. There are several types of neurons:
  - Sensory neurons carry messages from the extremities of the body back to the central nervous system.
  - Motor neurons carry signals from the central nervous system back to the parts of the body, such as the muscles, glands, and skin.
  - Receptors sense the environment of the body, such as light and sound, and send this information back to the sensory neurons.
  - Interneurons pass messages from the brain to the spinal cord.

The Parts of the Brain

Regardless of species, all mammals share these major parts of the brain.

- Brain stem – The brain stem is comprised of the medulla, the pons, and the midbrain. Together, these parts control both reflexes and involuntary functions of the body, such as blood pressure, heart rate, visceral function, and limb movement.
- Cerebellum – The cerebellum coordinates the movement of the limbs by digesting information from the vestibular system, where balance is controlled.
- Cerebrum – The cerebrum, contains the large fiber tracts, and deeper structures, such as basal ganglia, amygdala, and the hippocampus. In short, this region of the brain controls memory, emotion, and thinking.
- Thalamus – The thalamus is a messenger for the sensory pathways of the cortex. It determines which sensory information reaches the conscious mind and participates in information necessary for motor function.
- Hypothalamus – The hypothalamus controls the secretion of hormones from the pituitary gland. This part of the brain governs eating, drinking, lactation, sexual reproduction, growth, and almost all aspects of behavior.

Cerebral Cortex

The cerebral cortex covers most of the surface area of the brain. It can reach up to 465 square inches and is folded and grooved, called gyri and sulci, in order to fit inside the skull. The cortex is divided into lobes, which each serve a different function:

- Parietal lobe: The parietal lobe is responsible for all somatosensory operations. It processes stimuli and is associated with movement and recognition.
- Frontal lobe: The frontal lobe is involved in all motor skills, including speech and response. It also encases the memory and thought processes, such as learning and reasoning.
- Occipital lobe: The occipital lobe processes visual information from the eyes and relays the information to the parietal lobe. It interprets the upside-down images captured by the eye's lens and projected on the retina.
- Temporal lobe: The temporal lobe receives auditory signals from the ears and sends them to the parietal lobe and motor cortex. It is also involved with memory and speech.
- Amygdala: The amygdala controls emotions such as social behavior and sexual response.
- Basal ganglia: The basal ganglia control small, fine movements, such as the fingertips and toes.
- Limbic system: The limbic system also has a hand in emotional behavior, as it is influenced by hormones. It aids in visceral movement in the digestive tract and other body cavities.

Major Brain Dilemmas

Amnesia

The destruction of certain parts of the brain from an accident or illness can sometimes result in amnesia. There are many types of amnesia, but most are caused by damage to the temporal lobe of the brain in the hippocampal region.

- In most types of amnesia, destruction of the hippocampi results in an inability to remember anything new from the time of the destruction.
- Most often, events before the injury remain intact, as do prior intellectual abilities and knowledge.

Alice in Wonderland Syndrome

Also known as micropsia, Alice in Wonderland syndrome distorts the visual ability of a patient so that close-by objects appear tiny, as if they are being viewed through the back end of a telescope. The syndrome is associated with migraine headaches and is most often temporary in nature. It is thought that Lewis Carroll suffered from migraines, which perhaps explains why Alice, in his famed *Alice in Wonderland,* suffered from micropsia after ingesting medicine.

Foreign Accent Syndrome

After the onset of a stroke, tumor, or brain trauma, patients can sometimes suddenly begin speaking in their native tongue with a foreign accent, from French to South African. Researchers have found that a patient need not have prior recognition of the accent to adopt it, and that the phenomena results from damage to areas of the brain that produce language development. The trauma can change the tone, pitch, pronunciation, and speech pattern of the patient.

Pica

Pica is defined by a compulsion to ingest nonedible items, such as stones, cigarette ash, glass, paint, glue, or even hair. Its cause has been traced back to nutritional deficiencies and is often found among young children or pregnant women. The precise causes are unknown, but pica is prevalent in patients with brain damage or mental deficiencies. One serious type of pica, acuphagia, occurs when mental patients become drawn to swallowing sharp objects, such as glass, blades, and metal.

Alien Hand Syndrome

Also arising from brain trauma, alien hand syndrome occurs when a patient believes that he or she has lost control of motor functions of one hand. Often patients experience a complete lack of control over one hand, which can result in the unbuttoning of clothing that the opposite hand is attempting to button. Also known as Dr. Strangelove syndrome, the condition is somewhat rare and the exact cause is unknown. Patients report feeling some sensation in the "alien hand," though they have no ability to control it.

Synesthesia (Bless You)

A synesthete describes a person with synesthesia, a neurological phenomenon where one stimulation of a sensory or mental pathway creates an automatic experience within a secondary pathway. In one common form, a synesthete might attribute certain colors with numbers, or vice versa. In the synesthete's brain, each number or letter is actually colored a particular way. In another form, a synesthete might attach a personality or a location in space to a year, season, or month.

Myths About Memory

Myth: It is possible to produce an everlasting memory.
Fact: Although researchers sometimes use the term *permastore* in reference to the memory, there is no way to learn things well enough to make them absolutely impossible to forget. When memory strength is high, the lifetime of long-term memory can be longer than a human's natural life; however, no memory can remain safe indefinitely without repetition.

Myth: The more repetition, the stronger the memory.
Fact: Frequent repetition can actually prevent the effective formation of strong memories. The best way to build long-lasting memories is to review material in predetermined blocks of time, giving the brain only a particular allotted time to review before "breaking," such as in studying.

Myth: When memorizing, it is best to review material again after a long sleep.
Fact: Although sleep is necessary for learning, it is actually best to review material after three to seven days from the initial learning session. Spaced repetition has proved to be the optimal way to retain information. The computer program SuperMemo is based on spaced repetition and optimizes the length between learning and review to improve memory retention.

Myth: Large amounts of sleep are necessary for optimal memory function.
Fact: For effective learning and retention, well-structured sleep at the correct time is more important than length of sleep. Most individuals can sleep only five hours and feel refreshed. Many geniuses sleep very little yet take short naps throughout the day. Long sleep has been shown to correlate with many

diseases, and on average, a person who sleeps seven hours lives longer than one who sleeps nine hours. It is best to listen to the body for an indication of how much sleep is needed. When an individual is able to wake systematically without an alarm clock, sleep may be shorter yet more efficient and productive.

Myth: Memory worsens with age.
Fact: While it is true that we lose neurons with age, a well-exercised memory is resilient and shows fewer signs of aging than the heart, joints, and other major parts of the body. Researchers also believe that because of increased learning, and therefore training, memory can also continue to increase well into an advanced age.

Myth: One can learn information while sleeping.
Fact: It is nearly impossible to undergo productive learning while asleep. While one can consolidate memories and experience dreams and hallucinations while sleeping, the volume of knowledge that can actually be gained and retained during sleep is negligible. Many learning programs claim to allow individuals to save hours and work by learning with audio tools during sleep. The truth is that learning during sleep can actually disrupt sleep and has been shown to have negative health benefits in the long run.

High IQ and Vegetables

A 2006 Southampton University study found that children with high IQs were more likely to become vegetarians than children of average or lower IQ scores. The data showed that those who became vegetarians by the age of 30 had, on average, scored five points higher on an IQ test at age 10.

Common Phrases and Their Origins

Phrase: Pushing the envelope
Meaning: To challenge existing boundaries
Origin: The phrase originated in the United States Air Force test pilot program in the mid-20th century. The envelope refers to the capabilities of the airplane's performance, and pushing the envelope meant to fly beyond the plane's known or suggested limits.

Phrase: Pass the buck
Meaning: To turn over responsibility to someone else.
Origin: Certain card games use a marker known as a "buck." As players take turns as dealer, the buck is passed around to signify the current dealer. When the buck is passed on, so is the responsibility to deal.

Phrase: Bang for the buck
Meaning: Value for the price.
Origin: The phrase originates from Cold War times when the United States was deliberating the idea of buying new weapons. The United States Air Force claimed, at the time, that missiles such as ICBMs could do more damage to an enemy for the cost than a Navy aircraft carrier; hence, it had more "bang" for the buck.

Chaos Theory

Chaos theory was born in the 1960s from a desire to perfectly predict weather patterns. A meteorologist, Edward Lorenz, was working a weather prediction problem using a set of 12 equations to model weather. His system couldn't predict weather itself but did accurately suggest what the weather might be. In 1961, Lorenz wanted to look at a particular weather sequence again. He began in the middle of the sequence, instead of the beginning, and entered the numbers from his printout. When he checked his results, he found that the weather sequence had evolved in a drastically different way from the original. Eventually, he realized that he had entered the data only to three decimal points, when the original data was worked to six. From this, he derived that merely the tiniest change in a weather pattern, down to a fraction as small as a millionth, could drastically change a long-term pattern.

Today, the idea is commonly referred to as the "butterfly effect," because the variance in the starting points in the two curves of Lorenz's weather patterns were comparable to a butterfly flapping its wings.

Where Does *Chaos* Come In?

The name chaos theory comes from the fact that the systems the theory describes appear to be entirely disordered and unconnected. Chaos theory is really about finding the order that actually controls the apparently random data.

Quick Facts: Christianity

- Christianity is the most widespread religion in the world. There are an estimated 2.1 billion Christians on the planet.
- There are sixty-six books in the Bible. Thirty-nine are from the Old Testament, and twenty-seven in the New Testament.
- The only book of the Bible that does not contain the word God is Esther.
- Written in AD 95, Revelation is the youngest book of the Bible.
- There are seven suicides recorded within the books of the Bible.
- During the sixth century, it was tradition to congratulate anyone who sneezed, as it was believed that sneezing expelled evil from the body. During the great plague of Europe, the pope passed a law that required individuals to say "God bless you" when a person sneezed.
- In Old Testament times, the Mediterranean Sea was called the Great Sea.

The Vatican City is a landlocked territory made of a walled enclave inside Rome. It is the world's smallest independent state.

The Ten Plagues of Egypt

- Water turns into blood
- Frogs
- Lice, gnats
- Flies
- Cattle infected with disease
- Sores, boils

- Hail
- Locusts
- Darkness
- Death of the first-born child

The Seven Last Plagues – Revelation 16

- Sores
- Seas turning to blood
- Rivers turning to blood
- Heat of the sun scorches the earth
- Darkness
- The Euphrates becomes dry
- Earthquake

The Seven Fathers of the Church

- St. Athanasius
- St. Gregory of Nazianzus
- St. John Chrysostom
- St. John of Damascus
- St. Basil of Caesarea
- St. Gregory of Nyssa
- St. Cyril of Alexandria

Major Christian Pilgrimages

Jerusalem

Jerusalem is a major destination for Christian pilgrimages today, as it is the location of the crucifixion and resurrection of Jesus. According to Christian beliefs, Jesus was brought to Jerusalem not long after his birth and was cleansed in the Second Temple later in his life. The Last Supper is believed to have been held in Jerusalem, atop Mount Zion. Golgotha, the site of the crucifixion, is thought to be the main reason why Jerusalem has been a major Christian pilgrimage site for 2,000 years.

The Church of the Holy Sepulchre in Jerusalem, known as the Church of the Resurrection to Eastern Orthodox Christians, stands on a site that encompasses Calvary, where Jesus was crucified, and the tomb (sepulchre) where he was buried. A marble slab marks the place where Jesus' body was believed to have been laid.

Rome

Ancient roads such as the Via Francigena are important pilgrimage routes connecting Western Europe and Rome with harbors to Jerusalem. During medieval times, the Via Francigena was a major pilgrimage route to Rome. Many pilgrims still use this route today on foot, horseback, or by bicycle. Of course, a most popular pilgrimage spot for Catholics is the Vatican City, located in Rome. These locations make Rome the most visited Christian pilgrimage site in the world.

St. Peter's Basilica, designed and decorated by Michelangelo and other great artists, contains the relics of Saint Peter (the first pope), is the ceremonial center for the Catholic Church, and is located in Vatican City, Rome.

Lourdes

Nestled in the foothills of southwestern France, Lourdes is the second most visited Christian pilgrimage site, following Rome. With a population of about 15,000 inhabitants, Lourdes accommodates close to five million pilgrims and tourists each season. From March to October, the Sanctuary of Our Lady of Lourdes is the site of mass pilgrimages. The spring water found in the grotto there is believed to have healing properties, and miracles have been reported in the sanctuary.

Canterbury Cathedral

One of the oldest and most famous Christian structures in the world, the Canterbury Cathedral was the site of many famous events, including the assassination of Thomas à Becket, an archbishop of Canterbury who was murdered under the disputably misinterpreted orders of King Henry II. Many Christian pilgrims visit the cathedral to see Becket's shrine, which is believed to be a place of healing.

The second largest pilgrimage in the history of Christendom occurred in April 2005, after the death of Pope John Paul II. It was estimated that four million people traveled to the Vatican City to attend the funeral, adding to the near three million people already in Rome who ventured to see the pope's body.

Closed for Remodeling

Humor has long been a staple of storytelling, and literature has always had its share of pranksters. Writer and social activist George Bernard Shaw was no exception. The author of *Pygmalion*, Shaw often vented his anger at social injustice through sardonic novels and stage plays. The name alone of one such play, *Closed for Remodeling*, nearly ruined the Savoy Theatre in the London city of Westminster.

A vocal opponent of Britain's involvement in World War I, Shaw received great disapproval for his dissent and was nearly tried for treason by the British government. He responded angrily through his best outlet: his position as a celebrated playwright. From this point forward his plays would be consistently more critical of society and government. He created a scathing piece that condemned the so-called "Great War."

Throughout World War I, London's theaters had been closed, and crowds eagerly awaited the reemergence of their favorite pastime. In a mischievous reaction to his recent public criticism, the playwright donned his new play with the title *Closed for Remodeling* and waited. Everyone in the business was excited about the triumphant return of the theater, and the Savoy eagerly booked Shaw's newest piece. The show opened and, night after night, the turnout was atrocious. After three weeks of terrible box office receipts the stage manager of the Savoy Theatre discovered the culprit. The name *Closed for Remodeling*, posted all over London, was leading would-be patrons to believe that the house was indeed in a state of renovation and therefore closed to the public.

When approached by the producers of the show, Shaw denied any malevolence on his part. He agreed to change the name of the show to *Heartbreak House*, and the Savoy opened to a fervent audience. The show continues to be billed by that name.

The Sarcasm of George Bernard Shaw

- "Beauty is all very well at first sight, but whoever looks at it when it has been in the house three days?"
- "The fact that a believer is happier than a skeptic is no more to the point than the fact that a drunken man is happier than a sober one."
- "Martyrdom… is the only way in which a man can become famous without ability." – from *The Devil's Disciple*
- "It is dangerous to be sincere unless you are also stupid."
- "The reasonable man adapts himself to the world; the unreasonable one persists in trying to adapt the world to himself. Therefore all progress depends on the unreasonable man." – from *Maxims for Revolutionists*
- "A government that robs Peter to pay Paul can always depend on the support of Paul." – from *Everybody's Political What's What*

George Bernard Shaw was vexed his whole life at how difficult spelling was. In his will, he set aside a large amount of his wealth to fund a new alphabet with phonetic spelling. He also wanted someone to estimate the cost in man-hours of how much money was wasted writing and printing in English with an alphabet of only 26 letters instead of the 40 letters he would prefer to see used. Ultimately, £8,300 from Shaw's estate was given towards the development of the new alphabet, though the idea still hasn't caught on.

Facts About Islam

- There are at least 1.3 billion followers of Islam on the planet.
- The major sects and denominations of Islam are the Sunni and the Shi'a. Sufi is an aspect of Islam, not a sect.
- Religious professionals of Islam are known as sheikhs. In the Shi'ite denomination, they are known as imams.
- Muslims are strict monotheists, as they only believe in one god, whom they call Allah. Allah is the same God worshiped in Christian and Jewish faith.

The Five Pillars of Islam

- Confession of faith – *shahada*
- Daily prayer – *salat*
- Tax – *zakat*
- Fasting – *sawm*
- Pilgrimage – *hajj*

The Qur'an

Muslims follow the Qur'an, a sacred text they believe to be the divine word of Allah as written by the prophet Muhammad. The origin of the name Qur'an comes from the text itself, and though it has many translations, it is loosely translated to "recitation."

- The text has 114 chapters, and each is called a *sura.*
- Each sura is given a title that comes from a name or value discussed within the chapter. Muslims believe that Muhammad gave the suras their name under the command of Allah.

Major Islamic Holidays

- Ramadan – The holiday begins October 16th and lasts one month. Similar to the Jewish holiday Yom Kippur, Ramadan is a period of atonement and obedience to Allah. During Ramadan, Muslims are required to resist evil thoughts or actions, food and drink, and sexual intercourse from dawn until dusk.
- Eid ul-Fitr – The holiday is translated to mean the Festival of Fast-Breaking. It is similar to Christmas in the way it is celebrated, but it has strong religious significance. Gifts are given, along with donations to charity, and Muslims typically take off from school or work for the celebration, which lasts three days.
- Eid al-Adha – Also known as the Festival of Sacrifice, Eid al-Adha celebrates Abraham's willingness to sacrifice his son Ishmael to Allah. In the ancient story, Abraham is allowed to save his son and sacrifice a goat instead. Eid al-Adha lasts four days, beginning the day after the pilgrims descend from Mount Arafat in their annual pilgrimage to Mecca.

All About Buddhism

- Buddhism was founded in 520 BC in northeastern India.
- The fourth largest religion in the world, it has somewhere over 360 million followers.
- Buddhism is known as a nontheistic religion, as it does not teach followers to worship a particular god or gods. It is more like a body of philosophies and teachings.
- Buddhism is based on the theories and teachings of Siddhartha Gautama.

Profile of a Thinker: Sigmund Freud Father of Psychoanalysis

Born on May 6, 1856, in Moravia (now Czech Republic), Sigmund Freud grew up in Vienna. He entered the University of Vienna, where he stayed only a few months before moving on to perform research at the Physiological Institute of Ernst Wilhelm von Brücke. He received his M.D. in 1881 and focused on neurology and psychiatry.

Freud opened his own medical practice in neurology in 1886. He began treating his neurotic patients with hypnosis; however, he soon changed to the "talking cure"—having the patient talk through a problem—believing it was a more effective treatment.

In researching neurophysiology, specifically cerebral palsy, Freud concluded that William Little, the man who first identified the disease, was incorrect in his theory that the disease was caused by complications during the birth process. Freud believed that the complications were merely a symptom.

Developing a method for studying the unconscious mind is perhaps the most significant contribution Freud made. Researchers prior to Freud had documented the concept of an unconscious, or subconscious, mind, and Freud believed that dreams were the "royal road" to reach it. He believed that people who experience painful thoughts and feelings cannot banish them from their mind, but the memories can be pushed into the unconscious. He said that this repression in itself is an unconscious act. Freud identified three concepts of the unconscious:

- The descriptive unconscious: contains memories that the person is not subjectively aware of.
- The dynamic unconscious: made up of memories that are defensively removed from consciousness as a result of conflict.
- The system unconscious: the organizational zone; however, Freud replaced the idea of the system unconscious with the concept of the ego, super-ego, and id.

In *Beyond the Pleasure Principle* (1920) and *The Ego and The Id* (1923), Freud proposed that the psyche could be divided into three parts: ego, super-ego, and id. He believed each stage is a progression into adult sexual maturity.

Psychosexual development and awareness are the motivators for all aspects of a person's life, according to Freud. He presented this theory as the Oedipus complex, a sexual fixation on the mother, and the Electra complex, a sexual fixation on the father.

Freud's theories were controversial during his day, and they continue to be today. In 1930, he received the Goethe Prize in appreciation of his contribution to psychology and to German literary culture. Then three years later, the Nazis ceremoniously burned his books.

- Freud was an early user and proponent of cocaine as a stimulant and analgesic. He wrote several articles on the antidepressant qualities and believed that cocaine would work as a cure-all for many disorders, including "nasal reflex neurosis."
- The ashes of Sigmund Freud and his wife, Martha, are kept in a Greek urn that Freud received from Marie Bonaparte.

Quick Facts: Everyday Inventions

Rubber Tires

Air-filled rubber tires were used on bicycles several years before they were added to motorized vehicles. Invented by John Dunlop, the pneumatic tire was first tested on his son's tricycle and was later patented and mass-produced for cars and other vehicles.

Can Openers

The can opener was actually developed nearly 50 years after the invention of the metal can. Canned food was introduced by the British Navy in the early 19th century, and the can was made from iron. The cans were impractical, as they were much heavier than the food itself, and they needed to be opened with a chisel and hammer. The can opener was invented when thinner cans were introduced around the 1860s. Ezra Warner, from Connecticut, patented the first opener in 1858. The modern can opener, with grooves and a turning wheel, was invented in 1870 by William Lyman.

Video Killed the Radio Star

On August 1, 1981, the Music Television Network, the brainchild of James Lack and Bob Pittman, aired its first flick, "Video Killed the Radio Star," by the Buggles.

During the early years of syndication, the music videos weren't what they are today. They were more like choppy commercials for upcoming record releases. In fact, before the term "music video" came out, the three- to four-minute clips of singing and dancing were often called "promotional clips." The one thing MTV did for American music lovers in the end—they proved that a good video could make a terrible song a huge hit.

The Bad Guys of Political History

Mao Tse-tung
Death Toll: 40 million +
A founder of the Chinese Communist party, Mao Tse-tung founded the People's Republic of China in 1949. In 1915, he wrote the longest graphite ever recorded, which criticized the Chinese school system and Chinese society. His protest contained over 4,000 Chinese characters. As a later Chinese political leader, he was responsible for over 40 million deaths, most of which resulted from hunger and starvation in China during the Great Leap Forward. He took tens of thousands of lives during China's cultural revolution.

Peter the Great
Born in 1672, Peter the Great was a tzar and emperor of Russia during the 18th century. He was around six-foot-seven, and fought as a foot soldier in the battle against the Turks, as he believed that it was the only way for Russia to defeat the Turkish army. He had 11 children over the course of his life, and he even executed one of his sons in 1718 for treason.

Idi Amin Dada
Death Toll: 100,000–500,000
A former dictator of Uganda and heavyweight boxing champion, Idi Amin was one of the most notorious and bloody dictators in African history. He was a proponent of Hitler and often defended the Holocaust and the Germans involved. At one point, he offered to be the king of Scotland. It is rumored and reported that Idi Amin ate his opponents once he defeated them.

Pol Pot
Death Toll: Approx. 1.7 million
Pol Pot is the common name used to refer to Saloth Sar, leader of the communist movement Khmer Rouge in Cambodia. He was the prime minister of Cambodia from 1976 to 1979. During his rule, he imposed agrarian collectivism by which he moved city dwellers to the country to work in forced labor projects and collective farms. Between slave labor, starvation, executions, and neglect, Pol Pot is estimated to be responsible for anywhere between 700,000 to 1.7 million deaths in Cambodia. In 1979, when Vietnam invaded Cambodia, Pol Pot fled to the jungle to hide. He was arrested and imprisoned by other communist leaders. He died in 1998 while under house arrest.

Saddam Hussein
Death toll: Approx. 2 million
Saddam Hussein was president of Iraq from 1979 until 2003. He was largely involved in the coup that brought the Ba'ath Party to power. In power during the Persian Gulf War, Hussein remained popular among Arabs who disliked the West and its intervention in the Middle East. Saddam Hussein is reportedly responsible for countless deaths, both directly and indirectly. Combining Iraqis killed during both Gulf Wars, Kuwaitis, Kurds, and Shi'a Muslims and dissidents found in mass graves in Iraq, Hussein could be responsible for more than 2 million deaths. He was sentenced to death by hanging and was executed in December 2006.

The Deadliest Wars of the 20th Century

World War II (1939–45) - 20 million dead
World War I (1914–17) - 8.5 million dead
Korean War (1950–53) - 1.7 million dead
Chinese Civil War (1945–49) - 1.2 million dead
Vietnam War (1965–73) - 1.2 million dead

Record Holders: Planet Earth

- Highest mountain: Mt. Everest
  Mt. Everest grows nearly four millimeters per year, as two tectonic plates continue to push against each other.
- Highest waterfall: Angel Falls
  Located in Venezuela, the waterfall drops 3,212 feet.
- Hottest place on Earth: Azizia
  Located in Libya, Azizia reaches 136° Fahrenheit, or 57.8° Celsius.
- Coldest place on Earth: Vostok, Antarctica
  Vostok reached -129° Fahrenheit, or -89° Celsius, breaking the world record.
- Largest ocean: Pacific
  The Pacific takes up 32.6 percent of the earth's surface.
- Longest river: The Nile
  The Nile stretches 4,160 miles, or 6,695 kilometers.
- At 630 feet high, the tallest constructed monument in the world is the Gateway Arch in St. Louis, Missouri. The stainless steel arch designed by Eero Saarinen was constructed to commemorate the Louisiana Purchase. It was completed on October 28, 1965.
- Built to demonstrate the strength of iron, the Eiffel Tower in Paris, France, was the tallest building in the world in 1889. It is twice as tall as the Washington Monument. The tower is painted every seven years and takes 50 tons of paint to complete the job.
- Ka Lae (South Cape) Island in Hawaii is the southernmost point in the United States.
- The southernmost city is Hilo, Hawaii.
- The lowest point in the US is Badwater Basin in Death Valley, California. It is 282 feet below sea level.

Facts About Encyclopedias

- The word encyclopedia comes from two Greek words meaning "a circle of learning."
- The oldest known encyclopedia was written in Greece nearly 2,000 years ago but is no longer in existence.
- The oldest existing encyclopedia was written during the first century by Pliny the Elder, a Roman scholar. It is titled Natural History and consists of 37 volumes.
- The largest encyclopedia ever written is the 17th-century Yung Lo Ta Tien encyclopedia. It was bound in 11,100 volumes and completed by nearly 2,000 writers.

Copyright vs. Copyleft

- A typical copyright lasts for 70 years past the life of the original author.
- Ideas cannot be copyrighted. Only written material is copyrightable.
- A person "owns" the rights to his or her own written text, even if that person has not filed for a copyright with the Library of Congress. By registering a copyright with the Library of Congress, the rights to your work can be upheld in any court.
- A copyleft is the process of making a copyrighted work or program free to the public, or public domain. This allows the work or program to be shared, or, in the case of software, turned into proprietary software, if an individual wants to claim ownership of his or her changes.

A Plot to Know: Sense and Sensibility

In this Jane Austen masterpiece, Elinor is all sense (reason) and Marianne is all sensibility (feeling), or at least for most of the book they are. However, once each feels the pain of desertion from the man they love, they begin to see the wisdom in the other sister's point of view. Older sister Elinor loves Edward Ferrars, but she is too dignified and, well, sensible, to show it. He shares her restraint, which keeps him from telling her one tiny, important fact—he has been secretly engaged to Lucy Steele for, oh, about four years now. Oops. Meanwhile, Marianne meets the love of her life, John Willoughby, while running through a field in a storm. She twists her ankle, and, like a knight in shining armor, he comes to the rescue. Turns out, though, that this knight is a bit rusty. He harbors a few secrets of his own, which make his competitor for Marianne's affections, Colonel Brandon, all the more attractive as Marianne wises up and gets a little more sensible. Eventually everyone lives happily ever after, once they learn to balance out their reason with their emotions.

Jane Austen was so humble and shy about her writing that no one ever caught her with a pen in hand. "No matter how suddenly one arrives, she has heard the door close ... and hidden the white sheets," writes biographer Virginia Moore.

The Trouble with English

English is said to be one of the most difficult languages to learn, read, and write. In an international study, scientist Philip Seymour and a team from Dundee University compared reading comprehension ability of children from over 15 different European countries. Their findings showed that students learning romance languages, such as French and Italian, progressed further and quicker than students who studied Germanic languages, such as German and English. Children reportedly found English to be the most complex of all.

Researchers found dyslexia to be much more common in English-speaking countries because of the large volume of words with clustered consonants. For example, words like *yacht*, *sign*, and *bomb*.

The study found Finnish to be the easiest language for children to learn.

British practices usually do not include periods after such common abbreviations as Mr. and Mrs. Also in Britain, the period is called a full stop.

Stephen King

Before producing major films and best-selling novels, Stephen King began as a short story writer. He published his first full-length novel, *Carrie,* in 1973 and has enjoyed a booming writing career since. Over 50 of King's stories have appeared in film today, both on the big screen and television. King has capitalized on his uncanny ability to appeal to the fears of the mass public. A genius indeed!

King's Box Office Stories

Carrie, 1976

Carrie documents the story of a young girl with an overprotective mother. Carrie gets taunted at school because of her sheltered oblivion to teenage issues and eventually breaks down from the trauma, wreaking horror and havoc on her high school prom. The story was published as a novel, made into a box-office hit, and later became a Broadway play.

The Shining, 1980

The Shining tells the story of a family snowed in at an abandoned and haunted hotel for the winter. Overcome by cabin fever, the father, Jack, loses his mind and develops hallucinations and psychotic thoughts and behavior. In the climax of the movie, Jack comes after his family with an axe, prompted by the ghosts of the hotel to murder his family. The film was directed by Stanley Kubrick and is noted as one of the best horror movies of all time on countless lists.

Christine, 1983

Due to King's popularity in the 1980s, the movie *Christine* was in production before he even finished writing the novel. The film is about a boy and his possessed car. The car threatens to kill anyone who gets in her way. The film and story were never regarded as King's best but still had great popularity and success in the theaters.

Children of the Corn, 1984

From a book of stories entitled *Night Shift,* this film chronicles the children of Gatlin, Nebraska, who become brainwashed by a preacher named Isaac. The children are called to commit murders in the town and follow diligently. A young couple tries to interfere and angers the children, causing murder and mayhem. Seven sequels of the film were released, and the film is universally well known.

Firestarter, 1984

A couple receives a dose of experimental medicine while in college, and later their offspring is infected with the chemical. The daughter, played by Drew Barrymore, instinctually starts fires with her mind, causing mass chaos around her. It is rumored that King was unhappy with the results of the original production, and the film was reproduced in 2002.

Stephen King was accused of vandalism in Alice Springs, Australia, on August 15, 2007. He was secretly signing his books and managed to sign six books before a customer reported him to store manager Bev Ellis.

Medical Myths Busted

Myth: Eating chocolate and fried food causes acne.
Truth: In actuality, hormones are the real cause of acne. Acne occurs when there is a buildup of sebum, a waxy oil secreted from pores. The body uses sebum to stay lubricated, and its secretion is highly affected by hormones. The hormonal influence explains why teenagers show more signs of acne than adults or younger children.

Myth: A person can get a cold from cold weather.
Truth: Colds are caused by viruses, not weather. A person must come in contact with a virus in order to catch a cold. The infection typically happens when one inhales after a cough or sneeze of an infected person. Shaking hands, touching phones, and touching door handles are also common culprits. There is one correlation between weather and colds: during the winter, individuals spend more time inside, therefore more frequently coming in contact with viruses, which jump from person to person or can linger on objects.

Myth: Chewing gum takes seven years to digest.
Truth: Unfortunately, people have chewed on this myth for years, although it is entirely false and irrational. In fact, the myth has been around since the later 19th century, most likely because of a word once printed on the package: *indigestible*. Gum is comprised of flavor, sweetener, softener, and gum base, the latter ingredient being the only one that is *indigestible*. This means that the stomach cannot extract nutrients from the gum base, much like fiber. However, it is still passed through the body just like fiber, at the same speed, and usually comes out relatively unchanged.

Myth: A person can catch the flu from a flu shot.
Truth: Because vaccinations are actually created from the viruses themselves, they often get a bad reputation. However, a flu shot contains strands of an inactive virus. In essence, the part of the virus that can cause infection is dead, but the body still reacts and creates antibodies to stop the virus. The only time a person should avoid a flu shot is when that person has an allergy to eggs, as eggs are used in the construction of the vaccine. While it is possible to get the flu after receiving a flu shot, it is impossible for the virus to have come from the shot.

After taking a long stroll to inspect his estate on December 12, 1799—a chilly day of snow, sleet, and rain on Mount Vernon—George Washington came down with a bit of a sore throat. Two days later his condition worsened, and doctors predicted that his lungs and his throat were "shutting down." To try and treat his aches and pains, Washington's physicians had a bright idea—draining blood out of the former president's body and placing a strip of flannel soaked in ammonium carbonate around his neck.

Not surprisingly, the remedy failed to prolong Washington's life, but it was something other than needles (and the stench of the flannel) that kept him from being able to simply die in peace. He had an intense fear of being buried alive and made his secretary promise multiple times not to put his body in the ground less than three days after his death—just to be sure. Sixty-seven years old, Washington died while taking his own pulse. One of the last things he said was, "I die hard, but I am not afraid to go."

Several Severely Destructive Earthquakes

Earthquakes are one of the most destructive natural disasters that can occur. They can cause thousands of deaths and spur other natural disasters, such as tsunamis, fires, famines, and landslides. Earthquakes occur when the earth's tectonic plates shift and the fault slips.

The Richter Scale is a base-10 logarithmic scale used to measure an earthquake's strength. Its measurements can be negative or positive, and have no limit either way. A 5.0 tremor is roughly the same as a 32-kiloton blast, which has nearly the explosive force of the atomic bomb that the United States dropped in 1945 over the Japanese city of Nagasaki.

An increase in a whole number, such as going from 5.0 to 6.0, indicates a tenfold increase in the amplitude of the seismic waves of an earthquake. Some of the most powerful earthquakes in history are listed here.

- December 16, 1811: The New Madrid Fault
  The quake that shook the point where four US states meet—Missouri, Kentucky, Arkansas, and Tennessee—measured at least to 8.0 on the Richter scale. It is rumored that the tremors spread so far across the country that church bells rang in Boston from the force of the quake. The topography of the land was so affected that the Mississippi River flowed backward, as the land was lifted high enough to change the currents.

- April 18, 1906: The Great San Francisco Earthquake
  A 7.8 magnitude quake, this natural disaster caused approximately 3,000 deaths and over $500 million in property damage. Buildings in the San Francisco Bay area

crumbled to the ground, water lines broke, and the streetcar tracks that sewed the city were twisted into metal disasters. Most of the deaths of the tragedy were a result of a large fire caused by the tremor. The fire spread rapidly because with the busted water mains, there no way to control it. As far away as Oregon and Nevada, people felt the tremors from the earthquake for nearly one minute.

- October 5, 1948: Turkmenistan
  Over two-thirds of the population of Ashgabat, Turkmenistan, were killed in the 7.3-magnitude earthquake, a total of approximately 110,000 people. It was the most devastating quake to ever hit Central Asia at the time, and the city was reduced to rubble and ruin. In 2002, the government issued coins to commemorate the lost lives of the tragedy of 1948.

- May 22, 1960: Southern Chile
  A 9.5 on the Richter scale, this disaster was the strongest earthquake ever recorded in history. It was actually comprised of several quakes that struck together over several hours, causing a large tsunami to follow. The Chilean coast was completely destroyed, leaving landslides, volcano eruptions, and flooding to occur in the days following. Afterward, the tsunami moved across the Pacific Ocean and inundated Hawaii. Overall, the disaster was responsible for over 5,700 deaths in Chile, Hawaii, Alaska, Japan, and the Philippines.

- March 28, 1964: Alaska
  The most powerful earthquake to ever strike the United States, the quake that struck the Prince William Sound registered at 9.2 on the Richter scale. The quake itself only took 15 lives, but the tsunami to follow loomed nearly 200

feet over Alaska, killing over 100 more people and causing over $300 million in damage.

- July 27, 1976: China
  Measuring at 7.5 on the Richter scale, this quake was a major tremor that occurred along the Pacific's Ring of Fire, a belt that has endured a large amount of seismic activity and weather disaster. This particular quake hit Tangshan, a city near the northeastern coast of China. Of a population nearing 1 million, the quake caused between 250,000 and 655,000 casualties.

- December 26, 2004: Indonesia
  Off the western coast of Sumatra, a 9.1-magnitude quake and its subsequent tsunami killed over 230,000 people of 12 different countries in the Indian Ocean. Causing enormous, devastating waves in the Indian Ocean, the quake's full extent of damage is unknown. Scientists report that the tremor was so large that it shifted the earth's rotation on its axis by nearly one inch, a huge phenomenon.

Irony to Note

Keeping the world turning, irony does a good job of making a story truly stick.

- In January 1962, the group of artists later known as the Beatles performed a mediocre audition at Decca Records. Producer Mike Smith rejected them, stating that the company did not like their sound, and that groups of guitars were on their way out of the music scene. Smith was proved horribly wrong when the Beatles later signed with EMI Records and achieved lifelong fame and celebrity.
- At age 28, Beethoven became deaf and was unable to hear his own compositions.
- The second most popular song associated with baseball, "Take Me Out to the Ball Game" was written by two men who had never attended a baseball game.
- When the hatch door for the capsule of NASA flight *Liberty Bell 7* flew open prematurely, Astronaut Gus Grissom nearly drowned. After the incident, NASA engineers redesigned the hatch door for the flight *Apollo 1*, so that it would require force to open and hopefully prevent another similar accident from occurring. In a test of the capsule before its takeoff, Grissom and two other astronauts were killed when a fire started inside, and the men were unable to open the hatch to escape.
- In 1900, prisoner Charles Justice redesigned the electric chair with a better way of restraining a prisoner. He proposed the use of metal clamps to replace the traditional leather straps. The changes were made, and Justice was released on parole. He was later sentenced to death on a murder conviction. In November 1911, Justice was executed in the electric chair he had improved 11 years earlier.

Ken Jennings: A Jeopardy Master

Ken Jennings, holder of the record for the longest winning streak on *Jeopardy*, won 74 games before he was defeated by challenger Nancy Zerg. By this point Jennings had amassed $2.52 million in winnings. During his reign, ratings for the show increased by 22 percent, according to the Nielsen TV National People Meter, as people across America tuned in to witness for themselves how deep his trivial knowledge went. In keeping with the spirit of the show and Jennings's wealth of useless knowledge, here's some trivial facts about the big winner:

- Jennings won the rookie division of the American Crossword Puzzle Tournament in 2006.
- He appeared twice on NPR's *Wait, Wait, Don't Tell Me* program and twice on *The Late Show with David Letterman.*
- He is currently pressing networks to help him produce a potential game show titled *Ken Jennings vs. the Rest of the World.*
- He kept a plush Totoro toy from the movie *My Neighbor Totoro* in his pocket as a good luck charm.
- During game 53 of his streak, Jennings was given the clue "This term for a long-handled gardening tool can also mean an immoral pleasure seeker." Jennings quickly replied, "What's a ho(e)?" Host Alex Trebek replied "No," caught the audience's laughter, and said, "Whoa, whoa, whoa, they teach you that in school in Utah, huh?" The correct response was "Rake."
- He frequently gave answers in clever ways. Examples: "What are the munchies, man?" when given a clue about midnight food cravings, and "What be Ebonics?"

Famous Last Words of Literary Geniuses

- **Anton Chekhov**
  "It's a long while since I've drunk champagne."
- **Noel Coward**
  "Goodnight, my darlings. I'll see you tomorrow."
- **Emily Dickinson**
  "…the fog is rising."
- **Johan Goethe**
  "Open the second shutter so that more light can come in."
- **O. Henry**
  "Turn up the lights. I don't want to go home in the dark."
- **Heinrich Heine**
  "God will pardon me. That is His trade."
- **Henry James**
  "So it has come at last, the distinguished thing."
- **Karl Marx**
  "Go on, get out. Last words are for fools who haven't said enough."
- **W. Somerset Maugham**
  "Dying is a very dull, dreary affair. And my advice to you is to have nothing whatsoever to do with it."
- **Alexander Pope**
  "Here I am, dying of a hundred good symptoms."
- **Dylan Thomas**
  "I've had 18 straight whiskeys. I think that's the record."
- **James Thurber**
  "God bless, God damn."
- **Voltaire**
  "This is no time to make new enemies." (in response to a deathbed request for him to renounce Satan)

Literary Terms to Know

Problem play: A type of drama that became popular in the 19th century in which a social issue was dramatized in order to inspire the audience to action. Feminism, prostitution, and economic injustice are common themes addressed in problem plays.

Simile: A comparison using the words *like* or *as*. "Happy as a clam" is an example, as is "dumb as dirt."

Soliloquy: In real life, when an individual talks to himself, we often call it mental illness. In drama we call it a soliloquy. A famous soliloquy is Hamlet's speech that begins: "To be or not to be."

Stream-of-consciousness technique: A type of narration that takes a reader inside a character's mind. The words read as if they are random thoughts streaming through a character's psyche. Stream-of-consciousness is often written without punctuation or capitalization because most people don't think in grammatically perfect sentences. James Joyce and Virginia Woolf are two novelists known for this technique.

Tragedy: A story that touches on serious themes and results in an unfortunate situation for the main characters. Aristotle once said that the purpose of tragedy is emotional purging. Usually the protagonist of a tragedy begins in a high place (king, prince) and falls in some way, which makes the situation tragic.

Villanelle: A form of poetry consisting of 19 lines divided into six stanzas: five tercets (a group of three lines) and a concluding quatrain (a group of four lines). To make things more complicated, the first and third lines of the first tercet rhyme; these rhymes are repeated in all of the following tercets and in the final quatrain.

A good example is Dylan Thomas's poem "Do not go gentle into that good night":

Do not go gentle into that good night,
Old age should burn and rave at close of day;
Rage, rage against the dying of the light.

Though wise men at their end know dark is right,
Because their words had forked no lightning they
Do not go gentle into that good night.

Good men, the last wave by, crying how bright
Their frail deeds might have danced in a green bay,
Rage, rage against the dying of the light.

Wild men who caught and sang the sun in flight,
And learn, too late, they grieved it on its way,
Do not go gentle into that good night.

Grave men, near death, who see with blinding sight
Blind eyes could blaze like meteors and be gay,
Rage, rage against the dying of the light.

And you, my father, there on the sad height,
Curse, bless me now with your fierce tears, I pray.
Do not go gentle into that good night.
Rage, rage against the dying of the light.

A Plot to Know: A Tale of Two Cities

In this oppositional plot line, Charles Dickens contrasts Paris and London during the French Revolution. The story begins when Dr. Alexander Manette is released from eighteen years in the Bastille for having knowledge about the Marquis de St. Evrémonde assaulting a peasant girl. M. and Mdm. Defarge take Manette back to London to his daughter, Lucie. Years later they are asked to testify that they saw Charles Darnay, the nephew of Evrémonde, flee to England to escape trumped up charges of treason. Through a twin plot device, Darnay is saved by Sydney Carton who happens to look a lot like him. The two young men become buddies, and while both love Lucie, Darnay wins her hand. More years pass and once again false charges affect Darnay. He learns that a beloved old servant has been imprisoned in Paris, so he goes to the war-torn city to help. He is imprisoned and sentenced to die. Only his "twin," Carton, can save him, if he is willing to take his place on the guillotine. Do Darnay and Lucie live happily ever after, or does Darnay lose his head and Carton win Lucie's hand? You'll have to read the book to find out.

Useless Trivia

Charles Dickens was nearly caught vacationing with his mistress. Desperately trying to hide the fact that he was traveling with actress Ellen Ternan, who was rumored to have broken up his marriage, he told few people that he was involved in a serious train wreck on June 9, 1865. At first he rushed to aid the wounded, but when he realized press would soon arrive and discover him with Ellen, he grabbed the manuscript he was working on (the novel *Our Mutual Friend*) and left the scene of the accident.

Know the Language of Spies

It takes a lot of secrecy, intelligence, and wit to be a spy and not get caught. Below is some of the lingo of spies, translated for those who prefer to remain open to recognition.

L-Pill

An L-pill is a poisonous pill sometimes carried by spies for the purposes of suicide in the event of capture. For spies during World War II, sometimes L-pills contained enough cyanide to kill them instantly once ingested. The cyanide was stored in a glass capsule small enough to be hidden inside a fake tooth. If the spy bit into the capsule, it would kill him instantly.

Sheep Dipping

In CIA terminology, sheep dipping refers to the act of disguising the identity of a spy or agent by positing the agent with a legitimate organization. Using the clean credentials, the spy can then penetrate other organizations. As the term suggests, the agent is cleaned up so that his past is invisible, in much the same way sheep are cleaned with chemicals before shearing.

Brush Contact

A public meeting between two spies, in which they exchange documents or information without speaking or acknowledging one another, is called a brush contact. It can be pictured as one spy walking past another and exchanging briefcases. To a bystander, it might look as though the two simply bumped into one another by accident.

Dangle

A dangle is an agent who infiltrates one agency while seeking information for another. The agent goes to a second agency or organization and convinces them that his loyalties have changed, offering to be a double agent, or to leak information from his past organization. Once in, the dangle uses his new position to feed information back to his original loyalty.

Quiz: What's in a Name?

1. Mouth and Chunk were the nicknames of what characters in *The Goonies?*
2. Bill and Ted introduced several historical figures to Missy in *Bill and Ted's Bogus Journey.* Who were they?
3. Name all four Ghostbusters.
4. In *Labyrinth*, Sarah is trying to save her baby brother. What was his name?
5. In *Aliens*, what was Newt's real name?
6. Name the robot from the *Short Circuit* flicks.
7. In the 1980s cult classic film *Sixteen Candles*, what was the name of the exchange student kept by Sam's grandparents?
8. In *Tootsie*, what was the name of the woman played by Dustin Hoffmann?

Answers

1. Clark and Lawrence
2. Socrates, Billy the Kid, Joan of Arc, Sigmund Freud, Genghis Khan, Beethoven, Abraham Lincoln
3. Peter Venkman, Egon Spengler, Ray Stantz, Winston Zedmore
4. Toby
5. Rebecca Jorden
6. Johnny
7. Long Duck Dong
8. Dorothy Michaels

A Genius's Guide to Knowing Latin

What better way to sound like a genius than to sprinkle Latin words and phrases into conversation? The following is a quick guide to make sure you know your Latin abbreviations and phrases, and well enough to pronounce them correctly.

Latin Abbreviations

Ca. (circa): About or around. Indicates an approximate date.
Ex.: Chaucer wrote ca. 1370s.

Cf. (confer): Compare. Often found in literary annotations
Ex.: "Auntie Em" cf. *The Wizard of Oz.*

Et al. (et alia): And others
Ex.: Modernist writers include Joyce, Woolf, Lawrence, et al.

E.g.: (exempli gratis): For example
Ex.: Yeats wrote many great poems, e.g., "The Second Coming."

N.b. (nota bene): Take note or note well.
Example: One might pencil *n.b.* in the margin of a book next to an extraordinary line.

Viz. (videlicet): Namely.
Ex.: There are many great Victorian poets, viz., Robert Browning.

Latin Phrases

Ad nauseam: Overly repetitive, to the point of making one ill
Antebellum: Before the Civil War
Carpe diem: Seize the day
Ex libris: From the book collection of…
Finis: The end
In media res: In the middle of things
In situ: In position
In toto: Completely or wholly

Juvenilia: Works written when young
Magnum opus: Masterpiece
Modus operandi: How someone works, or a method of working
Mutatis mutandis: With necessary changes
Non sequitur: Does not follow an order, as in something completely random
Post scriptum: Written after (p.s.)
Tabula rasa: Blank slate
Verbatim: Word for word, exactly
Deus ex machina: Literally, "God out of a machine." This term describes a literary device where an improbable or unlikely character or situation is inserted into a story to resolve conflict.

Grammar Lesson

Verbals are words that start out as verbs but later become other parts of speech. The three types are infinitives, gerunds, and participles.

Infinitives are made of the word to, plus a verb: to go, to write, to begin. The infinitive may be used as a noun, as in this sentence, where it is the subject: To read has always been my favorite pastime.

Gerunds are verbs to which -ing has been added, also making them nouns. In this sentence, the gerund is the object of the verb. His favorite sport was running.

Participles are verb forms that act as adjectives. They also end with -ing and sometimes -ed, and modify nouns or pronouns. An example would be: The stomped ash was quickly extinguished.

Really Old Stuff to Note

Oldest City in the World

Archaeologists on a 2001 dig tapped in on an ancient city in western India off the coast of the Gulf of Khambhat. Submerged beneath the water, the city stretched 5.6 miles and, through carbon dating, was found to date back to 7500 BC This was a huge discovery; previously, the earliest cities were thought to be about 4,500 years older and located in Mesopotamia.

Oldest Tavern in America

The Bell in Hand Tavern, located in Boston, is the oldest and longest running tavern in the United States. It was established in 1795 and has never closed since. Famous customers at the bar have included President William McKinley and Paul Revere.

Oldest Company in the World

Based in Osaka, Japan, the Kongo Gumi Co., a construction business, was the longest operating company in the world. The business started in AD 578, when it built the Shitennoji Temple. It had a hand in building many famous temples and buildings around Japan, including the Osaka Castle in the 16th century. In 2006, after suffering financial trouble, Kongo Gumi was liquidated and purchased by Takamatsu Corporation.

Oldest Person to View the Earth from Space

American astronaut John Glenn became a national hero when he rode the shuttle *Friendship 7*, orbiting the earth three times. He was the third person to orbit the earth, and the first American. Glenn returned to space at the age of 77, to test the effects of space travel on an elderly body.

Oldest Person to Ever Live

Jeanne Louise Calment was born in 1875, and died 122 years later, making her the oldest person to ever live thus far. Born in Arles, France, a year before the invention of the telephone, Calment met Vincent Van Gogh when she was 13 years old.

Quiz: The Daily Grind

1. In *Office Space*, what was Milton's prized possession that Peter pulled from the rubble after Intitech burnt to the ground?
2. What job does Tom Hanks's character have in *Bachelor Party*?
3. In the movie *Notting Hill* what magazine does Hugh Grant's character say he works for in an attempt to get an "interview" with the movie star played by Julia Roberts?
4. What was Adam Sandler's occupation in *Big Daddy*?
5. In *Midnight Run*, what agency does Walsh (Robert De Niro) work for?
6. In *Beverly Hills Cop*, Axel Foley enters the hotel and uses an alias. Who does he say he works for, and who is he allegedly going to interview?
7. Who was the sponsor for *Wayne's World*?
8. In *The Karate Kid*, what color did Mr. Miagi make Daniel paint his house as part of his training?

Answers

1. The red stapler
2. He is a school bus driver.
3. *Horse and Hound*
4. Tollbooth worker
5. Mosconi Bail Bonds
6. *Rolling Stone* and is going to interview Michael Jackson
7. Noah's Arcade
8. Green

Two Really Bad Diseases Cured in the 20th Century

Malaria

Like a parasite, malaria attacks the liver and red blood cells, causing nausea and flulike symptoms and, if untreated, even seizures, coma, kidney failure, and death. Transmitted by mosquitoes, the disease infects between 350 and 500 million people every year. Because of new vaccines and medicines, the death rate for malaria has dropped over the last 100 years. While each infection used to be fatal, now only around 1 million cases per year are deadly.

H. Flu

H. flu, also known as Hib disease, is caused by the Haemophilus influenza type B bacteria. The infection is not related to any type of the influenza virus, but it can lead to bacterial meningitis, pneumonia, and serious infections of the bone, blood, and pericardium. A vaccine for the Hib disease was introduced in 1990 and achieved worldwide success. Even so, the disease is still responsible for 2 to 3 million infections each year, around 450,000 of which are fatal.

Before the advent of antibiotics, tuberculosis claimed the lives of many famous writers, including Jane Austen, Aubrey Beardsley, Anne Brontë, Charlotte Brontë, Emily Brontë, Stephen Crane, Franz Kafka, John Keats, D. H. Lawrence, Katherine Mansfield, and George Orwell.

More Literary Terms to Know

Haiku: Japanese-inspired poem of three lines: five syllables in the first line, seven syllables in the second, then five again. Fitted inside this tight structure is usually an image from nature.

Hamartia: Aristotle used this term to describe "some error or frailty," like greed or weakness, that brings about the downfall for a tragic hero, much like a fatal flaw.

Hubris: A gigantic ego. In Greek tragedy, this kind of pride typically ends in a disastrous event.

Hyperbole: A really big exaggeration, like "I'm hungry enough to eat a horse. No, make that a herd of horses."

Iambic pentameter: An iambic foot is one unstressed syllable followed by a stressed syllable, as in the word *regard*. Iambic pentameter is metrical pattern in poetry that consists of five iambic feet per line, so that the line sounds like this: du-Duh, du-Duh, du-Duh, du-Duh, du-Duh. Here's an example from John Keats: when I have FEARS that I may CEASE to BE.

Lyric: A brief poem that expresses the thoughts and feelings of a speaker. The important thing to remember is that the speaker is not necessarily the poet. Just because a poem is in the voice of a 19th-century firefighter doesn't mean traveled back in time to battle blazes, and nor should the poet reader assume he or she has. When William Carlos Williams writes the lines, "I have eaten the plums that were in the icebox," he may just be making that up. Sad poems don't necessarily come from sad poets. Same goes for angry or happy poems.

Melodrama: Basically, a literary soap opera, except they usually end happily.

Metaphor: A metaphor compares two things without using the word *like* or *as*. For example, the title *The Heart is a Lonely Hunter*, by Carson McCullers, employs the use of metaphor.

Ode: A type of lyric poem. Odes are usually serious and formal, such as Keats's "Ode on a Grecian Urn."

Oxymoron: This sounds like a type of insult, but no, it's a paradoxical phrase in which two opposite words are used together, as in "original copy" or "jumbo shrimp."

Paraphrase: To restate the idea of something in one's own words. Readers will often paraphrase a poem to help make sense of it or will paraphrase a quote to make it shorter and clearer.

Personification: A figure of speech in which human characteristics are given to nonhuman things. A writer might describe rain by offering that "the sky is crying." This helps readers identify with the situation in an emotional way.

Plot: The particular selection and arrangement of incidents in a story that helps unfold the narrative. The plot isn't simply what happens—it is the way the author puts those events in order. A story may proceed chronologically—first A happens, then B, then C. However, an author might plot the events differently—first we learn about C, and then we get the backstory of A and B.

Point of view: The perspective from which a story is told. A child's point of view will render a very different tale than an old man's, for instance. The point of view the author chooses affects how readers will respond to events. A first-person narrator speaks directly to the audience from within the story. A third-person narrator, on the other hand, presents a more neutral point of view, from outside the action.

A Plot to Know: Vanity Fair

When William Thackeray was writing this 1848 masterpiece, he said he wanted to create a cast of characters who were thoroughly greedy, haughty, and self-righteous. Only a few characters would exemplify any real humility, and we could learn from them. He succeeded in this book whose subtitle is "A Novel Without a Hero." Becky Sharp and Amelia Sedley are two friends from boarding school with vastly different backgrounds. The wily and scheming Becky was born into poverty, but she tries to seduce Amelia's wealthy, stupid brother, Joseph. When he won't marry her, she weds Rawdon Crawley, the son of her employer. Crawley's father disinherits him, but Becky still manages to live a life of luxury through her "friendship" with Lord Steyne. Eventually Crawley leaves Becky, and she is left with nothing but her wits to sustain her.

Meanwhile, Amelia marries George Osborne, who gets killed in battle. Living in poverty, she has to give up her only son, Georgy, to her father-in-law. When Mr. Osborne dies, he leaves little Georgy a fortune. Amelia finds happiness through her faithful son and through William Dobbin who has, for years, loved her from afar.

Little Smarty Pants

Children can be pretty sharp, and their accomplishments always impress the grownups who witness them. Not all of the triumphs of youth are biological of course; in fact quite a few children have tried their hand at writing throughout the years, and many have been published. None, however, gave their heart and soul to the publishing house while as young as Dorothy Straight.

Born in Washington, DC, in 1958, the young author penned her first, and apparently last, masterpiece at the tender age of four. One has to wonder if the original manuscript smelled of talcum powder and mashed peas. The book, *How the World Began,* began as a gift to her grandmother and ended up in print thanks to the generous (and possibly a little too excitable) people at Pantheon Books in 1964, just after Dorothy's sixth birthday. It doesn't appear that the book has ever been reprinted and the item is practically impossible to find for purchase. Less than 50 libraries and special collections throughout the United States have the text in their catalogs and although little Dorothy's entry has been excluded from the most recent Library of Congress catalog, a copy has been retained in the collection.

S. E. Hinton, born Susan Eloise Hinton, began writing *The Outsiders*, a novel about gangs and male rivalry, at age 15. She used her initials instead of Susan so that boys wouldn't disregard it as a book for girls. Since its publication in 1967, it has become one of the most popular books for young readers.

A Guide to Greek Gods

- Zeus (Roman: Jupiter)
  Zeus was King of Olympus and god of the sky. He was known for hurling thunderbolts, ruling the universe, and committing adultery.
- Hera (Roman: Juno)
  Hera was the wife and sister of Zeus. She was Queen of Olympus and the goddess of both marriage and childbirth. She punished the women that became Zeus' mistresses.
- Poseidon (Roman: Neptune)
  Poseidon was the brother of Zeus and the god of the sea. He carried a large trident (fork) and waved it to created tumultuous seas and storms, sinking ships. Poseidon was also the god of horses. He often disguised himself as a stud.
- Hades (Roman: Pluto)
  A brother of Zeus, Hades was god of the underworld. He pined after Persephone and eventually kidnapped her. He was also god of the dead and of wealth.
- Hestia (Roman: Vesta)
  Hestia was the sister of Zeus and goddess of the hearth. She was a protector of family, the home, and stability. She showed no interest in male gods Apollo and Poseidon and remained a virgin-goddess.
- Athena (Roman: Minerva)
  Smart and good with crops. Daughter of Zeus alone. She didn't have a mother. In fact, she just sprang from Zeus' head. This made her his favorite child. Goddess of wisdom, the city, and protector of agriculture, she could be tough like her father. He let her carry his special shield, the aegis. Anyone who looked at it turned into stone.
- Hephaestus (Roman: Vulcan)
  Really ugly but good with tools. He was the child of Hera.

She gave birth to him for revenge on Zeus for giving birth to Athena. Her vengeance was short-lived, however. Hephaestus was lame and considered so ugly that Hera threw him out of heaven. Despite his dysfunctional childhood, he grew up to be the god of the forge and fire and husband of Aphrodite.

- Ares (Roman: Mars)
  Ares was the god of war and the son of Zeus and Hera, both of whom hated him. He was famous among the Greeks for being a coward, as it was common for him to retreat in battle. The Romans, on the other hand, saw him as brave and heroic, and in Roman mythology, he was the lover of Aphrodite, goddess of love.
- Apollo
  Apollo was the son of Zeus and a Titan, Leto. He was god of light, arts, medicine, and music. When the mortal Cassandra wouldn't return his affections, he cursed her with the gift of foretelling the future. Though she was always honest, no one believed her prophecies, which was part of her lifelong curse.
- Artemis (Roman: Diana)
  Artemis was the twin sister of Apollo and the goddess of hunting. In her chastity, she protected young girls and was known for having a fiery temper. When a hunter, Actaeon, spied on her while she was bathing naked, she had him torn to pieces by his own dogs. In the temple at Ephesus, a statue depicts her with numerous breasts, symbolizing her as a goddess of childbirth.
- Aphrodite (Roman: Venus)
  Aphrodite was the daughter of Zeus and Dione, but in some stories she is said to have emerged from the foam of the sea. She was the goddess of love, and like her father, she found it difficult to remain faithful to her spouse. Renowned for her beauty, she cheated on Hephaestus with Ares, Hermes, Dionysus, and the handsome mortal Adonis.

- Hermes (Roman: Mercury)
  Hermes was the son of Zeus and the nymph Maia. He was messenger of all the gods and said to be the most cunning. He was famous for lying and stealing and became known as the god of commerce and the marketplace.

Quiz: Number Crunchers

1. How many days were the castaways on the mysterious island during the first season of *Lost?*
2. How many gigawatts of electricity did Doc Brown need to power the Delorion in *Back to the Future?*
3. What was the hottest possible temperature on the Klopek's furnace in *The 'Burbs?*
4. What was Dirty Harry's badge number?
5. Above what speed did the bus in the movie *Speed* need to go in order to keep from blowing up?
6. In *National Lampoon's Animal House*, what is Blutarski's grade-point average?
7. In *Stripes*, how much money does Ox (John Candy) pay to mud wrestle with women?
8. In *Monty Python and the Holy Grail*, what number must you count to before throwing the Holy Hand Grenade?

Answers

1. 44
2. 1.21 gigawatts
3. 5000 degrees
4. 2211
5. 50 mph
6. 0.0
7. $413.58
8. Three. No more, no less.

Inspired: Greek Muses

The ancient Greeks believed nine Muses inspired human creativity.

The Nine Muses

Calliope	Muse of epic poetry and eloquence
Euterpe	Muse of music or of lyric poetry
Erato	Muse of the poetry of love
Polyhymnia	Muse of oratory or sacred poetry
Clio	Muse of history
Melpomene	Muse of tragedy
Thalia	Muse of comedy
Terpsichore	Muse of choral song and dance
Urania	Muse of astronomy

Nine Facts

1. The early Greek poet, Hesiod, was the first to name the Muses in the *Theogony*.
2. Homer famously invoked the Muse in *The Iliad* and *The Odyssey*.
3. Like his epic predecessor, Virgil invoked the Muse at the beginning of the *Aeneid*.
4. In English poetry, one of the earliest invocations comes from Geoffrey Chaucer. In *The Canterbury Tales*, the Man of Law calls on the Muse of poetry to help him tell a moral story.
5. John Milton invokes the aid of a Muse at the beginning of *Paradise Lost*.

6. The earliest sites of the Muses' worship were Pieria, near Mount Olympus in Thessaly, and Mount Helicon in Boeotia.
7. In Roman, Renaissance, and Neoclassical art, artists often distinguished Muses by certain props so viewers could recognize them.

    - Calliope carries a writing tablet
    - Clio carries a scroll and books
    - Erato carries a lyre and a crown of roses
    - Euterpe carries a flute
    - Melpomene wears or holds a tragic mask
    - Thalia wears or holds a comic mask
    - Polyhymnia usually has a thoughtful look on her face;
    - Terpsichore carries a lyre
    - Urania carries a staff which she points at a globe.

8. Plato complimented the poet, Sappho, by calling her "the tenth muse." Since then, other female poets to earn that compliment have included Anne Bradstreet and Sor Juana Inés de la Cruz.
9. Muse comes from Latin *Musa*, from Greek *Mousa*. The name of Mnemosyne, the goddess of memory and mother of the Muses, comes from the Greek word mnïmosunï "memory," which comes from the Greek and Indo-European root men which means "to think." *Men* is the root word of amnesia, mental, and mind.

Speed Reading

A great deal can be said for taking the time to read a book critically. Exploring various points-of-view, questioning suppositions about the work, and considering the political or social implications underlying the text lead the reader to a heightened level of understanding. The comprehension rate accepted by scholars is around 400 words per minute, and according to researchers, reading beyond this rate results in a 50 percent comprehension loss. Don't tell that to the ever-growing army of speed-readers, however. They claim their increased reading rates have been accomplished without sacrificing the subtleties of the written word.

Whether the claims of comprehension and retention are true are false, the skill is of interest to many consumers. As with any product demand, a supply of products floods the market in the form of speed-reading courses and manuals. The businesses producing the materials claim that consumers can double or triple their reading speed without loss of comprehension, often for a high price. Some of the businesses selling speed-reading training materials declare that their customers will experience improvement up to 1,000 to 2,000 words per minute.

Speed Readers of History

Jacques Bergier - Best-selling author of *The Morning of the Magicians*

Howard Berg – Speed reading "celebrity" featured in the *1990 Guinness Book of World Records* and on *Live with Regis and Kathie Lee*

John F. Kennedy – 35th president of the United States

The Genius Club

Ever pondered what geniuses do with their spare time? Many of them join Mensa, the world's most famous high-IQ society. The apolitical, nonprofit organization, founded in 1946 by Englishmen Roland Berrill and Dr. Lancelot Ware, welcomes people of any race, religion, or background and requires its members to score in the 98th percentile or higher on standardized tests such as the Stanford-Binet. Membership currently consists of 100,000 geniuses in 50 countries worldwide.

Members of the society, known as Mensans, join primarily for networking and social reasons, although many of them are undoubtedly drawn by the prestige of belonging to a club of geniuses. According the the official website, Mensa International's purposes are "to identify and foster human intelligence for the benefit of humanity; to encourage research in the nature, characteristics, and uses of intelligence; and to promote stimulating intellectual and social opportunities for its members." The group regularly publishes multiple books and periodicals, including the monthly *Mensa Magazine*.Once inducted into the organization, members receive an invitation to local, national, and international events. The annual national meetings occur around the world, as well as the annual Mensa World Gathering. The events include activities typical to social clubs such as dances, costume contests, and games such as poker, chess, and double-deck cancellation hearts.

WWE professional wrestler Scott Levy, better known as Raven, is a member of Mensa and has a reported IQ of 143.

World Chess Champions

Undisputed world champions 1935–1993

Max Euwe	1935–1937	Netherlands
Alexander Alekhine	1937–1946	France
Mikhail Botvinnik	1948–1957	Soviet Union
Vasily Smyslov	1957–1958	Soviet Union
Mikhail Botvinnik	1958–1960	Soviet Union
Mikhail Tal	1960–1961	Soviet Union (Latvia)
Mikhail Botvinnik	1961–1963	Soviet Union
Tigran Petrosian	1963–1969	Soviet Union (Armenia)
Boris Spassky	1969–1972	Soviet Union
Robert J. Fischer	1972–1975	United States
Anatoly Karpov	1975–1985	Soviet Union
Garry Kasparov	1985–1993	Soviet Union/ Russia

FIDE world champions 1993–2006

Anatoly Karpov	1993–1999	Russia
Alexander Khalifman	1999–2000	Russia
Viswanathan Anand	2000–2002	India
Ruslan Ponomariov	2002–2004	Ukraine
Rustam Kasimdzhanov	2004–2005	Uzbekistan
Veselin Topalov	2005–2006	Bulgaria

Classical world champions 1993–2006

Garry Kasparov	1993–2000	Russia
Vladimir Kramnik	2000–2006	Russia

Undisputed world champions 2006–

Vladimir Kramnik	2006–2007	Russia
Viswanathan Anand	2007–	India

The Amazing Chinese Card Shuffler

When there is gambling to be done, there are millions of dollars to be made. Time is money and talk is cheap, but slow shuffling is not. Casinos hire dealers based on many qualities, one of which is quick and efficient shuffling. Over the last several years the nature of many games, not to mention the reasonable suspicion of casino managers, has led to the use of shuffling machines. For this reason, the card-slinger is slowly going the way of the buffalo. Nonetheless, the ability to shuffle a deck of cards in a flash is a sight to behold, and spectators love it when someone publicly performs the card-shuffling task at record-breaking speed, as did Zheng Taishun of China.

At a *Guinness Book of World Records* event on June 10, 2006, in Fuzhou City, China, Taishun displayed his superior card-shuffling prowess to the amazement of an eager audience. In fact, he did it so fast that several of the onlookers probably missed his display of skill. In only 39.28 seconds, Taishun placed a randomly shuffled deck of cards in order for all suits: Ace - King - Queen - Jack - 10 - 9 - 8 - 7- 6 - 5 - 4 - 3 - 2. The astonishing achievement landed him a position in the *2008 Guinness Book of World Records* over the previous champion, Kunihiko Terada of Japan, whose 2004 record was 40.3 seconds.

The accomplishment has granted Taishun some international acclaim, particularly among those who strive to usurp the man his position as the record holder. Little else is known about Taishun, but although his current occupation is not public information, it wouldn't be implausible to discover that in consequence of his extraordinary demonstration he scored a new career and relocated to the gambling hotspot of Macau shortly thereafter.

John Logie Baird
Inventor

Born in 1888, in Helensburgh, Scotland, John Logie Baird studied at Glasgow University, but he did not graduate because of the outbreak of World War I. The armed forces turned him down because of his poor health; however, he took the position of superintendent engineer of the Clyde Valley Electrical Power Company.

When the war ended he moved to the southern coast of England and started experimenting with making a television. By 1924, he was able to transmit a flickering image over a few feet. Then, in January 1926, he gave the world's first demonstration of his television at a meeting of 50 scientists in London. The next year his television was demonstrated over 438 miles of telephone line between London and Glasgow, and he formed the Baird Television Development Company. In 1928, he made the first transatlantic television transmission between London and New York and the first transmission to a ship in the mid-Atlantic. He also demonstrated the first color and stereoscopic televisions.

Unfortunately, he wasn't fast enough. In America, Marconi was developing an electronic system. When the British Broadcasting Company tried Baird's system alongside Marconi's system in 1935, Marconi's all-electronic television system won out. In 1937 Baird's system was dropped. Baird died in 1946, in Bexhill-on-Sea in Sussex.

- When Baird was in his 20s, he tried to make diamonds out of graphite and shorted out all the electricity in Glasgow.
- The Logie Awards, Australian television industry awards, honor John Logie Baird, who invented the first working television. The awards have been presented annually since 1959.

The Trivial Pursuits of Fred Worth and David Wall

The immensely successful Parker Brothers game Trivial Pursuit has entertained millions with its evaluation of the players' knowledge about general subjects and popular culture. For those unfamiliar with the game, it involves answering questions around the board and collecting pie pieces upon providing correct answers. Since its emergence onto the board game market in 1982, the game's creators, Scott Abbott and John Haney, have been involved in two major lawsuits concerning the game, one by trivia author Fred Worth and the other by a man named David Wall. In both lawsuits the Trivial Pursuit guys got all the pieces of the pie, therefore winning the cases.

The inventors of Trivial Pursuit pulled many of their facts from books written by Fred Worth, including one titled *The Trivia Encyclopedia*. In 1984, Worth sued them, claiming that a quarter of the Genius Edition came straight from his book and that he had included misinformation in an effort to catch anyone violating the copyright he had acquired for it. The game's creators did not deny the use of his books but stated that facts could not be protected by copyright. The court agreed, resulting in a Supreme Court appeal in 1988. The Supreme Court rejected Worth's claim.

In 1994, David Wall sued the inventors of Trivial Pursuit, claiming that, in 1979, he and a friend were hitchhiking when game-maker Chris Haney gave them a ride. According to Wall he told Haney about his idea for the game in detail. The alleged hitchhiking partner never testified. Haney denied ever meeting Wall. The final testimony was heard during the first week of 2007, and the Supreme Court of Nova Scotia ruled in favor of Haney and the other inventors of Trivial Pursuit.

A Good Name to Know: Sir Aaron Klug Crystallographic Electron Microscopy

Although born in Lithuania, Aaron Klug actually grew up in South Africa, where his family moved when he was two years old. He graduated with a degree in science from the University of Witwatersrand in Johannesburg and then moved on to graduate study in crystallography at the University of Cape Town. He completed his Ph.D. at Trinity College in Cambridge, England, in 1953.

- Klug won the Nobel Prize in chemistry in 1982 for the development of crystallographic electron microscopy and his work with nucleic acid-protein complexes.
- With crystallographic electron microscopy, he was able to take two-dimensional images of crystals from different angles and combine them to produce three-dimensional images, thus better determining the arrangement of atoms.
- Throughout his career, Klug's major focus has been on viruses. In the 1950s, he made significant discoveries in the structure of the tobacco mosaic virus, which destroys many crops, including tobacco, tomatoes, and ornamental flowers.

Klug was knighted in 1988 and appointed to the Order of Merit in 1995. In 2005, he was awarded the gold Order of Mapungubwe (Africa's highest honor) for exceptional achievements in medical science.

Remembering the '50s

The 1950s are remembered by many as "the good years" in America, probably as a result of the incredibly wholesome and heartwarming impressions left by shows such as *I Love Lucy* and *Leave it to Beaver*. The war was over, babies were being born, and mom's apple pie was cooling on the windowsill. Not everyone bought the hunky-dory vibe Hollywood was selling however, and much of the popular literature of the time records a different set of worldviews, as demonstrated by these bestsellers of the decade:

- *The Little Princesses* by Marion Crawford – A bestseller in 1950, this unauthorized biography of Princesses Elizabeth and Margaret resulted in the former employee of the British court being banished from court.
- *Courtroom* by Quentin Reynolds – A best-selling biography about Samuel Leibowitz, the defense attorney for the Scottsboro boys, the book shocked America by exposing American violence and racial injustice.

Useless Trivia

Often described as one of the most original musical geniuses of the 1950s, Bo Diddley has been playing guitar since his early teens. In 1955, at age 27, Diddley signed a record deal and put out his first singles, "Uncle John" and "I'm A Man." He soon became famous for influencing a rhythmic style called hambone, slapping your hands on your legs and chest while singing simple songs. He also invented rock's most foundational rhythm, the "Bo Diddley beat." The popular bass line has been picked up by decades of artists since then, including The Who, U2, and Bruce Springsteen. His square-bodied cigar box guitar, one he designed for himself while at school in 1945, remains his trademark instrument.

Could You Please Clarify, Mr. Lewis?

The fantasy series *The Chronicles of Narnia,* written by English author C. S. Lewis, is one of the most popular of children's literature. Over 100 million copies of the Carnegie Medal-winning series have been sold in 41 languages since the publication of the first novel in 1950. Librarians, parents, and children have canonized it for decades as quintessential material for young readers.

The Lion, the Witch and the Wardrobe, the first book of the series to be published, sets the stage for a story of seven installments involving a group of children who become central figures in the history of the fantasy realm of Narnia. Or does it? Although the sixth novel, *The Magician's Nephew,* was not published until 1955, many fans of the series believe it to be the beginning of the story. Written as a prequel to the previously published books, *The Magician's Nephew* describes the creation of the magical realm and therefore precedes the Narnian adventures of Lewis's primary cast of characters.

At its first American publishing by Macmillan, numbers were printed on books based solely on the order of publication year. The question did not concern Lewis, and he never publicly clarified his intent when crafting the series. However, in a letter to a young fan who sought illumination on the subject, the author agreed with the child's notion that *The Lion, the Witch and the Wardrobe* was indeed the proper text with which to begin the series. In 1994, Harper Collins acquired the publication rights for *The Chronicles of Narnia* and, by suggestion of a member of Lewis's estate, changed the order to reflect the chronological order of the story itself.

Proponents of the publication order insist that Lewis wrote the series book-by-book without the entire story in mind. He reflected this idea in a reply to the aforementioned youth. The other camp, however, believe the author to have been acting benevolently toward the young reader who sought affirmation in his opinion. Regardless of the order chosen by the reader, fans agree upon one certainty: *The Chronicles of Narnia* is an excellent read.

Publication Order	Chronological Order
• *The Lion, The Witch and the Wardrobe*	• *Magician's Nephew*
• *Prince Caspian*	• *The Lion, The Witch and the Wardrobe*
• *The Voyage of the Dawn Treader*	• *The Horse and His Boy*
• *The Silver Chair*	• *Prince Caspian*
• *The Horse and His Boy*	• *The Voyage of the Dawn Treader*
• *Magician's Nephew*	• *The Silver Chair*
• *The Last Battle*	• *The Last Battle*

A Good Name to Know: Wangari Maathai

The first woman in East and Central Africa to earn a doctorate degree, Kenya native Wangari Muta Maathai obtained a bachelor's degree in biological sciences from Mount St. Scholastica College in Atchison, Kansas, in 1964; a master's degree from the University of Pittsburgh in 1966; and a Ph.D. from the University of Nairobi in 1971. She taught veterinary anatomy and became chair of the Department of Veterinary Anatomy at the University of Nairobi.

Maathai joined the National Council of Women of Kenya, serving as chair from 1981 to 1987. As a part of her work with the council, she led the women in planting trees, a project that she turned into the Green Belt Movement, a broad-based, grassroots organization whose main focus is the planting of trees with women groups, in order to conserve the environment and improve their quality of life. She has helped women plant more than 20 million trees.

- Internationally noted for her devotion to the fight for democracy, human rights, and environmental conservation, Maathai has addressed the UN several times and spoken at special sessions of the General Assembly for the five-year review of the earth summit.
- She and the Green Belt Movement have received numerous awards, most notably the 2004 Nobel Peace Prize.
- In June 1997, Maathai was elected by *Earth Times* as one of 100 persons in the world who have made a difference in the environmental arena.
- In December 2002, Maathai was elected to parliament and appointed Assistant Minister for Environment, Natural Resources, and Wildlife.

Game Show Controversies

- No Whammies for Michael Larson – Before appearing on the now-defunct game show Press Your Luck, an unemployed ice cream truck driver named Michael Larson used a video recorder to learn the sequences used on the games board. He discovered that the games' configurations were not random, and he appeared on the show prepared to win. While on the show, he consistently hit "Big Bucks" and managed to accumulate $110,237 in winnings. The games producers discovered the ruse and determined that it did not qualify as cheating.
- Nude Gaming – In a short-lived television show called *Naked Jungle*, the British Channel 5 collaborated with actor Keith Chegwin and aired a show with completely nude contestants. Chegwin was also nude, and the show only appeared once.
- You've Won a Trip to (Previously) Beautiful New Orleans! – Shortly after Hurricane Katrina devastated New Orleans in August of 2005, a repeat of The Price is Right aired in which contestants were competing to win an all-expenses paid trip to New Orleans. After a mild reaction from viewers, broadcasters of the show at CBS pulled it from their programming, preventing a public outcry against them.

The Curie Family: Radioactivity

Pierre and Marie Curie developed an extensive study of radioactive isotopes during their careers, and their oldest daughter and her husband followed in the study.

Marie Curie

Maria Sklodowska was born in Warsaw, Poland, in 1867. She went to Paris in 1891 to study at the Sorbonne. There she received licenciateships in physics and mathematical sciences. She married physics professor Pierre Curie in 1895. She received her Ph.D. in 1903. After her husband's death, Marie took his place as professor of general physics at the Sorbonne, becoming the first woman to hold the position. She was also appointed director of the Curie Laboratory in the Radium Institute of the University of Paris.

Together, the couple achieved isolation of the radioactive substances polonium and radium. Marie played the major role in developing methods for the separation of radium from radioactive residues in sufficient quantities to allow for its characterization and study.

The United States backed the Curies' study. In 1921, US President Warren Harding, on behalf of the women of America, gave Marie one gram of radium in recognition of her service to science. And, in 1929, US President Herbert Hoover gave $50,000, on behalf of American friends of science, to purchase radium for use in the Curie Laboratory.

Marie received numerous awards during her career. With her husband, she was awarded half of the Nobel Prize for physics in 1903, for their study into the spontaneous radiation discovered by Becquerel, who was awarded the other half of the Prize. In 1911, she received a second Nobel Prize, this time in chemistry. She also received, jointly with her husband, the Davy Medal of the Royal Society in 1903. Marie Curie died in 1934 after a short illness, likely caused by overexposure to radiation during her research.

Pierre Curie

French-born Pierre Curie received his licenciateship in physics in 1878 and his Ph.D. in 1895 at the Sorbonne. He worked as faculty at the Sorbonne for his entire career.

His early interest was in crystallography. Together with his brother Jacques, Pierre discovered piezoelectric effects. Later, he turned his attention to magnetism, where he showed that the magnetic properties of a given substance change at a certain temperature—this temperature is now known as the Curie point.

After marrying Marie, Pierre began helping with her study of radioactive substances. Their work formed the basis for research in nuclear physics and chemistry. Pierre Curie was killed in a carriage accident in Paris in 1906.

Irène Joliot-Curie

Irène Curie, the oldest daughter of Pierre and Marie Curie, was born in Paris in 1897. She studied at the Faculty of Science in Paris and served as a nurse radiographer during World War I. She received her Ph.D. in science in 1925. A year later, she married fellow scientist Frédéric Joliot.

Throughout her career, Irène researched natural and artificial radioactivity, transmutation of elements, and nuclear physics.

Together, she and Frédéric were awarded the Nobel Prize in chemistry in 1935 for their work with the synthesis of new radioactive elements. The next year, Irène was appointed Undersecretary of State for Scientific Research.

In 1946, Irène became director of the Radium Institute. She took part in the creation and construction of the first French atomic pile in 1948. She was also instrumental in the establishment of the center for nuclear physics at Orsay.

In addition to science, Irène promoted the social and

intellectual advancement of women. She was a member of the Comité National de l'Union des Femmes Françaises and of the World Peace Council.

Frédéric and Irène had two children. Irène Joliot-Curie died in Paris in 1956.

Jean-Frédéric Joliot

As assistant to Marie Curie, Jean Frédéric Joliot not only studied science but also found his wife, Marie's daughter Irène. Frédéric was born in 1900, in Paris, where he attended the Ecole de Physique et Chimie. In 1925, he joined the Radium Institute as assistant to Marie Curie. He received his Ph.D. in 1930.

While serving as a lecturer in the Paris Faculty of Science, Frédéric joined Irène in studying the structure of the atom. Together, they also discovered artificial radioactivity, perhaps their most important work. They produced the isotope 13 of nitrogen, the isotope 30 of phosphorus, and, simultaneously, the isotopes 27 of silicon and 28 of aluminum. For this significant work, the couple received the Nobel Prize for chemistry in 1935.

In 1937, he became a professor at the Collège de France and left the Radium Institute. For his new laboratory, he commissioned the construction of the first cyclotron in Western Europe.

Frédéric also took an active part in political affairs and served as president of the World Peace Council for a time. When Irène died in 1956, he assumed her position as Chair of Nuclear Physics at the Sorbonne, while retaining his professorship at the Collège de France. He died two years later.

On a humanitarian note, Pierre and Marie's second daughter, Eve, married American diplomat H. R. Labouisse who became director of the United Children's Fund and received on its behalf the Nobel Peace Prize in 1965.

Albert Einstein

Born in 1879, in Ulm, Germany, Albert Einstein earned a Ph.D. in 1905 from the University of Zurich. As a professor of physics at universities in Zurich, Prague, and Berlin, Einstein became a well-recognized figure in the science community.

In 1916, Einstein published his theory of general relativity. Einstein had earlier theorized that distance and time are not absolute. He believed the rate that a clock ticked depended on the motion of the person looking at the clock. His theory of general relativity said that gravity and motion can affect time and space. In other words, gravity pulling in one direction is equal to acceleration in the opposite direction. This is an explanation of why a person is pushed back against the seat when a car accelerates.

In 1933, seeking to escape political oppression in Germany, Einstein immigrated to the United States. He accepted a position at the Princeton Institute of Advanced Study in New Jersey, where he taught until retirement in 1945.

During his retirement years, Einstein continued to work on his general theory of relativity.

- Einstein received the 1921 Nobel Prize in physics for his discovery of the law of the photoelectric effect and his work in the field of theoretical physics.
- He was instrumental in establishing the Hebrew University in Jerusalem.

Einstein was offered the presidency of Israel in 1952. He declined.

Sir Edward Appleton
1947 Nobel Prize for Physics

Born in 1892, in Bradford, West Yorkshire, England, Edward Victor Appleton attended Cambridge University, where he studied natural science. During World War I, he served in the Royal Engineers. Then he returned to Cambridge to research atmospheric physics, mainly using radio waves. In 1924, he accepted a position as professor of physics at London University, and he returned to Cambridge in 1936 as professor of natural philosophy.

- Appleton's research into the strength of the radio signals indicated a signal during the daytime was constant but varied at night, rising and falling in an almost regular manner. He believed that, at night, his radio received two waves, one traveling directly and the other being reflected by the atmosphere.
- Appleton was knighted in 1941 and received the Nobel Prize for physics in 1947.
- Two years later, he become principal and vice chancellor to the University of Edinburgh, a position he held until his death in 1965.

As he conducted more experiments to prove his theory, Appleton discovered a third atmospheric layer that reflected back shorter wavelengths in daytime as well as at night. They were reflected back with greater strength than the initial layer. Appleton realized that this was the atmospheric layer responsible for reflecting short-wave radio around the world. His findings led Robert Watson-Watt and his colleagues to develop radar, a crucial weapon in war.

A Name to Drop: Sir Alec Jeffreys

(Hint: Breakthroughs in DNA)

Born in 1950, Alec Jeffreys attended Oxford University, where he studied biochemistry and received his Ph.D. in 1975. Then, after studying for two years in Amsterdam, he moved to the University of Leicester, where he became a professor of genetics in 1987.

During his early research at Leicester, Jeffreys developed techniques for DNA fingerprinting and profiling, changing the way criminals are prosecuted. This technique became the basis for the United Kingdom's National DNA Database (NDNAD), launched in Britain in 1995.

Jefferys continues to teach and do research at the University of Leicester. He became a fellow of the Royal Society in 1986, was appointed as a Royal Society research professor in 1991, and was knighted in 1994. In 1996, he was awarded the Albert Einstein World Award of Science. These are only a few of the numerous honors he continues to receive.

"Our discovery of DNA fingerprinting was of course totally accidental.... But at least we had the sense to realise what we had stumbled upon."
—Alec Jeffreys

Charles Dickens and Maria Beadnell

Biographies lament on behalf of the great novelist Charles Dickens that he experienced a severe heartbreak at an early age when his beloved, and wealthy, Maria Beadnell discovered the truth about him. The young man, not yet as great a writer as he is known today, was hard working but penniless, was ambitious but altogether without heritage. Upon her realization about Dickens's background, she rejected him and left him with his heart in his hand.

The years went by, and the man began to write novels, eventually becoming one of the most famous men in Europe and the Americas. He also married, but the biographies proclaim that the marriage was not a happy one. Although it is difficult to prove, a cynical yet bitterly satisfying legend exists concerning Beadnell's return. According to legend, the lost love turned gold digger, upon connecting the admirer of her youth with the now internationally renowned writer, decided to pay him a visit. While the years gone by had affected Dickens profitably, as his wealth exploded and his celebrity grew to international acclaim, his old crush experienced growth of a different sort. Over the years, Maria Beadnell had gained considerable weight. So much weight, in fact, that Dickens didn't recognize her when she graced his doorstep one afternoon. Legend has it that the two enjoyed their visit together, and that Dickens found Beadnell just as charming as he had in his youth.

Dickens is known as one of the great novelists, yet he published his stories in serials. The anticipation caused by the popularity of the serials is comparable to that of the recent Harry Potter craze, and J. K. Rowling has often been publicly compared to this.

Thoughts on Dickens

- "Dickens is one of those authors who are well worth stealing." – novelist and essayist George Orwell, from *Charles Dickens*
- "My mother read secondarily for information; she sank as a hedonist into novels. She read Dickens in the spirit in which she would have eloped with him." – novelist Eudora Welty, from *One Writer's Beginnings*
- "I was walking on a Southern highway, and a friend driving in a pony carriage passed me, stopped and said, 'Have you heard that Charles Dickens is dead?' It was as if I had been robbed of one of my dearest friends." – novelist Margaret E. Sangster, from *An Autobiography from My Youth Up*

Useless Trivia

Dickens was a regular at his hometown boot-blacking factory, and while most children his age were playing cops and robbers, he worked ten hours a day gluing labels on jars of shoe polish in a room overrun with rats. His family was stuck in a debtor's prison, and Dickens's earnings, six shillings a week, were used to support them as they paid off their debts. The writer never forgave his family for making him work in such harsh, crowded factory conditions, and until his death in 1870, he made the plight of the working class a focus of his literature.

Thoughts on Shakespeare

- "Well, what the hell has he ever done for Colorado! Take it down and put my picture up there!" – mine magnate H. A. W. Tabor, on seeing a portrait of Shakespeare hung in Denver's Tabor Grand Opera House
- "Shakespeare wrote better poetry for not knowing too much; Milton, I think, knew too much finally for the good of his poetry." – philosopher and essayist Alfred North Whitehead, from *Dialogues of Alfred North Whitehead*
- "He [Shakespeare] was the man who of all modern, and perhaps ancient poets, had the largest and most comprehensive soul." – poet and essayist John Dryden, from *Essay of Dramatic Poesy*
- "I met and fell in love with William Shakespeare. He was my first white love…." – poet and novelist Maya Angelou, from *I Know Why the Caged Bird Sings*
- "Brush up your Shakespeare and they'll all kowtow." – singer Cole Porter, from the song "Brush Up Your Shakespeare"
- "The remarkable thing about Shakespeare is that he is really very good—in spite of all the people who say he is very good." – poet Robert Graves, when interviewed by *The Observer*
- "If we wish to know the force of human genius, we should read Shakespeare. If we wish to see the insignificance of human learning, we may only study his commentators." – essayist William Hazlitt, from the article "On the Ignorance of the Learned," printed in *Edinburgh Magazine*
- "If we tire of the saints, Shakespeare is our city of refuge." – poet Ralph Waldo Emerson, from *Representative Men*

Shakespeare Experimenting

According to an article in the *South African Journal of Science,* a recent excavation at the Stratford-upon-Avon homestead of the famous playwright William Shakespeare revealed some "far out" artifacts. The South African team unearthed 24 clay pipes, many of which contained trace amounts of both marijuana and cocaine. Of course, the appearance of centuries-old paraphernalia doesn't necessarily mean that Shakespeare himself used drugs. Taking into account some of the author's famous texts, however, many researchers find it easy to believe that he indulged for inspiration or possibly even pleasure. Phrases such as "noted weed" and "compounds strange" abound in his work, but this may be completely coincidental.

Useless Trivia

Shakespeare was an easy target for jokes when it came to his love life. He was rumored to have married Anne Hathaway when she was already three months pregnant, and his reputation among both women and men forever changed once critics read his works. Twenty-six of his sonnets appeared to be love poems to a married woman, referred to as the Dark Lady, and another 126 are addressed to a man, Fair Lord. Although Elizabethans commonly referred to their friendships as more aggressive types of love in poetry, critics believed Shakespeare was actually referring to sexual rendezvous. Some argue that the "speaker" in the poems does not necessarily have to be Shakespeare; he could have been writing in third person. Others disagree and insist he was indeed bisexual.

The I Ching

The *I Ching* (pronounced EE-Ching) is one of the oldest works of human literature. For centuries, people have consulted it to predict the future.

Brief History

I Ching translates as "The Book of Changes." The book is over 3,000 years old, but the philosophy behind it is even older. Chinese mystics developed keen sensitivities about the world around them through contemplative activities and meditation, and they recorded what they figured out. From one generation to the next they passed down these "ancient Chinese secrets," and by 1200 BC they began to get recorded. Eventually Confucius got in on the act, helping to codify some of the material. By the 17th century, Jesuit missionaries got interested in the *I Ching,* and in 1876 the first complete English language translation appeared.

How to Consult the Oracle

The *I Ching* is some fun reading in and of itself, but most treat it like an oracle that provides answers (however enigmatic) to their questions. It reveals how the forces of the universe are working at any given time. While there are many ways to approach the *I Ching,* the best way is to use three coins or sticks and toss them six times. Afterward, instructions included in most editions show how to develop a six-line figure known as a hexagram. There are 64 possible hexagrams. Each one tells something different about a situation.

The Hexagrams

A hexagram is actually composed of two trigrams (3 lines + 3 lines = a 6-line hexagram). The trigrams are divided into eight natural elements: Heaven, Thunder, Water, Mountain, Earth, Wind, Fire, and Lake. So, in any given hexagram, you might have a combination of Fire + Water (you can imagine this produces conflict) or Mountain + Earth (two elements that go together more smoothly). The combination of the two trigrams gives you your answer.

Wacky Writers

- Joseph Conrad had a serious gambling problem. His debts were so bad in 1878 that he tried to shoot himself, but survived.
- When he was feeling depressed, Graham Greene used to play Russian roulette.
- Vladimir Nabokov was an avid butterfly collector.
- Marcel Proust was so germ-phobic that if he dropped a pen on the floor, he refused to pick it up again.
- Wilkie Collins never married, but he had three illegitimate children with one woman all the while living with another.
- Lord Byron fathered a child with his half-sister Augusta Leigh.
- Hans Christian Anderson had a terrible fear of being burned to death. He used to carry a piece of rope with him to slide out a window whenever he spent the night away from home.
- Samuel Johnson once shaved off all of his arm and chest hair just to see how long it would take for it to grow back.
- T. E. Lawrence liked to be spanked with a birch rod.
- Nathaniel Hawthorne was such a good friend to Herman Melville that he dedicated *Moby Dick* to him.

A Good Name to Know: Edmond Halley

Born in 1656, in London, Edmond Halley attended Oxford University. While there he was intrigued by astronomer John Flamsteed's project to catalog the northern stars. Halley wanted to do the same for the Southern Hemisphere. He set out for the South Atlantic island of St. Helena in 1676 and returned to England two years later with 341 stars recorded according to celestial longitudes and latitudes. He also noted a transit of Mercury across the sun's disk.

Halley joined the scientists of the day in their quest to explain planetary motion. When Isaac Newton identified the orbit as an ellipse, Halley expanded on the work. The orbits of comets fascinated him. He showed that three comets recorded in 1531, 1607, and 1682 were so similar that they were returns of the same object—now known as Halley's Comet. He correctly predicted the comet's return in 1758.

In 1716, Halley devised a method for observing transits of Venus across the disk of the sun, allowing an accurate calculation of the distance of the earth from the sun.

The idea of cataloging stars came before Flamsteed and Halley. In 129 BC, Hipparchus, a Greek astronomer, cataloged 850 stars, assigning them a numerical scale of magnitude ranging from 1 as the brightest to 6 as the lightest, to indicate the star's brightness. Hipparchus' scale is still in use today, although it has been extended in range.

Literary Scandals

Lewis Carroll and Queen Victoria

The story: It has been long rumored that British writer Lewis Carroll once presented Britain's Queen Victoria with a mathematics text as a jest. Queen Victoria was tremendously impressed with *Alice in Wonderland* and *Through the Looking-Glass,* written by Lewis Carroll, the pseudonym of the mathematician Charles Dodgson. According to a well-known myth, the queen requested a copy of his next work, and he responded mischievously by delivering a copy of *An Elementary Treatise on Determinants.*

The truth: Dodgson held utmost respect for the British court. He undoubtedly felt honored by the queen's appreciation for his work, and when confronted 30 years later with the rumor of the prank, he stated that it was a "silly story," and that "it is utterly false in every particular: nothing even resembling it has occurred." By this point of course, the story was legend.

Virginia Woolf and the *Dreadnought* Hoax

Academia often lumps notable writers from distinct eras together into periods, but sometimes the grouping of like-minded artists spontaneously occurs because of similar locations and philosophies. In the early 20th century, one such group developed that included Virginia Woolf, the author of *A Room of One's Own.* Controversy surrounded the Bloomsbury Group, a collective of artists and writers, because of their hedonistic lifestyle and the antiwar sentiments they expressed during both world wars. While they spent much of their time engrossed in cultural endeavors, they also occasionally gained attention with high-profile pranks. One such incident occurred in 1910 and involved a few well-designed costumes, the newspapers, and a British naval vessel.

On February 10, 1910, the British navy received a telegram announcing the imminent arrival of a group of dignitaries who wished to tour a warship. Shortly thereafter, a group of well-dressed dignitaries from Abyssinia approached Britain's most secret warship, the HMS *Dreadnought*. After being introduced as princes of Abyssinia, the assembly embarked on an incredibly exclusive tour of the ship. In actuality, the gathering consisted of Woolf and other members of Bloomsbury dressed in fine costumes and phony beards. Woolf and her gang spoke in a mixture of Swahili and Latin, and managed to succeed in their ruse without attracting any unwanted attention from their tour guides. The pranksters immortalized their trick by having a photograph printed in the *Daily Mirror*. The picture embarrassed the navy, resulting in the caning of one of the participants and national attention for the group.

Useless Trivia

If marrying your 13-year-old cousin isn't enough of a red flag to prove you are nuts, then running around the streets of Baltimore in a panic attack—while wearing another man's clothes—should be. Edgar Allan Poe did both. On October 3, 1849, he was found wandering, delirious, and incoherent. He spent the next several days in and out of consciousness at Washington College Hospital and never got the chance to explain the episode before he died four days later. Unfortunately, Poe's physicians and acquaintances never agreed on a cause of death. Some said he had gotten miserably drunk, while others argued that they never smelled liquor on his breath. Every possible condition was considered, but the true tale of his demise may never be known.

A Name to Drop: Franz Kafka

(Hint: Writer)

The Story Behind the Stories

Franz Kafka was born in a Jewish neighborhood in Prague in 1883. As a Jew with German-Austrian ancestry, he encountered hostility all of his life. He studied law and then worked for fourteen years as a bureaucrat in a job he hated, all the while living with his domineering father, whom he described as huge and overbearing. Throughout his life, he suffered from tuberculosis, depression, and anxiety, which helps explain the troubled tone and religious and psychological questions of much of his writing. He never married, but was twice engaged to a woman named Felice Bauer. He only published a few stories during his lifetime. In fact, he left instructions to his friend Max Brod to burn all of his unpublished material after his death, including three novels. When he died in 1924, Brod disobeyed Kafka's wishes and published his fiction and diaries.

Critics debate whether Kafka's symbolic, surreal, Freudian works are religious allegories or representations of his own troubled mind. He is often aligned with the Existentialists because of the absurdity and hopelessness that permeates his fiction. His style is precise, dream-like, and even humorous at times. He is the master of weird, so that even if people have never read any of his stories, they usually know what the word "Kafkaesque" means.

The Stories

- "A Hunger Artist"—The title of this short story refers to a man whose craft is starving himself to the brink of death. In the good old days, crowds used to gather around him as he wasted away in a cage. As the years go by and people lose interest in his art form, he has to come to terms with suffering, art, and what it means to sell out to the public. (Ironically, Kafka himself died from starvation as he was being treated for tuberculosis. His throat was so sore he could no longer eat).
- "A Country Doctor"—This surreal tale describes the events of one night as a rural doctor tries to find a horse to make a house call. Mysterious horses appear, but as he rides off, his maid is placed in danger. He arrives to discover a patient who may or may not be dying. Can he rescue the patient and his maid, or are forces working against him?
- "The Metamorphosis"—Gregor Samsa wakes up one morning to the surprise of his life: he has turned into a giant insect! Will he be squashed underfoot by his family? Will he ever return to normal?
- "In the Penal Colony"—A condemned prisoner is subjected to a unique torture device, a machine that carves the victim's punishment in words deep into his flesh. He is literally "sentenced" to death.

A Name to Drop: John James Audubon

(Hint: Wildlife Artist)

Born in Saint Domingue (now called Haiti), in 1785, John James Audubon grew up in Nantes, France. At age 18, he moved to Pennsylvania, where he studied native birds, drawing them and conducting the first known bird-banding experiment in North America. He and his wife later moved to Kentucky, where Audubon ran a dry-goods store and spent his spare time drawing birds. In the early 1820s, he took a tour following the Mississippi River, drawing birds and taking notes. Even before he left on his tour, he had created an impressive portfolio.

In 1826, Audubon took his art collection to England where his paintings and descriptions of the birds of America made him quite successful. He soon became known as America's foremost wildlife artist. Before the end of his career, Audubon traveled the country several more times, searching for and documenting native birds. John James Audubon died in 1851, at age 66.

The Audubon Society was named in honor of the nation's most famous birder. George Bird Grinnell, one of the founders of the Audubon Society, wanted a name that would draw inspiration for the organization's work of protecting birds and their habitats.

John James Audubon painted 435 watercolors of birds during his lifetime. In 1819, he was jailed for bankruptcy.

Edgar Degas
Impressionist/Realist

Born in Paris, France, in 1834, Edgar Degas enrolled in the Lycée Louis-le-Grand, where he received a bachelor's degree in literature in 1853. At the insistence of his father, Degas enrolled at the Faculty of Law of the University of Paris, where he stayed only a few months before switching to the École des Beaux-Arts to study drawing. He moved to Italy in 1856 and studied the Renaissance artists, such as Michelangelo, Raphael, and Titian.

In 1872, Degas moved to New Orleans, Louisiana, where several of his relatives already lived. While there he painted *The Cotton Exchange at New Orleans*, his only work to be purchased by a museum during his lifetime.

In 1873, Degas returned to Paris and began using photography to capture action for his paintings and artwork. His paintings eventually made him financially comfortable.

Although his work is often described as impressionistic, Degas did not like the label and preferred to be called a realist. Undoubtedly he was influenced by the impressionist artists of his day; however, his early study of the old masters influenced his work so that his paintings distinctly differ from the pure impressionists of the day.

Degas mastered the techniques of oil painting as well as working in pastels. He was also an accomplished sculptor and printmaker. He spent the last years of his life nearly blind and often wandering the streets of Paris. Edgar Degas died in 1917.

- Degas served in the National Guard during the Franco-Prussian War.
- More than half of Degas' work depicts dancers.

Louis Bromfield: The Most Famous Farmer in America

Born in 1896, in Mansfield, Ohio, Louis Bromfield grew up with soil under his fingernails and become the most famous farmer in America.

He entered Cornell Agriculture College in 1914 and moved on to Columbia University, where he studied journalism. Upon graduation, Bromfield accepted a position with the Associated Press. During World War I, he received the Croix de la Guerre for his service as an ambulance driver for the French Army.

For 31 years, Bromfield wrote books and screenplays that captured the attention of critics and the public alike. In 1925, Bromfield published his first novel, *The Green Bay Tree*. The story of the struggle between farming and industry generated a great deal of attention. His next book, *Early Autumn*, received a Pulitzer Prize in 1927. Two years later he was awarded the O. Henry Short Story Award for "Scarlet Woman." His screenplays included *One Heavenly Night* and *Johnny Come Lately* starring James Cagney.

Bromfield spent the early part of his career in Paris but returned to Ohio in 1938. He purchased Malabar Farm and took on a second career as farmer and conservationist. He attained worldwide fame in the 1940s and 1950s for his soil experiments and conservation efforts while maintaining a rigorous writing schedule.

Louis Bromfield died in 1956. In the 1980s, Bromfield was posthumously elected to the Ohio Agricultural Hall of Fame.

Bromfield's home, Malabar Farm, was the location of the wedding of Humphry Bogart and Lauren Bacall.

William Henry Fox Talbot Pioneer of Photography

Born in 1800 in Melbury, Dorset, England, William Henry Fox Talbot attended Cambridge University and was elected a fellow of the Royal Astronomical Society. He was a man of varied interests, including mathematics, botany, and the Bible.

In the 1830s, people were already reproducing leaves and other objects, a process they called photograms, but Talbot wanted a machine that could actually reproduce sketches and not fade like the photograms did. He began work on this idea in 1833. He presented his "art of photogenic drawing" to the Royal Society in 1839.

During his career, Talbot developed the three elements of photography—developing, fixing, and printing. Initially, his photogenic drawings on light-sensitive paper took long exposure times; however, he accidentally discovered that there was an image after a very short exposure. He found he could chemically develop the exposure into a useful negative. He called his new, faster process calotype and patented the process in 1841. The following year Talbot was rewarded with a medal from the Royal Society for his work.

In 1844, Talbot published *The Pencil of Nature*, the first commercial book to be illustrated with photographs. Talbot's photogenic drawings were in competition with the daguerreotype process. The daguerreotypes won the popularity contest because of their quality, compared to Talbot's process, and their cost. Talbot is said to have asked too much for the rights to his patented process.

Talbot also made contributions to mathematics, astronomy, and archaeology. He died in 1877.

George Eastman
Eastman Kodak Company

Born in Waterville, New York, in 1854, George Eastman dropped out of high school when his father died and went to work in order to support his family. As the story goes, he was working in a bank at age 24 and was due for a vacation. He wanted to tour the Caribbean islands and bring back photographs, but photography equipment was too heavy and cumbersome. He decided to forgo his vacation and work on making a portable camera.

Eastman invented a dry-plate process for developing photographs, and, in 1880, established a photo development factory in Rochester, New York. Eight years later, he devised a way to make photography film out of paper and put it on a roll. He also developed a camera to use the film. In 1889, he started making film out of cellulose instead of paper.

Eastman used the name *Kodak* because he liked the letter K. He tried many alphabetical combinations for the letters in the middle, but he knew the beginning and ending letters would have to be K.

The first Kodak camera cost $25 and took 100 round photos, each two and a half inches in diameter. The cost of developing the film and returning the camera filled with new film was $10.

George Eastman House

Seventeen years after the death of George Eastman, his home in Rochester, New York, was opened as a photography museum. It is a prominent photography and motion picture archives and a leader in film preservation and photography conservation.

The Eastman Kodak Company, founded in 1892, was one of the first firms in America to establish a plant for large-scale production of a standardized product and to maintain a chemical laboratory. The company was also a pioneer in employee relations, creating a "progressive welfare program" including a profit-sharing plan. Within four years, 100,000 cameras had been sold.

In 1900, Eastman introduced the Brownie. The new-style camera cost only $1 and a roll of six-exposure film cost 15 cents. Color photography followed in 1928.

Suffering the pain and depression of a degenerative illness, George Eastman committed suicide in 1932.

A Photo to Drop

Harold Edgerton's stop-action "Coronet" milk-drop photo was featured in the first photography exhibit at the New York Museum of Modern Art in 1937.

In 1850, there were 77 photographic galleries in New York.

Harold Edgerton Stop-Action Photography

Born in 1903 in Fremont, Nebraska, Harold Edgerton attended the University of Nebraska and went on to get his Ph.D. at the Massachusetts Institute of Technology. He became professor of electrical engineering at MIT, where he served until his retirement.

- Edgerton developed the stroboscope, which used strobe lights to isolate fast motion, allowing people to view high-speed motion that had never been seen before. Soon people could see photographs of athletes, hummingbirds, and even bullets in action.
- In 1939, Edgerton began working on a way for the US Air Force to take nighttime aerial photography for reconnaissance. And using his photography techniques on the lighter side, he collaborated with MGM to produce the short film *Quicker than a Wink!*, for which he received an Academy Award in 1940.
- In 1953, Edgerton took his photography to great depths as he teamed with Jacques Cousteau in underwater exploration. Edgerton developed sonar devices for analyzing and profiling the bottom of the sea, and in 1968, he produced the first underwater time-lapse photography.

In addition to his Academy Award, Edgerton received the Medal of Freedom for his aerial reconnaissance work during World War II and the National Medal of Science in 1973. He was named New England Inventor of the Year in 1982.

Edgerton died of a heart attack in 1990.

Desi Arnaz Multicamera Setup

With wife, Lucille Ball, Desi Arnaz founded the film studio Desilu Productions. At this time, most television programs were broadcast live, and kinescope images (the result of placing 35-mm or 16-mm film cameras in front of a television monitor) were shipped to other time zones for broadcast at a later date. Needless to say, kinescope film was poor quality, but television audiences across the nation loved Lucy no matter what the quality of film.

- Arnaz came up with an idea to produce high-quality images of the *I Love Lucy* show. He developed the multicamera setup production style using adjacent sets. Some people were not supportive of Arnaz's idea. They told him that it would be impossible to allow an audience onto a sound stage. However, he was not easily deterred.
- He began working with the cameraman Karl Freund to design a set that would allow room for an audience and filming while also complying with fire and safety codes. His process was a success, and the use of film gave television stations in every state the ability to broadcast high-quality images of *I Love Lucy*.
- Arnaz's production method became the standard and is still used today for filming situation comedies.
- He is also credited with the invention of the rerun.

I Love Lucy was based on Lucille Ball and Richard Denning's popular radio program *My Favorite Husband.* When it was turned into a sitcom, however, Ball dumped Denning for her real life husband, Desi Arnaz.

Arnaz produced a number of television shows including:

- *December Bride*
- *The Texan*
- *Make Room for Daddy*
- *The Mothers-in-Law*
- *The Lucy Show*
- *Those Whiting Girls*
- *Our Miss Brooks*

Arnaz also was not easily deterred when it came to allowing Lucy to be pregnant on television. This was during a time when pregnancy was a condition to whisper about, but Arnaz pushed the network to its limit. He consulted a priest, a rabbi, and a minister, all of whom told him that there would be nothing wrong with showing a pregnant Lucy or even using the word *pregnant*. The network gave in and allowed Lucy's pregnancy to become part of the storyline, but Ricky (Arnaz's character) had to use the word *spectin* in his Cuban accent instead of *pregnant*.

The Many Characters of Daws Butler

Born in 1916, in Toledo, Ohio, Charles Dawson Butler was the voice of Yogi Bear, Huckleberry Hound, Mr. Jinks, Snagglepuss, Augie Doggie, Quick Draw McGraw, Hokey Wolf, Elroy Jetson, and other cartoon characters.

- As a teenager, Butler entered a local talent contest and won many of them. He did voice impressions of Rudy Vallee, Franklin Delano Roosevelt, and other well-known voices of the time.
- In addition to cartoons, Butler also wrote and produced radio and animated TV commercials and starred in the popular *Time for Beany*.
- Butler and friend Stan Freberg served as voices and puppeteers for the early 1950s children's show. Butler served as Beany and Beany's Uncle Huffenpuff.

Albert Einstein was a fan of *Time for Beany*. He is said to have never missed an episode. In fact, as the story goes, he once adjourned an important scientific meeting by announcing, "Pardon me, gentlemen, but it's *Time for Beany*!"

Two Famous Hollywood Voices

Mel Blanc

Born in San Francisco, California, in 1908, Melvin Blanc spent much of his youth in Portland, Oregon. Before becoming a cartoon voice, Blanc appeared on several radio programs including *The Jack Benny Program, The Abbott and Costello Show*, and *Burns and Allen*. He even had his own radio show, *The Mel Blanc Show,* which ran from September 1946 to June 1947.

Blanc began doing cartoon voices in 1936 for Leon Schlesinger Studios, which distributed Warner Brothers cartoons. Blanc's many cartoon voices included Bugs Bunny, Daffy Duck, Porky Pig, Foghorn Leghorn, Tweety, Sylvester, Yosemite Sam, *The Flintstones'* Barney Rubble, and *The Jetsons'* Mr. Spacely, just to name a few.

When Blanc ended up in a Hollywood hospital after a near-fatal car accident, he received get-well cards from fans addressed only to "Bugs Bunny, Hollywood, USA." Incidentally, doctors had little hope of Blanc's recovering from the coma caused by the accident. But one day a doctor decided to talk to Bugs Bunny. The doctor asked, "How are you today, Bugs Bunny?" and Blanc, who mentions the story in his autobiography, answered in Bugs' voice.

Blanc's last original character was an orange cat named Heathcliff in the early 1980s. He died in 1989, in Los Angeles, California.

"Knighty Knight Bugs" is the only Bugs Bunny cartoon to win an Academy Award.

June Foray

Born in Springfield, Massachusetts, in 1917, June Foray made her radio debut at age 12. When she was 17, she was in Hollywood, performing on some of the top radio programs of the day, including the *Jimmy Durante Show* and *Lux Radio Theatre*. Eventually, she played the role of Lady Makebelieve on her own kids' show.

In the 1940s, Foray began lending her voice to animated films.

- She played Lucifer the Cat in *Cinderella* and Granny, the owner of Tweety and Sylvester.
- She also spoke for Rocky and the sultry Natasha on *Rocky and His Friends* (later renamed *The Bullwinkle Show*) and *Dudley Do-Right's* Nell. Several characters on the *Fractured Fairy Tales* were played by Foray.
- She was also the original voice for Chatty Cathy.

How Do People Get a Star on the Hollywood Walk of Fame?

A tradition that began in the 1960s, stars attached to charcoal terrazzo squares honor the greats from the worlds of motion pictures, television, radio, recording, or live theater. The Hollywood Chamber of Commerce, based on nominations submitted during an announced two-month period each year, makes the selections. Professional achievement and community service are both taken into consideration.

Singer Gene Autry has the most stars on the Hollywood Walk of Fame. He received stars for all five categories—motion pictures, television, radio, recording, and live theater.

American Philosophical Society

Begun in 1743 as a way to encourage scholarly pursuits of the fine arts, the American Philosophical Society had a long list of influential and esteemed charter members. First and most influential was Benjamin Franklin.

Others on the roster were George Washington, John Adams, Thomas Jefferson, Alexander Hamilton, Thomas Paine, Benjamin Rush, James Madison, John Marshall, Marquis de Lafayette, Baron von Steuben, and Thaddeus Kosciusko. Early members came from varied backgrounds—doctors, lawyers, clergymen, merchants, artisans, and tradesmen—but each held an interest in natural philosophy.

Early on, the American Philosophical Society improved agriculture, manufacturing, and transportation, paving the way for economic independence in the United States. And in the 1760s, the society became internationally recognized when it participated with other countries in astronomical observations.

Today, members are elected to the society in recognition of extraordinary accomplishments in their fields of research. There are more than 900 members from around the world, with 85 percent of the membership residing in the United States.

John J. Audubon, Robert Fulton, Charles Darwin, Thomas Edison, Alexander von Humboldt, Louis Pasteur, Albert Einstein, Robert Frost, George C. Marshall, and Linus Pauling have all been members of the American Philosophical Society.

The American Philosophical Society Library is a major national center for research in the history of science and technology, as well as general US history to 1840. It houses over 200,000 volumes and bound periodicals, 7 million manuscripts, and thousands of maps and prints.

Women became a part of the society in 1789, with the Russian Princess Dashkova, president of the Imperial Academy of Sciences in St. Petersburg, becoming the first woman elected. Other female members include Elizabeth Cabot Cary Agassiz, Marie Curie, Gerty T. Cori, and Margaret Mead.

The American Philosophical Society supports five grant programs and awards seven special prizes and medals. The Magellanic Premium was established in 1786. As the oldest scientific prize given by an American institution, it recognizes discoveries related to navigation, astronomy, or natural philosophy. Other prizes include the Barzun Prize, which recognizes contributions to American or European cultural history; the Franklin Medal; the Jefferson Medal for arts, humanities, or social sciences; the Lashley Award for neurobiology; the Lewis Award, and the Moe and Phillips prizes, honoring papers in the humanities and jurisprudence.

The society's quarterly journal, the *Proceedings*, was begun in 1838. Among the first papers supported by the society were those of Benjamin Franklin, Joseph Henry, William Penn, Meriwether Lewis and William Clark.

Located in the heart of Pennsylvania's Independence National Historical Park, the society consists of three buildings. Philosophical Hall, the society's original home was completed in 1789. Library Hall, which houses the society's library, was completed in 1959. And, in 1981, the society purchased the historic Farmers' and Mechanics' Bank and renamed it the Benjamin Franklin Hall. This building provides meeting facilities and exhibition space.

- The first grant made by the American Philosophical Society was given to Thomas C. Poulter, a member of the second Byrd Antarctic expedition, to measure the depth of the polar ice cap.
- More than 200 members of the American Philosophical Society have received the Nobel Prize.

Notable Dropouts

Benjamin Franklin

A philosopher, author, publisher, scientist, founding father, and signer of the constitution, Benjamin Franklin accomplished a lot of things in his life. One thing he never finished, however, was school. The youngest in a family of twenty, Franklin dropped out of school at the age of ten, beginning his work in printing with his father and brother.

Bill Gates

Having been ranked the richest person in the world for several years, Bill Gates is the cofounder of Microsoft and an entrepreneurial genius. After reading an article in *Popular Electronics* about a microcomputer, Gates dropped out of Harvard and formed the company now known as Microsoft with his friend Paul Allen. He was only a college junior at the time.

Walt Disney

The Oscar-winning film producer and animation pioneer Walt Disney dropped out of school when he was 16 years old. He planned to join the army but was too young to enlist, so Disney joined the Red Cross by forging his birth certificate. He was sent to France to drive an ambulance, which he covered in the cartoon drawings that eventually became his animated characters. At the age of 58, after winning the Presidential Medal of Freedom and founding the Walt Disney Company, he was awarded an honorary high school diploma by his alma mater.

Charles Dickens
Author of many classics, such as *A Tale of Two Cities* and *A Christmas Carol,* Charles Dickens dropped out of school at the age of 12. He entered the workforce at a boot-blacking company and did factory work for ten hours per day. He later worked as a law clerk, stenographer, and journalist. He finally published his first novel, *The Pickwick Papers,* in 1836.

Thomas Edison
With over 1,000 patented inventions to his name, including the lightbulb, the motion picture camera, and the phonograph, Thomas Edison is one of the most famous and prolific inventors of all time. He was a recipient of the Congressional Gold Medal, and a selfmade multi-millionaire at an early age. Because of an illness during his youth, Edison began school late and dropped out after just three months of formal education. Edison's mother was a former teacher and home-schooled Edison for much of his youth.

The History of the Yo-Yo

The first US patent for the yo-yo was issued in 1866 to James Haven and Charles Hettrich. They called their toy a whirligig. In 1928, Pedro Flores opened the Yo-Yo Manufacturing Company in California, and within a year, he had opened two more factories, employed 600 workers, and made 300,000 yo-yos a day.

Entrepreneur Donald F. Duncan bought Flores's Yo-Yo Company in 1929. Within a few years, he decided to move his company to Luck, Wisconsin, to be near the source of maple wood used in making the yo-yos. The factory made 3,600 yo-yos per hour and caused Luck to be dubbed the Yo-Yo Capital of the World.

In 1955, when plastic became popular, Duncan contracted with the Flambeau Products Corporation in Baraboo, Wisconsin, to begin making his yo-yos. Then, in 1968, Flambeau purchased the Duncan name and trademarks. Today, they produce Duncan yo-yos at their Columbus, Indiana, plant. The Butterfly yo-yo, made by turning the two sides of the yo-yo around, was introduced in 1958.

Tom Kuhn is known as the father of the modern yo-yo. In the 1970s, he began improving on the yo-yo's design, coming up with the No Jive 3-in-1 yo-yo. His latest designs are the Silver Bullet and the Tom Cat, the two most expensive yo-yos on the market today. Kuhn was also the first to receive the Donald F. Duncan Family Award for Industry Excellence in 1998.

An Innovative Thinker

The inventive mind of Donald F. Duncan worked in mysterious ways. He not only made the yo-yo popular in the US, but he also came up with ideas for parking meters and the Good Humor bar, the "ice cream on a stick."

The World Yo-Yo Contest, begun in 1932 in London, England, is now held every year in Florida. People from around the world—the US, Mexico, South America, the UK, Taiwan, Singapore, Japan, Hong Kong, Korea, France, Germany, Switzerland, the Czech Republic, Hungary, Australia—compete in these contests.

A person who shoots marbles is known as a mibster.

Notes on Novels

- The first American novel to be adapted to the stage was *The Spy* by James Fenimore Cooper. It premiered in 1821.
- The first dime novel, published by Beadle's Dime Novels series, was *Malaeska, the Indian Wife of the White Hunter* by Ann S. Stephens. It sold 200,000 copies its first year.
- The first novel published in the United States was William Hill Brown's 1789 book *The Power of Sympathy*.
- The first novel published by an African American writer was *Clotelle*, published in 1853 by William Wells Brown.

The Invention of the Frisbee

On college campuses in New England during the 1940s, a student could either duck, get struck in the head, or catch the flying pie pan. A Connecticut bakery sold pies in pie tins with the company's name—Frisbie—stamped on the bottom. Some of the bakery's best customers were college kids. Students ate the pies and rescued the empty pie pans from the trash. They found, if thrown just right, the pie pan would fly through the air and be easily caught by another person. In order to keep from hitting someone in the head with a flying pie pan, the students called out "Frisbie" when they tossed the pan.

Said to be a very good year for UFO sightings, 1948 was also the year that Walter Frederick Morrison came up with an idea for a flying saucer made of plastic. He named his plastic disc a Pluto Platter. In 1955, Wham-O bought the rights to the Pluto Platter and later renamed it Frisbee. The next year, Morrison received a patent for the platter and subsequently received more than $1 million.

Today, children, adults, dogs, and even cats play Frisbee. Organized games include Ultimate Frisbee, Disc Golf, and Freehand. The competitive Ultimate Frisbee is now a college sport in many areas of the United States and is played competitively in organized leagues all over the world. Disc Golf and Freehand are recreational sports more suited to players of all ages and skill levels.

- The sloped edge of the Frisbee is called the Morrison Slope.
- The ridges around the edge of the Frisbee stabilize flight and are called Rings of Headrick, after their inventor Ed Headrick, who is known as the father of disc golf.
- There are almost 100,000 Ultimate Frisbee players in more than 40 countries.

Notorious Art Thefts

- The most notorious art theft in the world has to be the robbery of 1911 in Paris, France, at the Louvre. Employee Vincenzo Peruggia stole the famed Leonardo da Vinci painting *Mona Lisa.* Peruggia hid in the museum until it closed and then concealed the painting under a smock while he escaped. The incident transformed the *Mona Lisa* into perhaps the most well-known painting in the world. Two years later, Peruggia tried to sell the painting in Florence and was arrested. The *Mona Lisa* was returned to the Louvre with a whole new level of fame and notoriety.
- Edvard Munch's painting *The Scream* was lifted in 1994, when thieves, who stole in through the window, took it from the Oslo National Art Museum. The men tried to ransom the painting to the government of Norway but were caught within several months. Having left a piece of the frame at a bus stop, they left a trail behind them and were soon convicted.
- In late 2002, robbers stole two Van Gogh paintings from the Van Gogh Museum in Amsterdam after breaking into the building through the roof. The men worked so quickly that they had vanished before the police arrived, even after setting after the alarm system upon entry. Fortunately, the men left hair inside two hats in the museum and were convicted on DNA evidence. However, the paintings, the missing link to proving the two men's guilt, have never been recovered. *View of the Sea at Scheveningen* and *Congregation Leaving the Reformed Church in Nuenen* together are worth more than $30 million.
- In August 2003, two men joined a guided tour through Drumlanrig Castle in Scotland. They subdued a guard and stole Leonardo da Vinci's *Madonna with the Yarnwinder*. The

men convinced bystanders that they were police practicing a protocol; and escaped in a white Volkswagen. The painting is still missing, and the two men were never caught.

- In August 2004, two armed thieves entered the Munch Museum of Oslo, Norway, in broad daylight. Masked, they stole two Edvard Munch paintings, *The Scream*, and *The Madonna*, after threatening workers with their weapons. The two paintings combined were worth an estimated 100 million euros. In May 2006, three men were convicted to prison sentences, and the paintings were recovered. The painting that they stole was actually a different version of *The Scream* than was lifted before, as Munch had created four different versions of the painting.
- In February 2008, the art world was ransacked again—this time in two thefts in Switzerland within one week. On Wednesday, February 6, thieves broke into the Seedamm-Kulturzentrum cultural center in the town of Pfäffikon, stealing two Picassos, *Horse Head* and *Glass and Pitcher*, estimated to be worth $4.4 million combined. The following Sunday, three armed men stole Cézanne's *Boy in a Red Vest*, Monet's *Poppies Near Vétheuil*, van Gogh's *Blossoming Chestnut Branches*, and Degas' *Count Lepic and His Daughters*, worth an estimated total of $163 million, from the E. G. Bührle Collection in Zurich.

Notorious Banned Books

***The Catcher in the Rye*, J. D. Salinger**

School boards in the following cities have been challenged and protested for allowing *Catcher in the Rye* in the classroom:

- Pittsgrove, New Jersey (1977)
- Issaquah, Washington (1978)
- Middleville, Michigan (1979)
- North Jackson, Ohio (1980)
- Anniston, Alabama (1982)
- Morris, Manitoba (1982)
- New Richmond, Wisconsin (1994)
- De Funiak Springs, Florida (1985)
- Medicine Bow, Wyoming (1986)
- Napoleon, North Dakota (1987)
- Linton Stockton, Indiana (1988)
- Boron, California (1989)
- Waterloo, Iowa (1992)
- Duval County, Florida (1992)
- Carlisle, Pennsylvania (1992)
- New Richmond, Wisconsin (1994)
- Corona Norco, California (1993)
- Goffstown, New Hampshire (1994)
- St. Augustine, Florida (1995)
- Paris, Maine (1996)
- Brunswick, Georgia (1997)
- Marysville, California (1997)
- Limestone County, Alabama (2000)
- Savannah, Georgia (2000)
- Summerville, South Carolina (2001)
- Glynn County, Georgia (2001)

***Of Mice and Men,* John Steinbeck**
In 1989, the novel was challenged as a reading assignment for summer school kids in Chattanooga, Tennessee, because "Steinbeck is known to have had an anti-business attitude." The spokesperson added that "he was very questionable as to his patriotism."

***The Great Gatsby,* F. Scott Fitzgerald**
Baptist College, in Charleston, South Carolina, challenged the teaching of F. Scott Fitzgerald's classic novel in 1987 because of "language and sexual references in the book."

***Ulysses,* James Joyce**
The New York Post Office found *Ulysses* so offensive that in 1922, they burned all copies of it. Recalling how his book *Dubliners* had been burned years before, Joyce said, "This is the second time I have had the pleasure of being burned while on Earth. I hope it means I shall pass through the fires of purgatory unscathed." Advocates fought until the US ban was lifted in 1933. As if banning wasn't enough, the book was also burned in the US in 1918, in Ireland and Canada in 1922, and in England in 1923.

***The Sun Also Rises,* Ernest Hemingway**
This Hemingway classic faced widespread rejection. The book was banned in Boston, Massachusetts, in 1930, in Ireland in 1953, and later in Riverside, California, in 1963. The Nazis also burned it in bonfires in 1933.

Tolkien, Back to Work!

The negligence of responsibilities sometimes leads to greatness. Almost everyone has heard of *The Lord of the Rings,* even if they haven't read J. R. R. Tolkien's masterpiece of fantasy fiction. Because of the immense popularity of the film adaptation of the three-part series, Frodo has become a household name and someone who doesn't know about Gollum obviously lives in a cave. The recent sensation is a renaissance of the excitement that occurred half a century before. At the time the author published his trilogy, he also worked for *The Oxford English Dictionary,* but according to legend, he wasn't working enough.

During his tenure at Oxford, Tolkien began writing texts about a fantasyland known as Middle-earth, including *The Hobbit* and *The Lord of the Rings.* A language scholar at Pembroke College, Tolkien had duties that included etymological work on the dictionary, as well as giving lectures on Old and Middle English. The basis for the trilogy roots itself in Tolkien's infatuation with language; a point demonstrated by the presence of fictional language within the texts. During the years following the publication of Tolkien's novels, it came to Oxford's attention that for the past several years his promises of academic publications had been neglected. Upon the overwhelming success following the publication of the trilogy's final book, *The Return of the King,* in 1955, Oxford understood why the promises hadn't been fulfilled. Tolkien received a polite reprimand from Oxford. He responded quickly with a lecture on Celtic in the English language, which he presented on October 21, 1955, one day following the publication of the trilogy's finale.

The Bell Ringer's Savior

A church bell ringer is a vocation no modern genius would pursue. On pleasant days in the 18th century, it was an honest enough career path, but heaven forbid that the sky display its powerful fury. For centuries people believed that lightning and its combustive force existed as a demonstration of God's will. With a booming cacophony, light demons filled the air, crashing into churches and homes. The method for frightening away these demons with reverent resonance came in the form of ringing church bells. Much to the dismay of the unfortunate soul whose duties included noisily distracting the devils, lightning had a taste for bell towers, regardless of reverent efforts. Many a ringer met his maker in the line of pious duty.

Not everyone thought that the sky's great crashes and illuminations represented a supernatural force. One such thinker was Benjamin Franklin. In the mid 1700s, curious minds began experimenting to discover the properties of electricity. In 1743, Franklin met a man in Boston named Dr. Archibald Spencer, whose public demonstrations were thought by many to be magic. Inspired by Spencer, Franklin began conducting his own tests of electricity. Soon, after numerous mildly shocking experiments, he began to draw several comparisons between electricity and lightning, based on their respective colors and course of movement. Much to the amusement of the esteemed Royal Society of London, Franklin sought to prove that what had long been thought to be God's wrath not only resembled electricity, but in fact was electricity.

One stormy afternoon in June 1752, Franklin's opportunity arose. Armed with a silk kite curiously crafted with a protruding metal rod, he and his son William set out to a field near their home, possibly passing a justifiably apprehensive bell ringer on their short journey. Once the kite was sailing into the darkening skies, the duo took shelter in a nearby shed to keep dry the silk string separating Franklin and a metal key tied to the cord. Franklin had experienced mild electric shocks in previous controlled experiments within his workshop. His hypothesis about lightning would be proven if he received a similar shock by touching the key, which would conduct the anticipated current.

Minutes passed and the pair noticed that the kite string had begun to fray. Because he was certain that his success was imminent, but also anxious of being electrocuted, Franklin cautiously touched his knuckle to the metal key. Upon contact he received a familiar jolt that assured him that he had been correct… lightning is electricity!

Franklin's pragmatic lightning research led to the lightning rod, a useful device designed to draw the sky's violent charges away from ships, homes, and church towers. In past experiments with electricity, Franklin had determined that electricity traveled more effectively in some materials than others, particularly metals and water. With this knowledge in mind, he assembled a long metal shaft connected to a wire. By placing the rod at the peak of a home and burying the wire, the electrical charge carried by bolts of lightning was safely rerouted. For years after, the groundbreaking invention spared buildings from flame and their inhabitants, and perhaps a few bell ringers, from electrocution and death.

More Notorious Banned Books

***One Flew over the Cuckoo's Nest,* Ken Kesey**

In 1974, five people in Strongsville, Ohio, sued the board of education to remove Kesey's book. They claimed it was pornographic and that it "glorifies criminal activity, has a tendency to corrupt juveniles and contains descriptions of bestiality, bizarre violence, torture, dismemberment, death," and, perhaps most heinous of all, "human elimination."

***The Grapes of Wrath,* John Steinbeck**

In 1939, the East St. Louis, Illinois, public library burned copies of John Steinbeck's novel. In the same year, the Buffalo, New York, public library banned it because of its "vulgar words." In 1973, eleven Turkish book publishers went on trial for "spreading propaganda" with it. More recently, it was challenged in 1991 in the Greenville, South Carolina, schools because the book uses the names of God and Jesus in a "vain and profane manner along with inappropriate sexual references."

***To Kill a Mockingbird,* Harper Lee**

In 1977, the book was temporarily banned because the appearance of the words "damn" and "whore lady" in the novel. Then, in 1980, the Vernon Verona Sherill, New York, school district deemed it a "filthy, trashy novel." In the following year, the Warren, Indiana, township schools decided that the book does "psychological damage to the positive integration process" and "represents institutionalized racism under the guise of good literature." In 1985, the book was kept on an eighth-grade reading list in the Casa Grande, Arizona, elementary school district despite protests by the National Association for the Advancement of Colored People, who argued that the book was not appropriate for junior high readers. As recently as 2004, the Stanford Middle School in Durham, North Carolina, was challenged for allowing the book to be taught because of the use of the word "nigger."

***The Color Purple*, Alice Walker**

In 1984, *The Color Purple* was challenged as appropriate reading in an Oakland, California, high school honors class because of its "sexual and social explicitness" and its "troubling ideas about race relations, man's relationship to God, African history and human sexuality." Nine argumentative months later, the weary Oakland Board of Education allowed its use. The word "smut" was used to describe the book after it was banned in the Souderton, Pennsylvania, area school district in 1992. Finally, a group who called themselves Parents Against Bad Books in Schools challenged the novel in the Fairfax County, Virginia, school libraries in 2002. No one, however, seems to have challenged the name Parents Against Bad Books in Schools.

Forbidden books have been around for a long time. The first *Index of Forbidden Books* came out in 1559, published by the Sacred Congregation of the Roman Inquisition. It was revised up until 1948.

Thoughts on Beethoven

- "If Beethoven had been killed in a plane crash at the age of 22, it would have changed the history of music, and of aviation." – British playwright Tom Stoppard
- "Life can't be all bad when for ten dollars you can buy all the Beethoven sonatas and listen to them for ten years." – journalist William F. Buckley
- "Beethoven always sounds to me like the upsetting of a bag of nails, with here and there an also dropped hammer." – art critic John Ruskin
- "Everything will pass, and the world will perish but the Ninth Symphony will remain." – anarchist Michael Bakunin, quoted in Edmund Wilson's *To the Finland Station*
- "I like Beethoven, especially the poems." – Beatles drummer Ringo Starr
- "A colossus beyond the grasp of most mortals, with his totally uncompromising power, his unsensual and uningratiating way with music as with people." – conductor Yehudi Menuhin in *Unfinished Journey*
- "Beethoven forces you along, and bows and bends you to his will." – writer Sir George Grove in *Beethoven, Schubert, Mendelssohn*
- "If anyone has conducted a Beethoven performance, and then doesn't have to go to an osteopath, then there's something wrong." – conductor Simon Rattle

The Top Albums of History

According to the Recording Industry Association of America, these are the best-selling albums of all time:

1. *Eagles/Their Greatest Hits 1971–1975,* Eagles
2. *Thriller,* Michael Jackson
3. *Led Zeppelin IV,* Led Zeppelin
4. *The Wall,* Pink Floyd
5. *Back in Black,* AC/DC
6. *Greatest Hits Volume I & Volume II,* Billy Joel
7. *Double Live,* Garth Brooks
8. *Come on Over,* Shania Twain
9. *The Beatles,* The Beatles
10. *Rumours,* Fleetwood Mac
11. *Boston,* Boston
12. *The Bodyguard* (soundtrack), Whitney Houston/Various Artists
13. *The Beatles 1967–1970,* The Beatles
14. *No Fences,* Garth Brooks
15. *Hotel California,* Eagles

Some of the Most Commonly Misspelled Words (Spelled Correctly)

cemetery
conscience
conscious
definitely
embarrass
guarantee
inoculate
liaison
maintenance
minuscule
occurrence
perseverance
privilege
receipt
separate
sergeant
twelfth
until

Oxymorons

An oxymoron is a combination of two or more words that contradict one another. The following are a few examples:

- Constant variable
- Exact estimate
- Only choice
- Act naturally
- Old news
- Original copy
- Same difference
- Alone together
- Jumbo shrimp

Pleonasm

Pleo-what? Pleonasm occurs when a person uses more words or word-parts to express an idea than are necessary. Some examples are:

- Null and void
- Terms and conditions
- Tuna fish
- Down south
- Face up to the facts

Where to Live, and How Long?

There are many factors that are believed to contribute to overall life expectancy. Of all factors, wealth is the biggest contributor, and the reason makes perfect sense: an increase in wealth means an increase in access to health care, information, and safety. Particularly affluent countries tend to have the lowest rates of violent crime and the highest life expectancies. The following countries have very high life expectancies:

Country: Andorra
Location: Between France and Spain
Life Expectancy: 83.51
Andorra became a popular tourist location after World War II, making it a thriving economy with particular focus on health care and nutrition.

Country: Macau
Location: Island in the South China Sea
Life Expectancy: 82.19
Reaping the benefits of Chinese tourism, Macau is a thriving economy that derives much of its wealth from gambling profits. The government uses the proceeds of the large casino industry to invest in public health care.

Country: Singapore
Location: Island off the Malay Peninsula
Life Expectancy: 81.71
Thanks to heavy government planning for the large elderly population in the 1980s, Singapore now has extremely top-rate health care facilities for the elderly, resulting in a rise in life expectancy.

City: Hong Kong
Location: China
Life Expectancy: 81.59

With diets based on rice, vegetables, and lean proteins, citizens of Hong Kong boast some of the lowest obesity and dietary-based cancer rates in the world, knocking out their risk for two of the major causes of death around the world.

Country: Japan
Location: East Asia
Life Expectancy: 81.25

Much like Hong Kong, Japan has a quite low obesity rate. At just three percent, it boasts one of the lowest obesity rates in the world and has a healthy diet of fish, vegetables, and rice to thank. Studies have also shown that the Japanese tend to be healthier because they stop eating when they are approximately 80 percent full, and they walk or bike far more than the citizens of Western countries.

Country: Switzerland
Location: Western Europe
Life Expectancy: 80.51

A historically neutral country, Switzerland has remained relatively isolated from armed conflict, a contributing factor to high life expectancy. Furthermore, the Swiss have an extremely high standard of health care, a stable economy, and a relatively healthful diet compared with the rest of the West.

Shel Silverstein

"Recited, Sung, and Shouted"

Known for his poetry, illustrations, plays, screenwriting, and songwriting, Shel Silverstein is somewhat of an anomaly in the international literary scene. Born in 1930 as Sheldon Allan Silverstein, the famous writer's work has been distributed to tens of millions of readers internationally, and he is often referred to as the most beloved children's author of all time.

As a G.I. in Japan and Korea during the 1950s, Silverstein began drawing his first cartoons. Never planning to write for children, he took up other hobbies such as guitar playing and songwriting. In the early '60s, Silverstein was introduced to Harper Collins editor Ursula Nordstrom, which led to Silverstein's publication of *The Giving Tree*. After selling more than five million copies, Silverstein's first book still tops bestseller lists in children's literature.

Where the Sidewalk Ends was published in 1974 as Silverstein's first book of poems. The book was instantly popular, and was followed by *The Light in the Attic* in 1981, which broke records on the *New York Times* bestseller list, where it stayed for 182 weeks. Silverstein continued writing songs, poems, and stories until his death in 1999.

Successful at many arts, Silverstein's talents at songwriting paid him well. His song "A Boy Named Sue" was a hit for Johnny Cash, and "I'm Checking Out", which he wrote for a film called *Postcards from the Edge* was nominated for an Academy Award in 1991. Silverstein won a Grammy in 1984 for Best Children's Album with *Where the Sidewalk Ends*. Silverstein wrote songs for Waylon Jennings, Mel Tillis, and Jerry Reed.

Interesting Facts About a Few Famous Minds

The lives of geniuses, artistic or otherwise, are sometimes envied by many who aspire to live a life of grandeur. It might be interesting to find out that they weren't always so glamorous. Below are some of the once-held day jobs of notable musicians, authors, actors, and more:

- E.B. White was once a salesman of roach powder.
- Bette Midler worked in a factory chunking pineapple.
- Billie Holiday was a prostitute at one time.
- Madonna worked as a coat check girl in her younger years.
- Christo scrubbed away at a garage car wash.
- Cyndi Lauper cleaned kennels at a veterinary office.
- Warren Beatty sprayed for pests as an exterminator.
- William Shakespeare sold real estate.
- Jack London worked making burlap in a jute mill for $1 per day and at an electrical company shoveling coal.
- Boris Pasternak worked at a chemical factory during World War I.
- Agatha Christie was a pharmacist during World War I.
- At 17, Ernest Hemingway was a reporter for the *Kansas City Star.*

A Few Seriously Independent Females

- Jane Austen remained single all of her life, reportedly once saying that the thought of marrying a man made her feel squeamish.
- Louisa May Alcott was noted as saying, "I'd rather be a spinster and paddle my own canoe."
- Zora Neale Hurston reported that she could never stay married because all men seemed to interfere with her writing. She even accused her first husband of putting hexes on her.

Ready, Aim, Misfire

When it came to protecting Franklin Roosevelt's wife, Eleanor, from any harm, he simply was not able to overcome her stubborn independence. Eleanor refused to be escorted by Secret Service agents, so government officials gave her lessons on how to use a personal handgun. But after a trip with her to the FBI firing range, then-FBI Chief J. Edgar Hoover had his doubts. "Mr. President," he said, "if there is one person in the US who should not carry a gun, it's your wife. She cannot hit a barn door."

Aristotle: Founder of Logic

Born in 384 BC at Stagirus, a Greek colony and seaport on the coast of Thrace, Aristotle traveled to Athens, the intellectual center of the world, when he was 17 years old. He joined the Academy and studied under Plato, attending his lectures for 20 years. When Plato died, Aristotle moved to Mysia and then on to Mytilene. At Mytilene, Aristotle began tutoring the 13-year-old Alexander (later known as Alexander the Great). He eventually set up his own school at the Lyceum in Athens.

Things to Know

- Known as the founder of logic, Aristotle practiced what is today called inductive reasoning. He conducted detailed observations and documented his findings. He is said to be the first to classify animals into two groups—a task that could not have been accomplished without inductive reasoning.
- Aristotle wrote "dialogues" for his students and composed many other philosophical treatises. Out of an estimated 150 works, only 30 survive. His writings touch on a myriad of topics, including biology, politics, physics, mathematics, and more.
- When Alexander died, the government in Athens was overthrown, and Aristotle was forced to flee to Chalcis, where he lived until his death in 322 BC.

Claude Monet
Impressionist

Born in 1840, in Paris, France, Claude Monet moved with his family to Normandy when he was five years old. In 1851, he enrolled in Le Havre, a school for the study of art. There he began making charcoal caricatures that he sold for 20 francs.

In the late 1880s, Monet began painting the same subject in varying light. The first of these series paintings was *Haystacks,* which he painted from different points of view and at different times of day. Claude Monet died in 1926 at the age of 86.

- In 1980, Claude Monet's home in Giverny was opened for public tour. Today it attracts tourists from all over the world.
- In 2004, Monet's London, the Parliament, Effects of Sun in the Fog sold for $20.1 million.

Monet attempted suicide by throwing himself into the Seine River.

The Doubleday Myth vs. the Real Origin of Baseball

In 1905, Albert Goodwill "A. G." Spalding formed a commission to investigate the origins of baseball. After several years of research and deliberation, the commission declared that Abner Doubleday had invented the sport. This was the beginning of the Doubleday Myth.

Spalding had been a baseball player before he started his sporting goods supply company. As a true fan of the game, he wanted to believe that baseball was a purely American game. Sports writer Henry Chadwick claimed that baseball was an offshoot of the British game rounders. This claim caused Spalding to set out on a quest to prove baseball was a purely American game.

Having heard about the commission and its purpose, Abner Graves, a retired miner, sent a letter to the commission. He said that Abner Doubleday created baseball in 1839 when he was a student at Green's Select School in Cooperstown, New York. The commission and Spalding were delighted with this personal account and accepted it as fact. The men thought Doubleday, being the major general who had fired the first shot of the Civil War at Fort Sumter, was certainly the patriotic sort who should be credited with inventing "the great American pastime." However, Doubleday was a student at West Point in 1839, not the Green's Select School. Growing up, he was more interested in map-making than sports.

Nevertheless, in 1939, the Baseball Hall of Fame was established in Cooperstown, New York, to celebrate the sport's centennial. However, Abner Doubleday was not credited with the invention of baseball; a man named Alexander Cartwright was. Before the opening of the Hall of Fame, Cartwright's grandson presented several old diaries proving that his grandfather had invented baseball in 1845.

Three Notable Baseball Stadiums

Fenway Park

Boston's Fenway Park opened on April 20, 1912. The original April 18th opening was postponed because of rain.

The biggest baseball crowd at Fenway ever was 47,627 for a Red Sox–Yankees doubleheader on September 22, 1935. That record will not be broken because of current fire laws and league rules limiting the number of people the stadium can safely hold. Today Fenway Park can hold just over 36,000 fans.

The original hand-operated scoreboard is still used. Scores from other American League games are posted there now during Red Sox games. Behind the manual scoreboard is a room where the walls are covered with signatures of players who have played at Fenway. In 1975, Fenway Park's first electronic scoreboard was installed. One seat in the right-field bleachers is painted red to mark the spot where the longest measurable home run ever hit inside Fenway Park landed: Ted Williams's 502-footer on June 9, 1946.

Wrigley Field

Wrigley Field in Chicago was first known as Weeghaman Park. It is the second-oldest ballpark in the majors behind Boston's Fenway Park. It was named Wrigley Field in 1926 after William Wrigley Jr. purchased the Cubs from Weeghaman. When it was first constructed, the stadium could seat 14,000 fans. The original scoreboard is in tact.

Traditionally, Wrigley Field places a flag with a *W*, for win, or an *L*, for loss, atop the scoreboard after a game. Ernie Banks's uniform number, 14, and Ron Santo's number, 10, are on flags that fly from the left-field foul pole. Billy Williams's number, 26, and Ryne Sandberg's number, 23, fly from the right-field foul pole.

Rickwood Field

Rickwood Field in Birmingham, Alabama, is the oldest baseball stadium still in existence in the nation. It opened in 1910 and was the first concrete and steel stadium in the minor leagues. The park was home to the minor league Birmingham Barons and Birmingham Black Barons of the Negro Leagues.

The stadium is still used once a year for an exhibition game. The Birmingham Barons now play at Regions Park in Hoover, about 13 miles away.

Hall of Fame outfielder Willie Mays played for the Birmingham Black Barons from 1948 to 1950. Rickwood has hosted many other noted players throughout the years, including Ty Cobb, Christy Mathewson, Honus Wagner, Burleigh Grimes, Babe Ruth, Rogers Hornsby, "Shoeless" Joe Jackson, Pie Traynor, Stan Musial, and Leroy "Satchell" Paige.

Rounders

Sports historians pretty much agree now that the British ballgame rounders was the predecessor of American baseball.

The game has always been more popular with school children than adults. Four posts surround a pentagon-shaped field. When a batter hits a ball thrown by the pitcher, he is to run to the four posts. Each team has nine players, and nine outs make an inning. A match consists of two innings.

A Poet to Know: E. E. Cummings

Edward Estlin Cummings, born in 1894 in Cambridge, Massachusetts, was the son of a renowned political science and sociology professor at Harvard University. It is said that the "preaching voice" that Cummings adopts in many of his poems is a voice inspired by his father, who left Harvard in 1900 to become an ordained minister. Cummings attended Harvard and studied languages, particularly Greek. He was introduced to the writings of Ezra Pound who became one of his major influences.

After college, Cummings joined an ambulance corps and met William Slater Brown. Brown was arrested for writing incriminating letters and was sentenced to a concentration camp. Cummings refused to be separated from Brown, and the two were sent to the La Ferte Mace concentration camp together. They were later freed because of the political pull of Cummings' father.

After the event, Cummings wrote *The Enormous Room*, an account of his time at the concentration camp. It was published, along with many other pieces of work over the next decade, and Cummings began to focus on his writing and painting. In 1926, Cummings' father was killed suddenly in a car accident; his mother was gravely injured. Cummings wrote about the incident and moved to transform his poetry to define more serious aspects of his life, something said to be influenced heavily by his father's passing.

Cummings died in 1962 from a cerebral hemorrhage. Three volumes of his poetry were published posthumously; he left behind 25 books of poetry, prose, drawings, plays, and stories, all completed during his short, 68-year lifespan.

The Chronicles of Narnia by C. S. Lewis

Written by C. S. Lewis, *The Chronicles of Narnia* is a seven-novel series of children's books. With over 100 million copies sold in over 40 languages, it is Lewis' most well-known work. Though there are many Christian parallels in the Narnia series, it was not originally intended to be a biblical allegory. The stories instead have a literal meaning, chronicling the lives of a group of children who influence the history of a fictional land. While the stories are full of adventure and vivid ideas, they also present traditional Christian ideas in a way that is accessible to young readers. Also evident in the series is the influence of Greek and Roman mythology and British fairy tales.

The books feature children from the human world who magically find their way to Narnia, where they are summoned to help a lion named Aslan restore the well-being of Narnia. In *The Lion, the Witch and the Wardrobe,* the children join forces with other creatures to defeat the White Witch who has controlled Narnia for a century. This book is perhaps the most famous and has been made into several films and animations.

Certain Christian organizations have criticized the books for suspected pagan themes and supposed heretical depictions of Christ as a lion. Also, many argue that Lewis portrays mythological creatures in a positive light, suggesting the promotion of paganism. Dissenters argue that the stories are not intended to be a biblical allegory but only loosely borrow many images and concepts from mythology, the Bible, and fairy tales.

A Good Name to Know: C. S. Lewis

Born in Belfast, Ireland, Clive Staples Lewis grew up writing and illustrating adventurous stories about animals. With his brother, Warnie, Lewis created a mythical world called Boxen, which was ruled by animals. As a teenager, he began to write operas and epic poetry and developed a serious interest in Norse mythology, which later influenced his most famous work, *The Chronicles of Narnia*. Lewis is well known for the Christian parallels in his works and is widely studied by scholars of literature and Christian symbolism.

C. S. Lewis was a close acquaintance of J. R. R. Tolkien, the author of *The Lord of the Rings*. They taught together at Oxford University and led a literary group called the Inklings. During his friendship with Tolkien, Lewis converted to Christianity. He began doing radio broadcasts about Christianity and gained a wide following of listeners. He had been an atheist from age 13 to age 31, as during those years he viewed religion as a chore. His interests drifted toward the occult and pagan ideas. During his years at Oxford with Tolkien, however, Lewis was reunited with Christianity. In 1931, he joined the Church of England, although Tolkien was a devout Catholic and had encouraged Lewis toward Catholicism. Lewis died in November 1963 and was buried in the churchyard of Holy Trinity Church in Oxford.

November 22, 1963, marked the deaths of three notable men of history. On the same day that C. S. Lewis suffered a fatal collapse, Aldous Huxley died of cancer, and John F. Kennedy was assassinated.

How Does a Paternity Test Work?

DNA testing is often employed to determine the biological father of a human being. Two main types of DNA testing are used when deciphering paternity:

- PCR (polymerase chain reaction): A sample of DNA is taken from the donor and then reproduced by a lab and highlighted with fluorescent tags. The section of DNA is then compared to determine a match.
- RFLP (restriction fragment length polymorphism): DNA is taken from a sample and broken down with enzymes. Then, an electric current is used to separate the DNA by size. Once segregated, DNA probes are used to identify the strands and find a match.

Most DNA samples are taken from either blood or saliva samples, though DNA can be found in nearly every cell in the body. Blood and saliva both yield high concentrations of DNA and are easy to test.

A prenatal paternity test, conducted before a child is born, can be performed in a sterile medical environment by a physician. A prenatal DNA extraction can pose a small risk to an unborn baby, and therefore many physicians are hesitant to conduct the test.

Ethanol

Ethanol, which comes from plants, is a renewable fuel that is rapidly moving to the front burner of fuel research. Most ethanol is made from corn and other sugary plants, created through the process of fermenting the plant sugars into alcohol.

E85

Pure ethanol cannot be used for transportation fuel, but it can be blended with gasoline and other substances to create an efficient and earth-friendly alternative to traditional fuel. E85 is a blend of 85 percent denatured ethanol and 15 percent gasoline. E85 can be used in special engines designed to burn the particular properties of ethanol gas, called flex fuel vehicles. Flex fuel is only offered in special markets but is becoming more common around the world.

A higher percentage of gasoline is added to flex fuel sometimes during colder winter months to ensure that an engine can still start in harsh climates.

FFVs

Flex fuel vehicles were introduced as early as the 1880s. Henry Ford designed a car that ran on ethanol, and later built a Model T in 1908 that could run on either ethanol or gasoline.

Modern FFVs can only run on a blend of ethanol and gasoline, with the maximum percentage of ethanol topping out at 85. Cars, trucks, and SUVs are now made as FFVs and require the same maintenance and have the same efficient qualities of regular gas-powered vehicles.

One drawback to driving an FFV is that the ethanol-gasoline blends, such as E85, contain less energy than gasoline, reducing fuel efficiency by around 20 percent. The cost of E85, however, is usually lower than pure gasoline and is more easily replenished and earth-friendly to produce.

One of the biggest benefits of E85 and FFVs is the fact that replacing gasoline with ethanol will reduce the demand for foreign oil, at least for the Western countries in Europe and North America. The United States is currently the world's largest ethanol producer, as most ethanol is extracted from corn, a major agricultural product of both the United States and Mexico.

E85 also reduced greenhouse gas (GHG) emissions by nearly 15 to 20 percent when compared to the production and use of gasoline. E85 is less volatile than gasoline and therefore emits far les gases such as carbon monoxide and other carcinogens upon evaporation.

There are nearly 6 million FFVs on the road today in the United States alone.

Biodiesel

Biodiesel is a fuel that is extracted from agricultural products like vegetable oils. Most biodiesel in the United States is produced from soybean oil, but a large number of recycled cooking oils, plant oils, and animal fats can be used to make the product.

A process called "esterification" is used to make biodiesel. Industrial alcohol, such as methanol or ethanol, is used to convert the oils into a fuel that can be used to power a motorized vehicle. Additionally, most diesel engines can be run on biodiesel without any special modifications to the hardware.

B5

While B100 is pure biodiesel, B5 is the most common biodiesel blend, consisting of 5percent biodiesel and 95 percent regular diesel fuel. Registered with the EPA, biodiesel is legal to use on and off road.

- Approximately 600 fleets of trucks in the United States use biodiesel blends to fuel their engines. Biodiesel can be more expensive than petrodiesel, but no extra maintenance is involved in the transition between the two fuels.
- Like ethyl-based fuels, biodiesel can help reduce the Western dependence on foreign oil as well as reduce greenhouse gas emissions and environmental contamination.

Little-Known Facts About the Arms Trade

The global arms trade involves the proliferation, sale, and technological advancement of weaponry and war resources.

Shocking Facts

- The United States spends over $400 billion every year on the procurement of weapons. This total is almost as much as the rest of the world's expenditures combined.
- In recent conflicts, more than 80 percent of casualties have been civilian, and close to 90 percent of these deaths are caused by small arms.
- The United Nations, a global organization set up after World War II to preserve peace and international cooperation, has a budget that is only two percent of the world's military expenditure.
- The most recent data about the arms expenditures of the United States is from 2005. It showed that the US military budget was close to 29 times as large as the combined expenditures of six rogue nations, including Cuba, Iran, Libya, North Korea, Sudan, and Syria.
- Arms and military expenditures are the largest business in the world, with a global expenditure of around $1 trillion every year.
- The United States, France, Russia, and Britain spend the most money on arms trade of any nations in the world.

The Diamond Trade

The global diamond trade is one of the bloodiest businesses in the world, continuing to fund civil wars all over the globe. Human rights campaigners have warned that international standards and regulations of the diamond trade tend to disappear as major diamond-selling holidays such as Valentine's Day and Christmas approach.

- An eight-year civil war in Liberia has been continuously funded by the illegal diamond trade. Diamonds are smuggled and sold in the international market, providing wealth and resources to rebel factions and regimes.
- Globally, marketers of diamonds are required to provide a store policy about the sale of conflict diamonds, alerting customers of the legality of the diamond. But in a street survey in 2006, it was found that only 18 percent of stores surveyed could provide proof of a conflict diamond policy; 22 percent admittedly did not have any such policy in their store.
- A report by Global Witness revealed that diamonds were being smuggled out of the Ivory Coast of Liberia and sold in international markets. Laborers were forced to work in diamond pits in the northern part of the country, extracting enough diamonds to produce nearly 300,000 carats per year—worth over $25 million.

Buying Clean Diamonds

Shoppers should always be wary when buying diamonds and ask appropriate questions before completing a sale. A customer can ask the vendor to produce a policy on conflict diamonds, to provide the location from which the diamonds were purchased, and to offer a written guarantee from the store's diamond supplier verifying that the diamonds are conflict-free.

The ABCs of Cloning

Cloning can seem fairly complicated, but when broken down into simple terms, it is quite understandable.

DNA Cloning

In order to clone a gene, a DNA fragment of the gene must be extracted from the chromosomal DNA. This is done using enzymes that basically pull apart the DNA strand. They are then connected with a plasmid that has been cut apart with similar enzymes. This fragment of DNA connected with the plasmid is called a recombinant DNA molecule. When introduced with the appropriate host cells, the DNA will then reproduce with the host cell DNA. Ta da! Cloning.

Plasmids can hold up to 20,000 base pairs of foreign DNA.

Reproductive Cloning

Reproductive cloning is the process of creating an animal that contains the same nuclear DNA as another. Using the somatic cell nuclear transfer (SCNT) process, genetic material from the nucleus of the donor cell is transferred to an egg whose nucleus has been removed. The egg containing the DNA from the donor must then be treated with electrical currents to stimulate the cell division process. Once the egg reaches a suitable stage of development, it must be implanted into a host animal, where it continues to develop until the birth stage. Boom! A cloned sheep.

Fast Facts About Cloning

- The first animal ever cloned was a tadpole in 1952.
- Since the first cloned mammal, Dolly the sheep, many large and small animals have been cloned, including, goats, mice, pigs, rabbits, cats, and cows.
- Attempts to clone certain animals, such as dogs, chickens, and monkeys, have been unsuccessful. It is believed that certain species may be more resistant to somatic cell transfer than others.
- Reproductive cloning is actually highly inefficient. Nearly 90 percent of attempts at cloning fail to produce desired results in offspring, and a successful procedure might take nearly 100 nuclear transfers. Furthermore, cloned animals tend to have low immune system function and high rates of disorders, tumor growths, and infection.
- Because of the many risks and the inefficiency of animal cloning, most scientists believe that cloning humans would be ethically irresponsible.

Therapeutic cloning, or embryo cloning, involves the production of stem cells, via embryos, that can be studied and used to develop treatments for Alzheimer's, cancer, and other diseases.

Amino Acids, Proteins, and Enzymes—Oh My!

Amino acids are the building blocks of protein cells. Linked together, they create chains and form proteins that play important roles as messengers, enzymes, and hormones. When a cell is provided energy through carbohydrates, the amino acid acts as a builder. They are named as such because they contain an amino group, NH_2, and a carboxyl group, COOH. There are essential and nonessential amino acids.

- Essential amino acids must be eaten and can be found in foods such as milk, meat, and eggs. These three foods are called complete proteins because they contain all the essential amino acids.
- Many vegetables, such as soybeans, contain some amino acids, as they are high in protein. Once the body breaks down these amino acids, they are sent into the blood stream to begin their building work in the body's cells.
- Proteins are amino acid chains folded up onto themselves. The immune system recognizes proteins because of their globular size and shape.
- Nonessential amino acids are produced by the body, which finds them inside chemicals, such as aspartic acid, pyruvic acid, glucose, and many others.

Nonessential Amino Acids

- Alanine
- Arginine
- Asparagine

- Aspartic Acid
- Cysteine
- Glutamic Acid
- Glutamine
- Glycine
- Proline
- Serine
- Tryosine

Essential Amino Acids

- Histidine
- Isoleucine
- Leucine
- Lysine
- Methionine
- Phenylalanine
- Threonine
- Tryptophan
- Valine

Enzymes

Enzymes are proteins with interesting jobs in the body. By helping break down and create new proteins, enzymes take an active role in the immune system and other important roles of the body. The body knows to recognize them because, like other protein chains, they are folded into interesting shapes.

MSG and Tryptophan

MSG stands for monosodium glutamate, a salt inside the essential amino acid of Glutamic Acid.

- A salt is a molecule that is held together by opposite charges.
- In MSG, one sodium atom is basically stuck to glutamate, the amino acid.

MSG can affect hormone response and production in the body by affecting the hypothalamus. When glutamate is in excess, which can happen in the consumption of MSG, the body will begin to convert glutamate into other amino acids. Because the body absorbs MSG so quickly, receptors become excited, thinking there is an overdose of glutamate present. Areas of the brain can be inhibited or even damaged by this overload of glutamate detected by the body.

- In studies involving lab rats, scientists have found that MSG causes obesity in some cases because it inhibits hypothalamic appetite suppression, causing rats to ingest higher amounts of food. The same effect has not been documented in humans, yet.
- In the United States, the FDA requires foods containing MSG to be documented on the ingredient list of the product.

Tryptophan

Tryptophan is an essential amino acid, meaning that the body has to extract it from food. A common source of tryptophan and tryptophan-related myths is turkey. Many believe that eating turkey on Thanksgiving causes drowsiness because of the high levels of tryptophan absorbed. This is an explanation of how the amino acid works.

- Tryptophan helps the body produce niacin, a B-vitamin that entices serotonin production. Serotonin is a chemical that functions as a calming agent in the brain, encouraging healthy sleep. This explains why most believe that eating turkey will speed the production of serotonin and, in turn, make them sleepy.
- In actuality, tryptophan's sleep-inducing effects only really work when the amino acid is absorbed alone, such as on an empty stomach. When turkey is eaten with other foods, other amino acids and chemicals are absorbed, and relatively no effect will occur from the tryptophan present.
- Of course, if a person desires to feel the drowsy affects of turkey, one way to achieve the sleep-inducing effects is to have a light snack of turkey before bed, without any other foods.

Excess Amino Acids

The body has an intricate system of transforming amino acids when a certain type is in excess. The processes, called transamination and deamination, involve removing nitrogen from the atoms and converting the acids to fuel for storage. Both processes mainly occur inside the liver.

For example, if the body has too much of the amino acid aspartate, which is found in artificial sweeteners, the aspartate can be converted into glutamate. This sort of transformation can present a problem for those with liver dysfunction or diabetes whose bodies respond differently to glutamate.

NATO

NATO, which stands for the North Atlantic Treaty Organization, is the most powerful defense alliance in the world. Formed in 1949, NATO aimed to protect the freedom and civilization of its membering countries by promoting stability worldwide. An agreement was formed to state that an attack on one NATO country was to be treated as an attack on all NATO countries, each forming an alliance to respond and come to one another's aid.

Timeline

NATO currently has 26 members and several applicants for future memberships. Over time, countries have been added to the alliance.

- The Treaty of Brussels, which was signed in 1948 between Belgium, the Netherlands, France, Luxembourg, and the United Kingdom, is often considered to be the precursor of NATO's development.
- The treaty resulted in the Western European Union, but soon it was realized that the United States' involvement was needed in order to combat the military power of the Soviet Union. Talks were initiated, which led to the signing of the North Atlantic Treaty in 1949.
- The North Atlantic Treaty was signed by the five Treaty of Brussels nations, as well as Canada, the United States, Italy, Norway, Portugal, Denmark, and Iceland.
- In 1952, Greece and Turkey joined the treaty.
- In 1954, the Soviet Union proposed to join NATO in order to help preserve peace in Europe. Every single country inside NATO rejected the proposal.

- In 1955, the Soviet Union created the Warsaw Pact, a counteralliance to NATO. It quickly dissolved in 1991, when the USSR broke apart.
- In 1999, the Czech Republic, Hungary, and Poland gained NATO membership.
- Estonia, Latvia, Lithuania, Slovenia, Slovakia, Bulgaria, and Romania became NATO members in 2004, inducted at a ceremony in Washington, D.C.
- In 2008, Croatia, Bosnia, Serbia, and Montenegro are expected to join the NATO alliance. They are already members of NATO's Partnership for Peace alliance.

NATO has one civil and two military budgets. Each member nation allocates money into the budget using a cost-sharing formula. Each nation also provides resources for the organization's daily expenditures and needs.

The G8

The Group of Eight, set up during the oil crisis and recession of the 1970s, was created to ensure the stability of global economic issues and challenges. In 1973, the Library Group was formed between senior financial officials of the United States, Europe, and Japan. Two years later, the French joined in, and the group decided to meet annually. The countries, France, Germany, Italy, Japan, the UK, and the US, became known as the G6, and later the G7 and G8 when Canada and Russia joined.

- Though G8 members decide on policies related to economics and finances, compliance with the decisions is completely voluntary, as there is no real international law enforcement body.
- A different country holds the presidency of the G8 each year and is responsible for hosting the annual meeting, the G8 Summit. In 2006, Russia hosted the summit, and in 2007, Germany held the meeting in Heiligendamm.
- The G8 has been criticized as an organization that lacks representation by major economies such as China and India, and it is regarded by some as a body that only represents the elite industrialized nations of the world, ignoring the well-being of many other states.
- There have been disagreements within the G8 over the US war in Iraq, the Kyoto treaty, and international concerns such as global warming.

What Is Narcolepsy?

Commonly portrayed in film and popular culture, usually in a comedic way, narcolepsy is a well-known concept, but most likely, the facts and causes of the disorder are not widely understood.

Narcolepsy causes a person to have trouble staying awake, even during the day. Commonly called sleep attacks, the symptoms can occur even when a patient has slept enough during the night and does not feel tired. However, the sleep pattern of a person with narcolepsy is somewhat self-perpetuating and can severely affect their work and social life.

There are two main types of sleep. During rapid eye movement sleep, or REM sleep, the eyes move quickly and involuntarily behind shut eyelids. Most people dream during REM sleep, and have no control over muscle movement. During this time, a person cannot act out a dream he or she is having, as the body is limp. NREM sleep, or nonrapid eye movement sleep, occurs right when a person falls asleep. REM sleep follows, in a normal sleeping pattern, a few stages later.

A person with narcolepsy has a different pattern of sleep and often enters REM sleep right when he or she falls asleep, not after NREM sleep. Also, they can enter REM sleep while awake, causing them to experience any of the following difficulties:

- Loss of muscle control, sometimes resulting in a collapse of the body
- Loss of speech and movement, called sleep paralysis
- Vivid dreams during waking hours, much like hallucinations
- A sleep attack at any time during the day. The conditions do not necessarily have to be calm or quiet—a narcoleptic can

fall asleep while driving, eating, talking, or even while being physically active. This inconvenience can cause injuries, social difficulty, depression, and impaired memory and concentration. Often narcoleptics have trouble distinguishing between being asleep and being awake.

Currently, there is no cure for the disorder. Medicines can help with sleep patterns and deter the severe symptoms of narcolepsy, but a narcoleptic patient must continuously be wary of his or her safety and the possibility of losing waking consciousness at any time.

Useless Trivia

Some people say there's nothing a good night's sleep can't cure. J. R .R. Tolkien hated those people—he spent most of his marriage sleeping in a different room than his wife because she couldn't stand his snoring.

How Does a Pacemaker Work?

The pacemaker's ability to control the heart can be attributed to a tiny computer chip that reads and computes information from the heart 24/7. The pacemaker contains a generator that sends electrical pulses into the heart, correcting its rate and rhythm. The chip is responsible for calculating all information from the body and thereby determining the pulses that need to be sent into the heart by the generator. A wire is connected to the heart and feeds this crucial info back to the chip. That wire holds sensors that listen to the body's movement, blood temperature, breathing rate, and many other factors.

A doctor can also use the computer chip's recordings of the heart to set a pacemaker for a particular individual. To boot, the pacemaker can be programmed by a physician without even using needles or directly contacting the pacemaker.

- A single-chamber pacemaker carries pulses from the generator directly into the right ventricle of the heart.
- In a dual-chamber pacemaker, pulses are sent between the right atrium, the right ventricle, and the generator. The contractions of each chamber are determined by the electrical pulses from the generator.
- In a triple-chamber pacemaker, pulses are carried between an atrium, the generator, and both ventricles of the heart. This style of pacemaker is necessary for especially weak heart muscles and helps coordinate the timing of all chambers of the heart and their respective function.

There are two styles of programming for pacemakers, and each works in a different way.

- A demand pacemaker monitors the rhythm of the heart. The device only stimulates the heart with pulses when it detects that the heart is skipping beats or pulsing too slowly.
- A rate-responsive pacemaker speeds or slows the heart rate depending on physical activity. This pacemaker reads the signals from the entire body, from sinus rate, blood pressure, and all factors determining activity level. Patients who need a pacemaker that will constantly reset their heartbeat use rate-responsive pacemakers, as they are full-time workers.

There can be anywhere from one to three wires in a pacemaker, depending upon the model.

Hezbollah

The most powerful military force in Lebanon, Hezbollah formed in 1982 with financial support from Iran. Also called the Party of God, the organization is Shi'a Muslim and also serves as a large political force in the Lebanon parliament.

Hezbollah's military wing is called the Islamic Resistance and is believed to have well-trained fighters and missile capabilities that pose threats to Israel, its main target.

- The main initiative of Hezbollah is to dissolve the nation of Israel, which members believe occupies Muslim holy land unrightfully. Hezbollah was created in the early 1980s in response to the Israeli invasion of Lebanon. The group currently draws heavy support from the Lebanese because of its involvement in Israel's withdrawal from South Lebanon in the year 2000.
- Hezbollah has also gained support for providing health care and social services throughout Lebanon. They have a television station, al-Manar, which is widely received by the Lebanese, with support from Iran and Syria.

Hezbollah has been subject to many attacks, bombings, and kidnappings. Organizations such as the CIA, the UN, and Israeli military groups have targeted Hezbollah leaders in the recent past.

In a car bombing in 1985, the CIA allegedly attempted to assassinate Hezbollah leader Mohammad Hussein Fadlallah. The attempt failed, however, and Fadlallah survived.

The United Kingdom considers the military part of Hezbollah to be a terrorist organization but views its political party as a legitimate force.

Notable Young Achievers

Temba Tsheri

At the age of 16, Temba Tsheri, a boy from Nepal, reached the top of Mt. Everest with a hiking group from France. He was the youngest person to ever climb Mt. Everest, which stands at 29,035 feet and claims several climbers' lives per year.

Ruth Elke Lawrence

At the age of 11, Ruth Lawrence passed an entrance exam and was admitted to Oxford to study mathematics. She was the youngest person ever to attend the prestigious college and had to be accompanied to class by her father. Then, she graduated the program in just two years, while most students take three. Lawrence currently teaches at Hebrew University in Jerusalem.

Tatum O'Neal

In 1974, ten-year-old actor Tatum O'Neal won an Academy Award for her roll in the film *Paper Moon*, making her the youngest actor to ever win an Oscar. After such early success, her career turned to focus mainly on television.

Balamurali Ambati

Born in 1977, Balamurali Ambati graduated from NYU at the age of 13. He then went on to Mount Sinai's School of Medicine, from which he graduated four years later, becoming the youngest doctor in the world in the year 1995. Currently teaching and researching in the field of ophthalmology, Ambati has won countless awards and received many honors for his medical achievements.

Arfa Karim Randhawa

Born in Pakistan, Arfa Karim Randhawa passed the exams necessary to become a Microsoft certified professional (MCP) before the age of ten. After asking Bill Gates for a job with Microsoft, she was granted an internship, as Gates felt it was necessary for her to stay in school longer. She is an MCP in Windows programming and is proficient in the C++ and C# programming language.

A Few Other Child Prodigies

Jean Piaget –	Published an essay on the albino sparrow at age 11.
Dylan Scott Pierce –	Became a professional wildlife artist at age ten.
Zhu Da –	Published poetry by age 7; later became a painter.

Useless Trivia

The Shirley Temple of the 1930s, who grew famous alongside fellow singing actress Judy Garland, Deanna Durbin was the highest paid actresses of her time. She won a juvenile Oscar for her work in the 1936 flick *Three Smart Girls*—the same year Garland won for *The Wizard of Oz*, but in 1939, at just 17 years old, she left Hollywood for a little peace and quiet. Today she is a widower and protects her right to privacy in Paris, where she continues to refuse all requests for interviews.

The Cannes Film Festival

References are often made in popular culture to the Cannes Film Festival, one of the world's most famous film festivals. However, few really know the origin and significance of the festival and the awards given to film directors all over the world.

- The first Cannes Film Festival occurred in 1939, but after the beginning of World War II, the festival was postponed until the 1950s, after the war was over.
- Since the 1960s, Cannes has been recognized as the world's most prestigious film festival.

Seven Major Sections

- In Competition: Films competing In Competition have been nominated for the Palme d'Or prize, a major honor that is coveted by filmmakers all over the world. A Palme d'Or prize can help a movie climb to the top of the box office. The films that are In Competition are referred to as Official Selections and are screened at the famous Lumière Grand Theatre.
- Out of Competition: Films that are Out of Competition have made enough of a stir to be screened at Cannes but are not offered space on the official Cannes program. In the Out of Competition portion of the festival, highly respected filmmakers are also allowed to prescreen works in progress. Martin Scorsese prescreened his film *Gangs of New York* at Cannes in 2002, while the movie was still in production.
- Un Certain Regard: As a major side event of the festival, Un Certain Regard is a portion that showcase films that are not up for any awards or prizes. The section allows filmmakers

to present their work and gain possible worldwide exposure and reviews that they might not otherwise have.

- Cinefondation: The Cinefondation portion of the festival allows filmmakers to showcase short films. Close to fifteen short films are screened, and a jury selects three for best-film awards.
- Marche du Film: Marche du Film is the market portion of the festival, where film dealers and industry leaders travel to Cannes from all over the world to trade, buy, and sell film rights. Any filmmaker can enter a film into the Marche du Film by paying a registration fee.

Award-Winning Trivia

- The first Academy Awards ceremony to be telecast was the 25th, in 1953.
- The 1st Academy Awards were presented in 1927.
- Between 1931 and 1969, Walt Disney collected 35 Oscars.
- In 1969, *Midnight Cowboy* became the first and only X-rated production to win the Academy Award for Best Picture. Its rating has since been changed to R.

A Plot to Know: A Doll's House

If this 1879 Henrik Ibsen play were written in the 1970s, it could have been called "I Am Woman, Hear Me Roar." *A Doll's House* tells the story of Nora, the pampered, sheltered wife of the patronizing Torvald. His pet names for her include "songbird" and "little squirrel," which tells you all you need to know about him. He fell ill early in their marriage, and in order to get the money to pay for his medical bills, Nora forged some papers. His pride would have been wounded if he had known that she had squirreled away the cash necessary to save him, so Nora never tells. Unfortunately, her secret is discovered by Krogstad, a disgruntled employee of Torvald's bank. He threatens to blackmail Nora. Eventually Torvald discovers the truth about her "crime." Never mind the fact she saved his life. He berates her so harshly that by the time he tries to apologize for his cruel words, she is outta there. The play ends with her slamming the door, leaving Torvald in the dust.

Henrik Ibsen's Crazy Habits

- Henrik Ibsen began writing everyday at 4:00 a.m.
- He wrote with a pet scorpion on his desk.
- He had an affair with a 27-year-old when he was 63.

Sunnis and Shi'as

In the religion of Islam, Muslims are split into two main denominations—Sunnis and Shi'as. The divide occurred after the death of the prophet Muhammad, when Muslims were in argument over who should take on the role of leading the Muslims in the future. Though both sects share the fundamental principles of Islam, they have differences in belief about the doctrine, laws, rituals, and organization of the religion. Both, however, believe that Muhammad was the last living prophet, and both follow Allah as their sole god.

- The majority of Muslims around the world are Sunnis—close to 90 percent in fact.
- Certain extremely conservative groups of Sunnis preach hatred and disgust for Shi'as in their doctrines.
- Shi'as are often the poorest of Muslim societies.
- Because of Hezbollah's influence across Lebanon, Shi'as have gained wide-reaching respect across the country.

Sunnis

Sunni Muslims are self-regarded as the traditional, orthodox branch of Islam. They believe in the teachings of all the prophets named in the Qur'an, but consider Muhammad to be the final and most important prophet. The name Sunni comes from the phrase *Ahl al-Sunna,* which means "the people of the tradition." The tradition to which the phrase refers is the practices based on teaching of the prophet Muhammad. Sunnis follow a system of Islamic law, and most Sunni teachers are stateregulated.

Shi'as

Shi'as began as a political faction called *Shiat Ali*, which translates to "party of Ali." Ali was the son-in-law of Muhammad, and the Shi'as claimed the right to him as the leader of their sect. In a struggle over who would become leader of the Muslims after Muhammad's death, Ali was killed. In the wake of this event, Shi'as began rituals of grieving and martyrdom, casting themselves away from the Sunnis as victims. Ever since the divide, there has been a bloody and tumultuous history between the Shi'as and Sunnis.

There are an estimated 170 million Shi'a Muslims, representing around ten percent of all Muslims in the world. Shi'a Muslims are found in the countries of Iran, Iraq, Bahrain, and Yemen.

Quotes from Muhammad

Even as the fingers of the two hands are equal, so are human beings equal to one another. No one has any right, nor any preference to claim over another.

Do not consider any act of kindness insignificant, even meeting your brother with a cheerful face.

A man's true wealth here after is the good he does in this world to his fellow man.

Shall I not inform you of a better act than fasting, alms, and prayers? Making peace between one another: enmity and malice tear up heavenly rewards by the roots.

The Darfur Conflict

The Country

Darfur is a province in the west of Sudan, which is the largest country of Africa. Darfur is roughly the size of France. The majority of the population of Darfur is black African, and the country is under Arab control.

The Conflict

The Darfur Conflict began in 2003. For a long time, tensions between black African farmers and Arab herders have created opposition groups and boiling conflict around Darfur. In 2003, rebel groups began attacking the government in a violent revolt. Over two million citizens of Darfur had to flee their homes to escape the violence.

The government's retaliation of the revolt wreaked havoc on the country. Military aircraft bombed entire villages, and militias would then ride though the desecrated villages and rob, rape, and steal. Survivors and refugees believe that the violence was part of a deliberate attempt to rid Darfur of the black Africans. These refugees live in camps across Darfur, hiding from the violence, and many have crossed the border into Chad to escape. Foreign aid agencies have entered Darfur from all over the world to help the refugees, but many report that the spreading of violence has made it difficult to remain inside the country.

- A peace deal was signed in 2006 by the African Union in order to end the conflict. Part of the agreement was that the government would disarm the Janjaweed militia, but the disarmament was slow in taking off. The government of Sudan signed the peace agreement to help rid Darfur of violence, but little has been done on their part as well.

- The African Union has sent nearly 7,000 soldiers into Darfur to monitor the ceasefire outlined in the peace deal.
- Britain and the United States have pushed the United Nations to become involved in the peace mission for Darfur, but the Sudanese government has forbidden the UN from its territory, making things rather difficult.

There are many estimates of the number of casualties that have occurred as a result of the Darfur conflict, but all are well into the hundreds of thousands. The UN reports that at least 450,000 have died as a result of violence, disease, and starvation caused by the wars in Darfur.

Scientists report that the scale of climate change that has occurred in Darfur because of manmade global warming is unprecedented around the world. Some believe that this drastic climate change is a partial cause, or contributor at least, of the Darfur conflict. The rapid desertification of the land and fast reduction of rainfall because of drying, heating climates has caused migration and turmoil between farmers, herders, and landowners.

The Arab League

The Arab League is a voluntary association of Arab-speaking countries that seeks to strengthen relationships between member nations and serves to protect the common good of Arab nations. The league was founded in Egypt in 1945, at the end of World War II, when many Arab nations were still under colonial rule.

- The Arab League has 22 member states, including Palestine.
- The population of the league reaches nearly 300 million, across an area totaling nearly 5.25 million square miles.
- A council rests at the top of the Arab League, comprised of representatives from each state. Every nation has one vote, no matter the nation's size, and meetings are held twice per year.

Amr Moussa, a popular charismatic diplomat in the Arab world, currently holds the title of secretary-general of the Arab League. As the leading member, the secretary-general is elected by nomination from at least two member states and is then selected by a council to serve for a five-year term. Moussa has served as an ambassador in India and to the United Nations. He served as Egypt's foreign minister before becoming head of the Arab League.

The European Union

The European Union is a compilation of European democratic nations that seeks to transform Europe into a sort of single body, with common currency, open trade, and a common foreign security policy.

- The Treaty on European Union was signed in 1991, officially beginning the European Union.
- The Union is governed by a council of ministers, with each individual member country represented by several members. A commission and a parliament are also governing sections of the EU, regulating the currency and holding regular elections.
- In recent years, many formerly communist countries have joined the EU. There are currently 27 members:

Austria	Cyprus
Belgium	Czech Republic
Bulgaria	Denmark
Estonia	Malta
Finland	Netherlands
France	Poland
Germany	Portugal
Greece	Romania
Hungary	Slovakia
Ireland	Slovenia
Italy	Spain
Latvia	Sweden
Lithuania	United Kingdom
Luxembourg	

Any individual country, once part of the EU, must ratify the constitution in order for it to take effect.

Mouthing Off About Music

- "Of all noises, I think music is the least disagreeable." – poet and essayist Samuel Johnson
- "I hate music, especially when it's played." – comedian and jazz musician Jimmy Durante
- "Hell is full of musical amateurs." – novelist and playwright George Bernard Shaw
- "The music business is a cruel and shallow money trench, a long plastic hallway where thieves and pimps run free, and good men die like dogs. There's also a negative side." – journalist and novelist Hunter S. Thompson
- "The public doesn't want new music; the main thing it demands of a composer is that he be dead." – composer Arthur Honegger
- "A composer is a guy who goes around forcing his will on unsuspecting air molecules, often with the assistance of unsuspecting musicians." – composer Frank Zappa
- "Rap music… sounds like somebody feeding a rhyming dictionary to a popcorn popper." – novelist Tom Robbins
- "All music is folk music. I ain't never heard no horse sing a song." – jazz musician Louis Armstrong
- "I don't like country music, but I don't mean to denigrate those who do. And for the people who like country music, denigrate means 'put down.'" – comedian Bob Newhart
- "It is not hard to compose, but what is fabulously hard is to leave the superfluous notes under the table." – Johannes Brahms

Unusual Facts About Johannes Brahms

Johannes Brahms spent much of his life composing in Austria and spending time with composer and pianist Clara Schumann. He is most remembered for "Lullaby and Goodnight" and for his first symphony, which conductor Hans von Bülow referred to as "Beethoven's Tenth." Here are a few more tidbits on the composer:

- Brahms once fell asleep while composer Franz Liszt was playing piano for him.
- He played with tin soldiers until he was almost 30 years old, and he carried candy in his pocket to give out to neighborhood children.
- Schumann was his best friend, and he spent two years of his life helping her raise her children.
- The Third Symphony supposedly came to him during a meal in which he was enjoying fresh asparagus and champagne.
- Brahms was known for the red-and-white-checkered underwear that was almost always visible underneath his baggy pants. He often forgot to cinch his pants when conducting, and audiences regularly witnessed him tugging at his pants when they began to fall down during performances.

Wi-Fi

Wi-fi stands for wireless fidelity, which describes a group of standards for the movement of data over a wireless network. Much like a walkie-talkie, information is encoded into a radio frequency and sent to a receiver. The difference, though, is that wi-fi can transfer a much larger amount of data in a shorter time than a walkie-talkie, making it fast, efficient, and highly mobile.

- Strategically placed antennas create wi-fi hotspots, or outlets that are able to receive the radio waves that power the wireless network.
- An Internet connection is provided by a server, and then antennas are connected to that server either wirelessly or by cable.
- A computer equipped with wireless capabilities can connect with the server and access the Internet, as long as it is within the "hotspot," or within reach of the radio waves.

Wi-fi hotspots are growing larger and larger, to the point that some entire cities are going wireless or are creating zones so large that the Internet can be reached wirelessly from anywhere within the city. Many campuses and schools have already transformed into wi-fi zones.

The Risks of Wi-Fi

While wi-fi is convenient and easy to access, it also has its downfalls. Currently, wireless capabilities make it possible for large numbers of people to access networks and servers. This opens up the threat for viruses and worms to be spread at a much quicker rate. Security is one big reason that critics are skeptical of how wireless technology will be controlled.

Another criticism of wi-fi is the profitability. While it costs very little for a business such as a restaurant or coffee shop to set up a wireless router, business owners have caught on to the practice of charging customers to access the wireless Internet. Many locations, however, offer free wi-fi in open networks. Analysts have warned that wi-fi could be the cause of another "dotcom crash," because of the lack of hardware and regulations involved with the relatively new technology.

New Wonders of the World

The New Open World Corporation's New Seven Wonders of the World

Great Wall of China – China

Petra – Jordan

Christ the Redeemer (statue) – Brazil

Machu Picchu – Peru

Chichen Itza – Mexico

Colosseum – Italy

Taj Mahal – India

Great Pyramid – Egypt

American Society of Civil Engineers' Seven Wonders of the Modern World

Channel Tunnel – Strait of Dover, between England and France

CN Tower – Toronto, Ontario, Canada

Empire State Building – New York, NY, US

Golden Gate Bridge – Golden Gate Strait, north of San Francisco, California, US

Itaipu Dam– Paraná River, between Brazil and Paraguay

Delta Works – Netherlands

Panama Canal – Isthmus of Panama

Plastic Electronics

Plastic electronics are electronics fashioned from organic polymers, rather than silicon. Organic polymers can be used to make a plethora of electronic materials, given that they are highly conductive. Discovered in the 1960s, these polymers can be used to create solar panels, bin bags, LEDs (light-emitting diodes) in screens, and many other products.

- Semiconductors have traditionally been created from inorganic substances, which contain no carbon. Silicon is one of the most popular inorganic materials used in electronics, but it must be processed at extremely high temperatures in expensive facilities, hence the desire to replace it with organic materials.
- Polymers can be printed using simple inkjet printers, much like the production of wallpaper, posters, and magazines. This process is cheap, quick, and easy, whereas printing on silicon chips is highly complicated and expensive.
- Currently, high-speed computer chips are produced using silicon and require extremely pure materials and meticulous design methods. These silicon products are printed in components that are nanometers (billionths of a meter) in size. Currently, scientists are working with plastic materials in an attempt to print them in sizes small enough to replace the silicon chip.

The introduction of plastic electronics could lower the cost of computer chip production, making electronics cheaper for consumers and faster and easier to create.

String Theory

String theory is a class of thinking in which everything in the universe can be explained by the relative tension on strings. Like musical notes that come from plucking the strings of a guitar, particles are said to be affected by the tension on a string. Unlike a guitar, though, the strings of the universe are not attached to anything, but floating. They are, instead, acted on by the tension of gravity.

String theory is, in essence, a microscopic theory of the way gravity works. Instead of viewing a particle as a point, it is viewed as a loop on a string. Take an electron for example—a string theorist would view an electron as a loop on a string that oscillates in different directions. When viewed under a microscope, at a particular oscillation of the string, the viewer might see an electron. But if the string were to oscillate in a different way, the viewer might actually see a quark, or a photon. In reality, the particle is not a photon, quark, or electron, but actually a string. String theory holds that the universe is actually just...strings!

While there is no empirical proof that string theory is correct, many scientists believe that the theory actually represents a feasible explanation of how the universe works.

String theory is sometimes called the Theory of Everything, as it attempts to explain that everything in the entire universe can be viewed as one thing.

Interesting Facts About Wolfgang Amadeus Mozart

One of the greatest composers of the 18th century, Wolfgang Amadeus Mozart accomplished much before his death at age 35 in 1791. He is remembered by historians as an incredible talent and child prodigy, as well as a little irresponsible and immature. The latter descriptions may come as no surprise, however, when taking his unusual circumstances into account. Due to his immense talent, the early years of Mozart's life bear little resemblance to a common childhood:

- Age 3 – Imitated his sister's piano playing
- Age 4 – Composed his own music and studied violin
- Age 5 – Practiced music by candlelight late into the night
- Age 6 – Went on a musical tour of Europe, playing for upper-class families and nobility
- Age 7 – Proposed marriage to Marie Antoinette
- Age 8 – Composed his first symphonies
- Age 11 – Composed his first opera

As an adult Mozart maintained an unusual life, and legend states that he wrote music almost constantly. Activities combined with composition included eating, spending time with friends, and playing pool.

According to many accounts, Mozart held his wife's hand with one of his hands while she was in labor and composed with the other.

Common Sayings and Their Origins, Part III

Saying: A bird in the hand is worth two in the bush.

Meaning: It is better for one to have a small advantage or victory than the slight chance at a bigger one.

Origin: In the Bible (Ecclesiastes IX to be exact), one can find the following adage: "A living dog is better than a dead lion." Later, in 1530, Hugh Rodes' *The boke of nurture or schoole of good maners* quotes, "A byrd in hand—is worth ten flye at large." Clearly, the adage has evolved over time, and now there are even many pubs across Western society named *The Bird in Hand.*

Saying: The apple of my eye

Meaning: Literally, the central portion of the eye; figuratively, something cherished most, above all other things.

Origin: The phrase first appeared in a work by King Alfred of Wessex entitled *Gregory's Pastoral Care*. In modern English, its first use is noted in *Old Mortality* by Sir Walter Scott: "Poor Richard was to me as an eldest son, the apple of my eye." The adage also appears in Deuteronomy 32:10.

Saying: Baker's dozen

Meaning: Thirteen, rather than twelve.

Origin: It is believed that in medieval times, English bakers would often give out an extra loaf of bread when selling one dozen in order to avoid being accused of short-selling a customer. The practice seems to have begun centuries before the phrase was coined.

Saying: Blonde bombshell

Meaning: A glamorous, beautiful blonde woman.

Origin: The phrase was first used in reference to actress Jean Harlow about her role in the 1933 film *Bombshell.* A review of the film with the advertisement stated, "Lovely, luscious, exotic Jean Harlow as the Blonde Bombshell of filmdom," coining the phrase that has been used to describe foxy blondes ever since.

Vivaldi: The Red Priest

Italian composer Antonio Vivaldi, known as the Red Priest because of his red hair and robes, influenced many of Europe's greatest composers. He spent most of his life performing in a church in Venice. Applause was forbidden within the house of God, but audiences who came great distances apparently showed their appreciation through loud coughs and enthusiastic nose blowing. Vivaldi provided the world with one of its most loved compositions, *Four Seasons*, in which he included sounds that replicated the natural noises of chirping birds, barking dogs, and howling winds.

Empiricism and Rationalism

Rationalism and empiricism both ask the questions of epistemology, or the theory of knowledge. For example:

- What is the nature of knowledge?
- How can knowledge be gained?
- What are the limits or parameters of knowledge?

Empiricism holds that all knowledge is simply experience, not truth. The term, when used in a scientific matter, refers to observational methods of research. Empiricism is often contrasted with the theory of rationalism, which holds that the mind can ascertain truths in a direct way, without relying on observation or the senses. Empiricists tend to view knowledge in a manner that emphasizes probability and tentative discovery, rather than absolutism and truth. Conversely, rationalists are far more dogmatic in thinking, applying discoveries to absolute knowledge and certainty.

Rationalism, on the other hand, holds the view that truth can be discovered and affirmed directly. Rationalists seek to face all skepticism and counter it, in order to establish absolute certainty in knowledge and truth.

The philosophy of Descartes, Spinoza, and others is often called continental empiricism because it was predominant in the countries of continental Europe, while Empiricism wa popular in the island nation of Britain.

A Few Empiricists:
John Locke
George Berkeley
David Hume

A Few Rationalists:
Socrates
René Descartes
Emmanuel Kant

Hinduism at a Glance

- Hinduism is the world's third-largest religion, following Christianity and Islam.
- Because it has evolved from thousands of religious groups, it does not have a single founder or a single morality code.
- Its origins trace back to 4000 to 2200 BC, possibly making it the world's oldest religion.
- Hinduism's primary texts are known as the Vedas, which consist of the Rig Veda, Sama Veda, Yajur Veda, and Atharva Veda, and contains ancient hymns, incantations, and rituals.
- The Ramayana is another important text and contains stories about the hero Rama.
- There are two major divisions of Hinduism: Vaishnavaism regards Vishnu as the ultimate deity, and Shivaism regards Shiva as the ultimate deity.
- The Four Aims of Hinduism are broken into two parts: *pravritti*, those who are in the world, and *nivritti*, those who renounce the world.
- Pravritti has three goals:

– *Dharma*, righteousness in their religious life, is the most important.

– *Artha* is success in their economic life.

– *Kama* is gratification of the senses.

- Nivritti has one goal. *Moksa* is liberation from *samsara*.
- The three major Hindu deities are Brahma, the Creator; Vishnu, the Preserver; and Shiva, the Destroyer.

Sir Humphry Davy

Born in 1778, in Penzance, Cornwall, England, Humphry Davy first worked as an apprentice to a surgeon. Then at age 19 he moved to Bristol to study science. While there he experimented with laughing gas (nitrous oxide) and published his results in 1800. This work garnered the attention of the Royal Institution, and the following year, he was hired as an assistant lecturer in chemistry.

- He became a great success at the university, with his lectures drawing members of the fashionable London society.
- He became a fellow of the Royal Society in 1803 and was awarded its Copley Medal in 1805.
- In his further research, Davy used the newly invented battery to isolate potassium, sodium, calcium, strontium, barium, and magnesium, inventing the new field of electrochemistry.
- His exemplary work led to his being knighted in 1812.
- He invented what became known as the Davy lamp in 1815 after learning of the dangers facing miners who used candles for light in the dark mines.

Davy received many honors during his career, including a gold medal presented by Napoléon I, appointment as a baronet in 1818, and the presidency of the Royal Society of Science from 1820 to 1827. Sir Humphry Davy died in 1829 in Switzerland.

Edison and the Lightbulb

Thomas Edison didn't invent the lightbulb—he just made it work. More than a dozen people were working on their versions of the lightbulb. Joseph Swan had already placed lightbulbs in homes in England. And American inventor Hiram Maxim had a bulb that would burn for 24 hours straight.

So what was the big deal for Edison? He developed a total electric system—the bulbs, the wires, the fuses—all the elements necessary to satisfy customers. He had a plan to install underground wires and light up all of lower Manhattan.

New and Approved

Edison improved on Alexander Graham Bell's telephone by designing a carbon transmitter (mouthpiece) that improved the sound of the speaker.

Lightbulb Trivia

- Macy's department store in New York City became the first store to use incandescent lamp lighting in 1883.
- In 1888, the Hotel Everett on Park Row in New York City became the first hotel to be illuminated by electric light. There were 101 electric lightbulbs.
- New York theaters were the first to take advantage of using lightbulbs to spell out messages on their marquees.
- The world's largest lightbulb is in Edison, New Jersey. The lamp shaped like a lightbulb stands on top of the 131-foot Edison Memorial Tower. The tower itself stands on the site of Edison's famous Menlo Park Lab.

Household Games with Household Names

Parcheesi

One of the oldest trademarked American games, Parcheesi appeared in the US in 1867, when John Hamilton claimed a copyright for the American adaptation of the Indian Cross and Circle game Pachisi. He called his game Patchessi. By 1874, Hamilton had sold the copyright to a game-maker who registered the trademark Parcheesi.

Monopoly

Charles Darrow began selling Monopoly to individuals in 1933. He modeled his game after the 1904 Landlord's Game. There were so many design errors that Parker Brothers rejected the game when he offered it to them, but he went on to sell 5,000 handmade sets. When he couldn't keep up with the demand, he went back to Parker Brothers, and they struck a deal. In its first year of commercial production, Monopoly became the best-selling game in America. Today more than 250 million sets have been sold in 81 countries and in 27 languages.

Mind-Blowing Monopoly Facts

- More than 500 million people have played Monopoly.
- The longest game of Monopoly lasted 1,680 hours.
- Monopoly sets were used to conceal contraband smuggled into POW camps during World War II.
- Braille Monopoly was introduced in the 1970s.
- Neiman Marcus created an all-chocolate version of Monopoly in 1978. It retailed for $600.
- More than 5,120,000,000 green Monopoly houses have been made since 1935.

Facts to Drop About Modern Toys

- The Slinky toy came about by accident. In the 1940s, a spring fell off Richard James' desk. He watched it tumble end-over-end across the floor and shared the phenomenon with his wife. She called the sprightly spring a Slinky. It takes 63 feet of wire to make a Slinky.
- Play-Doh first entered the market in the 1950s as wallpaper cleaner. More than 700 million pounds of the toy-modeling compound have been produced.
- Mr. Potato Head was the first toy advertised on television. Before 1987, he smoked a pipe; however, in that year he kicked the habit and surrendered his pipe to the US Surgeon General at an official White House ceremony.
- The first electric Lionel train was designed as a window display to draw window shoppers into a toy store. It was not for sale until demand became so great that the toy shop owner had to start making them for sale.
- Every year 119,000 pounds of yellow paint and 5.1 million pounds of sheet metal are used to make Tonka trucks and other Tonka vehicles.
- Silly Putty was created in an attempt to find a substitute for rubber during World War II. Today, over 1,500 pounds of Silly Putty are produced each day; that's more than 20,000 eggs.
- Monopoly was banned in China and Russia and outlawed in North Korea and Cuba.

What is the total amount of money in a standard Monopoly game?

Answer: $15,140

The Jewel of Southern Black Baseball

The Birmingham (Alabama) Black Barons was a popular team after World War I. They were charter members of the Negro Southern League and shared the Birmingham Barons' ballpark, Rickwood Field.

- Satchel (Leroy) Paige, one of the world's greatest pitchers, was a Birmingham Black Baron. He was joined by other great players, including Lorenzo (Piper) Davis; Artie Wilson; Jehosia Heard; Bill Greason; and "The Say Hey Kid," Willie Mays.
- The Black Barons, dubbed "the jewel of southern black baseball," enjoyed fame and popularity at home and on the road. Then in 1946, when Jackie Robinson broke the color barrier by signing with the Brooklyn Dodgers, the era of black baseball soon came to an end.
- Two years later, in 1948, the Black Barons and the Homestead Grays played the last Negro League World Series.
- The Black Barons disbanded in 1963 as Birmingham's focus diverted to the Civil Rights Movement.

- Burleigh Grimes was the last legal major league spitball pitcher.
- Fans know Willie Mays as "The Say Hey Kid," but his friends and teammates know him as "Buck."
- In March 1984, President Ronald Reagan posthumously awarded Jackie Robinson the Presidential Medal of Freedom.

Facts to Drop About Baseball

- The first official baseball stadium was established in 1862, at Union Grounds in Brooklyn, New York. The price to attend a game at the stadium was 10¢.
- Yankee Stadium was called the House That Ruth Built. Babe Ruth hit the first home run in the ballpark during the first game played in the stadium.
- In 1935, President Franklin Roosevelt threw the light switch for the first National League night baseball game. He was in the White House, 600 miles away from Crosley Field. That year, seven night games were played.

Presidential Fans

In 1910, William Howard Taft, the 27th US president, began the tradition of the presidential "first pitch" of baseball season. Since then every president except Jimmy Carter has opened at least one season of baseball during his tenure.

Woodrow Wilson was such a fan that in 1915 he became the first president to attend a World Series Game.

An Innovative Idea: Gatorade

In 1965, scientists at the University of Florida were called on to solve a problem for the school's football team, the Florida Gators. It seems the Gators were having trouble with exhaustion and muscle cramps when playing and practicing in the hot southern Florida climate. The researchers' task was to find a way to alleviate the dehydration that the team was experiencing. The result was Gatorade.

Sports drinks like Gatorade help the body in two ways. They provide an extra dose of electrolytes to replace those lost when exercising, and the carbohydrates in the drink provide extra energy.

When the football team began drinking the new electrolyte-replacement beverage, their performance almost immediately increased. They could outplay heavily favored opponents even in oppressive Florida temperatures. The first year the team drank Gatorade, they achieved their first winning season in more than a decade. The next year, 1967, the Florida Gators again played stronger and longer, winning the Orange Bowl for the first time ever in the history of the school.

- When other schools found out about the electrolyte-replacing drink, they ordered large quantities for their own teams. Today, more than 70 Division I colleges provide Gatorade for their football players during games.
- In 1983, Gatorade became the official sports drink of the NFL. Since then, the NBA, AVP, PGA, Major League Baseball, and Major League Soccer have claimed it as their official drink too.

Ergonomically Correct Gatorade

When researchers were confronted with the task of allowing sports players to hydrate quickly and re-enter the game in as little time as possible, they turned their thoughts to bottle design. The scientists who accepted the challenge were by then experts in ergonomic design, having already created the ergonomic computer mouse.

After hours of research and design they developed the ultimate sports bottle—the E.D.G.E. The Ergonomically Designed Gatorade Experience is easy to hold and has a precision-fit mouthpiece. The twist-open top makes hydrating even quicker.

- The Gatorade Sports Science Institute was established in Barrington, Illinois, to evaluate and research athletes, nutrition, and exercise programs. The institute also provides educational materials for sports health professionals.
- The Gatorade In-Car Drinking System (GIDS) was developed to help race car drivers remain hydrated while racing. Temperatures inside race cars can reach as high as 130°F.

Increase Your Golf IQ Score

- Scotland's Leith Links held the world's first recorded golf competition in the late 1700s.
- Less than 7 percent of US golfers play left-handed. Even players who are left-handed in their daily lives prefer the right-handed golf swing.
- The South Carolina Golf Club in Charleston was the first golf club established outside of the United Kingdom. Players started using the course in 1786.
- J. J. McDermott was 17 years old in 1911. In that same year, he became the first native-born American to win the US Open. He remains the youngest winner to date.

Quotes on Golf

I have a tip that can take five strokes off anyone's golf game: it's called an eraser.
—Arnold Palmer

Golf is a game that is played on a five-inch course—the distance between your ears.
—Bobby Jones

The first time I played the Masters, I was so nervous I drank a bottle of rum before I teed off. I shot the happiest 83 of my life.
—Chi Chi Rodriguez

Through years of experience I have found that air offers less resistance than dirt.
—Jack Nicklaus, on why he tees his ball high

The Powder Puff Derby

Prior to 1929, women were flying airplanes and performing tricks and even Hollywood stunts. But 1929 was an important year in women's air history. It was the year that women got into the act of airplane racing.

Twenty women entered the Women's Air Derby, which began on August 18 in California and ended August 27 in Cleveland. Competitors included Amelia Earhart, Louise Thaden, Opal Kunz, and other experienced pilots. Thaden won the race, and Earhart placed third.

Will Rogers, who was one of the spectators that day, commented that it looked like a powder puff derby since each woman dabbed powder on her nose before setting out for Cleveland.

That day, one pilot died from carbon monoxide poisoning, and one was hospitalized with yellow fever. One pilot ran into a car that was parked on a landing strip, and another ran into a steamroller that was working at the edge of a runway.

Today, many high schools and universities hold powder puff football games as fund-raisers, where the genders reverse their typical roles. The girls play flag football, and the guys often dress up as cheerleaders.

Fast Facts About Female Pilots

- Amelia Earhart was married to book publisher George Putnam.
- Louise Thaden, winner of the Powder Puff Derby, made history again 60 years later when astronaut Lt. Col. Eileen Collins carried Thaden's cloth flying helmet with her on a space flight.
- Later, when Collins went to the Russian space station Mir, she took early female pilot Bobbi Trout's pilot certificate, which had been signed by Orville Wright.
- Lt. Col. Eileen Collins was the first woman to pilot a space shuttle in 1995.
- Bobbie Trout and Pancho Barnes, who both flew in the Powder Puff Derby, established the Women's Air Reserve, WAR. They took first-aid courses and trained in navigation and military maneuvers so that they could use their piloting skills to help injured people. The WAR staff included doctors, nurses, pilots, and parachutists who could quickly fly to the scene of a disaster and provide medical assistance.

Born in 1924 to a wealthy banker named Prescott Bush, George H. W. Bush went on to become the youngest pilot in the Navy when he was just 18 years old. After his plane was shot down during a WWII bombing mission in 1944, Bush returned home to Connecticut and married sweetheart Barbara Pierce, who once said Bush was the first man she ever kissed. The couple had six children (one died of leukemia at just three years old), and Bush enrolled at Yale University. There, he played baseball and became a member of an elite secret society known as Skull and Bones.

Fascinating Details About Johann Sebastian Bach

Johann Sebastian Bach is known as one of the greatest composers of history. Thought to be a serious musician as well as a deeply religious man, the composer is remembered for his gifted dedication to the organ and the Christian God.

- Bach once wished to terminate his employment with a duke, and the man refused. When Bach requested with such persistence that his contract end, the duke finally imprisoned him. While in jail, he wrote 46 pieces of music.
- According to legend, one evening while walking home, Bach was attacked by six of his students, one of which he had referred to as a "nanny-goat bassoonist." The students demanded an apology from the composer, but he refused. Rather than withdraw his insult, Bach drew a knife in self-defense. Luckily, the police arrived to divide the brawlers before any serious violence occurred.
- Bach reportedly walked 250 miles from Arnstadt to Lübeck to visit the father figure of German organists, Dieterich Buxtehude.
- Bach's parents were both dead by the time he reached the age of 10, and he was financially independent by the age of 15.
- Because he loved coffee so much, Bach once wrote a cantata about it.
- Bach had 76 male relatives who were musicians, 53 of which were named Johann.
- Bach wrote his *Goldberg Variations* as a commissioned piece for an insomniac millionaire. The composition was intended to help the patron relax. The piece led to the largest payment the composer ever received.

Talkin' Bach

- "Since the best man could not be obtained, mediocre ones would have to be accepted." – Leipzig mayor Abraham Platz, commenting on appointing Bach as the cantor of St. Thomas School, quoted in Werner Neuman's *Bach*
- "Bach almost persuades me to be a Christian." – English critic Roger Fry, quoted in Virginia Woolf's *Roger Fry*
- "Why waste money on psychotherapy when you can listen to the B Minor Mass?"– composer Michael Torke
- "Study Bach: there you will find everything." – composer Johannes Brahms
- "If Bach is not in Heaven, I am not going!" – journalist William F. Buckley
- "It may be that when the angels go about their task praising God, they play only Bach. I am sure, however, that when they are together en famille they play Mozart." – theologian Karl Barth
- "I would rather play Chiquita Banana and have my swimming pool than play Bach and starve." – Cuban musician Xavier Cugat
- "Mozart tells us what it's like to be human; Beethoven tells us what it's like to be Beethoven; and Bach tells us what it's like to be the universe." – novelist Douglas Adams
- "Now there is finally something from which one can learn something." – Wolfgang Amadeus Mozart, upon hearing a Bach motet

Paddle Tennis: An Innovative Accident

Frank P. Beal thought he could teach other kids how to play tennis if he reduced a typical tennis court by one-half and replaced the tennis ball with a sponge rubber ball and the racket with a wooden paddle. In 1898, he introduced his friends to paddle tennis.

For 23 years, kids in Beal's hometown, Albion, Michigan, had all the fun to themselves. Then, when Beal moved to New York to become a minister, he introduced the children at the church to paddle tennis. The game caught on quickly and kids of all ages were playing paddle tennis in the street and on special courts set up in parks and on playgrounds.

After World War II, paddle tennis became popular in California and has since spread across the nation. In 1978, the first national paddle tennis championships were played.

Table tennis is the second most popular sport in the world. In the US alone it is played by more people than baseball or football. What is the most popular sport in the world? Soccer.

Board Games: Pieces to Know

- The first major manufacturer of games in the US is said to be W. and S. B. Ives of Salem, Massachusetts.
- The company published at least two dozen games in the mid-1800s. Parker Brothers bought the company in 1887.
- Their Mansion of Happiness is said to be the first American board game.
- Milton Bradley created a pocket-sized game pack for soldiers who fought in the Civil War to carry around with them.
- In the mid- to late-1800s, John McLoughlin created beautiful, handcrafted card games. His games are known as some of the most beautiful games made in the US. In 1920, his company was bought out by Milton Bradley.
- The games industry helped Americans through the Depression years of the 1930s. Games and movies were inexpensive entertainment that many families were able to participate in. Jigsaw puzzles became popular during this time.
- The oldest family-owned game company still conducting business in the US is the Pressman Toy Company, which opened in 1921.
- Games historian Bruce Whitehill is also known as the Big Game Hunter. He has the world's largest collection of antique American games, with some dating from 1843.

Judaism at a Glance

Judaism is one of the three major Abrahamic Religions. Worldwide more than 18 million people consider themselves Jewish. Unlike most religions, Judaism does not have a strict outline of beliefs, but most Jews follow the Thirteen Principles of Faith as outlined by 12th-century Rabbi Maimonides:

1. God exists.
2. God is one and unique.
3. God is incorporeal.
4. God is eternal.
5. Prayer is directed to God alone.
6. The words of prophets are true.
7. Moses' prophecies are true and he was the greatest of the prophets.
8. The Written Torah and Oral Torah were given to Moses.
9. There will be no other Torah.
10. God knows the thoughts and deeds of men.
11. God will reward the good and punish the wicked.
12. The Messiah will come.
13. The dead will be resurrected.

Judaism focuses on relationships and a person's actions. Jews also believe that everything was created by God; that one shouldn't spell the name or title of a deity in full; that God is neither male nor female and is omnipresent, omnipotent, omniscient, just, merciful, holy, and perfect; and that we are all God's children and were created in his image.

Judaism teaches that the Messiah, or Moshiach, will eventually come. Unlike Christianity, Jews do not believe that

Jesus was the Messiah. Some see him as a moral leader, while others insist he was a false prophet.

The Jewish texts are made up of the Tanakh and the Talmud. The Tanakh, which is made up of the Torah, the Nevi'im, and the Ketuvim, contains the Jewish scriptures. The Talmud is comprised of the Mishnah and the Gemara and contains Jewish stories, laws, medical knowledge, and other material.

Jewish Holy Days

- Days of Repentance
- Hanukkah
- Passover
- Purim
- Rosh Hashanah
- Sabbath
- Shavuot
- Sukkkot
- Tisha B'av
- Tu B'Shevat (Tu Bishvat)
- Yom Hashoah
- Yom Kippur

Children are considered adults when they reach a specific age. Boys enter Bar Mitzvah on their 13th birthday, and girls enter Bat Mitzvah at 12.

Apocrypha

At the time of Christ, two versions of the Old Testament were in circulation, a Hebrew version and a Greek version. The Greek version is known as the "Septuagint." Several books appear in the Septuagint that do not appear in the Hebrew version. The early Christians, most of whom spoke Greek, used the Septuagint, which included these books, collectively known as the Apocrypha:

1. Esdras
2. Tobit
3. Judith
4. additions to Esther
5. Wisdom of Solomon
6. Ecclesiasticus
7. Baruch
8. Song of the Three Children
9. Susanna
10. Bel and the Dragon
11. The Prayer of Manasseh
12. 1 Maccabees
13. 2 Maccabees

The Apocrypha continued in common use among Christians until the Reformation, when the Hebrew canon was chosen as the Protestant Old Testament. However, today Catholic and Orthodox Churches continue to use the Septuagint. The only theological significance of the Apocrypha is that the books of the Maccabees support prayer for the dead, which Protestants dispute.

The Dead Sea Scrolls

Discoveries throughout time have confirmed the Bible's authenticity. The most recent of these discoveries is the Dead Sea Scrolls. They were first discovered in 1947 when a goat-herder threw a rock into a cave and broke open a clay pot that contained scrolls wrapped in linen. Excavations until 1956, to find additional scrolls continued in eleven caves located on the northwest shore of the Dead Sea near the ancient site of Qumran. Over 800 scrolls were found covering both biblical and non-biblical topics. The Scrolls are believed to be written as early as the 2nd century BC thru 1st century AD This makes the Dead Sea Scrolls the oldest biblical manuscripts known to date. The majority are written in Hebrew, but some are in Aramaic and Greek. Copies of a portion of every book of the Old Testament have been found, with the exception of Esther. This includes almost 40 copies of Psalms, over 30 copies of Deuteronomy, and over 20 copies of both Genesis and Isaiah. The scroll containing Isaiah is over a thousand years older than any other known copy. A large portion of the scrolls are written on animal hide, others on papyrus (paper-like material), and one is on joined together copper sheets. This Copper Scroll is a list of hiding places in Israel that some believe are the locations of hidden treasure of the Temple at Jerusalem. The longest of the scrolls was found in cave 11 and is referred to as the Temple Scroll. It presently is 26.7 feet long, but was originally over 28 feet. Numerous scrolls have been displayed in various locations all over the world, but most are kept in the Shrine of the Book at the Israel Museum or in the Rockefeller Archaeological Museum; both are in Jerusalem. Thousands of books and publications have been written not only containing the text of the scrolls, but also their impact on history, society, and religion. The discovery of the Dead Sea Scrolls has been regarded as the greatest biblical and archeological find in the 20th century.

Holy Relics

Since the beginning of Christianity, believers have viewed "relics" as a means to come closer to a person who was deemed divine and therefore form a closer bond with God. Holy relics pertain to the saints' bodies and belongings and are enshrined in churches around the world. Traditionally, a martyr's relics are the most prized among the saints. Some saints' relics are known for their extraordinary incorruptibility or miracles linked to them. Relics can be categorized into first-class (items directly associated with Jesus Christ or the physical remains of a saint), second-class relics (an item that the saint wore or possessed), and third-class (either a piece of cloth touched by the body of a saint after his death or a piece of cloth touched to the shrine or reliquary of the saint).

Note that many, if not all, of the following relics are linked to legends that have passed through the centuries, obscuring the authenticity of both the story and the items at hand.

- The **Shroud of Turin** is a linen cloth bearing the image of a man who appears to have been crucified. Intense debate has ensued over the centuries as to whether the shroud is part of the cloth that covered Jesus' body when he was laid in the tomb or a piece of art from the Middle Ages. It is kept in the royal chapel of the Cathedral of Saint John the Baptist in Turin, Italy.
- The **Sudarium of Oviedo** or Shroud of Oviedo is a bloodstained piece of cloth, claimed to be the cloth that was wrapped around the head of Jesus after he died. It is kept in the cathedral of Oviedo, Spain.
- The **Holy Prepuce** is said to be the Holy Foreskin of Jesus. Throughout history, a number of European churches have claimed to possess this foreskin, which has been the source of various miraculous powers.

- The **Holy Lance** (also known as the Spear of Destiny, Holy Spear, Lance of Longinus, Spear of Longinus, or Spear of Christ) is said to be the lance that pierced Jesus' side while he was on the cross. There have been many relics in many churches that are claimed to be parts of the Holy Lance.
- The **Seamless Robe of Jesus** (or Holy Tunic, Holy Coat of Trier, Holy Coat of Trèves) is the robe said to have been worn by Jesus before his crucifixion. The Roman Catholic Church traditionally claims that the robe is housed in the Cathedral of Trier, Germany.
- The **Holy Chalice** is said to be the cup in which Jesus served the wine during the Last Supper. There are several contenders with claims of being the true chalice, including the Jerusalem Chalice, Genoa Chalice, Valencia Chalice, and, more recently, the Antioch Chalice. The **Holy Grail** is also associated with the Last Supper and is said to possess miraculous powers, although folklore has created many different stories as to what the Holy Grail actually is.
- According to early literature, the Empress Helena (mother of Constantine, the first Christian Emperor of Rome) discovered in the fourth century the hiding place of the three crosses used at the crucifixion of Jesus and the two thieves. A miracle revealed to her which of the three was the **True Cross**. Many churches claim to possess fragmentary remains of the cross.
- The **Iron Crown of Lombardy** is a royal crown within which a thin band of iron is said to have been hammered out of one of the nails from the True Cross. According to tradition, the nail was first given to Emperor Constantine I by his mother Helena after she discovered the cross. It is kept in the Cathedral of Monza near Milan, Italy, the capital of modern Lombardy.

The Green Eggs and Ham Bet

Who says gambling is a bad thing? The story of *Green Eggs and Ham,* listed by the *New York Times* as a best-selling book of the 1960s, began as a bet. Since its publication in 1960, the book has become one of the most popular children's books of all time and has made the name Dr. Seuss synonymous with quality children's literature.

In the mid-1950s, Dr. Seuss, born Ted Geisel, began producing children's books for Random House. Upon the birth of a series called Beginner Books, he began creating numerous children's books that incorporated vivid artwork, nonsensical words, and rhymes with unusual meter, resulting in immediate successes. Because of the sensation surrounding his first books, his publisher rapidly began to recognize Dr. Seuss as a major asset to the company. He developed a partnership and friendship with the businessman behind Random House, Bennett Cerf. In 1960, the friendship resulted in a small wager. Cerf challenged his writer-artist friend that he could not produce a Beginner Book using only 50 different words. Geisel, as Dr. Seuss, set to the task without delay. In time he had created a storybook titled *Green Eggs and Ham,* a story about an enthusiastic character named Sam who successfully encourages an irritable and unnamed friend to try something new. Dr. Seuss' undertaking proves as fruitful as Sam's: the story includes precisely 50 different words.

Dr. Seuss is uncontested as the champion of the wager; however, it seems he never received his winnings from Cerf. It is doubtful that receipt of the prize concerned him; the financial success of the book remains to this day far beyond any of Dr. Seuss' other publications. As of 2004, only three books had outsold *Green Eggs and Ham*: *The Poky Little Puppy* (1942), *The Tale of Peter Rabbit* (1902), and *Tootle* (1945.)

A Poet to Know: Langston Hughes

Langston Hughes began writing poetry when he was a mere eighth grader. His father discouraged poetry as a career and agreed to later pay Hughes' tuition to Columbia University only if he pursued a career path in engineering. Hughes soon dropped out of the program but continued writing poetry, publishing his first piece in *Brownie's Book,* titled "The Negro Speaks of Rivers."

- He later published poems, essays, and stories in many magazines. His essay titled *The Negro Artist and the Racial Mountain* appeared in the *Nation* in 1926, stirring controversy and gaining him widespread attention. The essay discussed the "false integration" of black writers or poets, arguing that many black writers wanted to write like white writers. Hughes criticized this trend.
- Hughes' controversial and outspoken attitude toward race in writing gained him popularity and acclaim, leading to over sixteen books of poetry, three collections of short stories, four volumes of "documentary" fiction, twenty plays, two novels, three autobiographies, and countless musicals, children's poems, and magazine articles.
- Some of his more famous collections of poetry include *The Big Sea, The Dream Keeper,* and *One Way Ticket.*

Langston Hughes died of cancer in the spring of 1967, leaving five plays to be posthumously published. His block of residence on East 127th Street in Harlem, New York, was renamed Langston Hughes Place in his honor.

Really Old Things: The Oldest American Toy Company

Founded in 1922 by Jack Pressman, the Pressman Toy Company enjoyed its first big success in 1928, when it acquired the rights to Chinese checkers, which is still on their product list. The toy company was also among the first to begin licensing toys such as the Dick Tracy and Little Orphan Annie playthings in the 1930s, even introducing a line of Snow White toys in 1937 to accompany the release of the first full-length animated feature film, *Snow White and the Seven Dwarfs*. In 1955, the Pressman Company capitalized on the popularity of Walt Disney's *Mickey Mouse Club* and offered a full line of Disney-themed games, toys, and activities.

Throughout the years, the company has remained family owned—first under the direction of Jack and his wife, Lynn, and now in the capable hands of son Jim. In keeping with the times, Pressman has begun issuing games patterned after television shows such as *Wheel of Fortune, Jeopardy, Who Wants to Be a Millionaire, Amazing Race,* and *Deal or No Deal*.

Facts to Drop During Game-Night

- A deck of playing cards sold for $143,550 at Sotheby's in London in 1983. The cards, dating back to 1470, are the oldest complete hand-painted set.
- Twister was first called Pretzel. It was created to advertise a shoe polish company.
- Jenga, a Hasbro game, is a Swahili word meaning "to build."
- In 1400 BC, Egyptians played a game that resembles today's checkers.
- John Spilsbury, a map-maker living in England, invented the jigsaw puzzle in 1767. Of course, his first jigsaw puzzle was a map of the world.

Where Are Thomas Paine's Bones?

In his last will and testament, Thomas Paine requested that he be buried at a Quaker gravesite. Unfortunately, the Quakers required membership to their denomination for that particular privilege. At the time of his death in 1809, the establishment did not recognize Paine as a member of their order, although he had once been one.

The author of the call to arms titled *Common Sense*, Paine spent his early years in Thetford, England, as a young Quaker. Quakers, also known as the Society of Friends, have, since their establishment in the 17th century, practiced the Peace Testimony. The belief of peace teaches that mankind should not act in violence and, therefore, should object to all war. As an adult he became one of the more outspoken men in New England, having emigrated there in 1774 under the guidance of Benjamin Franklin. Over the next couple of years he busied himself with lobbying settlers against the injustice of British rule over the colonies in the Americas and rallying support for rebellion. This was not the first of his indiscretions against the fold and certainly not the last.

Paine left the church in the early years of his life, claiming that as a child he had heard a sermon that led him to see Christianity as exceedingly malicious. Paine would pronounce himself to be a part of the growing deist community. As a deist, he proclaimed that God exists but has no participation in the events following creation, and he also believed that reason is supreme to faith. Deist belief contradicts the conventional orthodoxy of the various denominations of Christianity, and eventually Paine produced scathing publications against the religious establishment. The greatest of these was *The Age of Reason*, written while he was imprisoned by the Montagnards in France.

Regardless of the rationalization behind his preference for a Quaker burial, documents illustrate that Paine wished it so. Throughout his life, Paine embarrassed and infuriated the religious establishment, so that George Washington, who some historians proclaim to also have been a deist, thought him overzealous. Consequently, the Quakers refused the request for a burial within their lands when he died in June 1809, and Paine's body was buried in New York with only six mourners in attendance.

A few years after his death, an admirer of Paine's legacy named William Cobbett exhumed the controversial figure's corpse. The intention to relocate Paine's remains to the man's native soil was born in the desire to provide him with a heroic burial. As fate would have it, Paine's deceased body never made it to England, and to this day its location remains uncertain.

From Paine's Own Blasphemin' Mouth

- "I do not believe in the creed professed by the Jewish Church, by the Roman Church, by the Greek Church, by the Turkish Church, by the Protestant Church, nor by any Church that I know of. My own mind is my own Church." – *The Age of Reason*
- "The Bible is such a book of lies and contradictions there is no knowing which part to believe." – *The Age of Reason*
- "Priests and conjurors are of the same trade." – *The Age of Reason*

Unusual Terms of Classical Music

Aleatoric (adj) – describes pieces that, through improvisation and randomness, involve chance as an element in their composition

Castrato (n) – a male vocalist of the 17th and 18th centuries, castrated during his early years to avoid the effects of puberty on his voice

Devil's interval (n) – medieval term for tritone, an interval that spans three whole tones. It is the same as an augmented forth or diminished fifth

Heckelphone – a woodwind instrument that is more or less a baritone oboe, popular in the early 20th century

Incidental (adj) – describes pieces that are written for supplementary use in a dramatic work

Polyphony (n) – the combination of multiple rhythmically diverse musical voices

Prima donna (n) – leading soprano of an opera

Quodlibet (n) – a piece involving the polyphonic sounding of multiple popular and well-known melodies

Sackbut (n) – a brass instrument of the Renaissance that ultimately evolved into the trombone

Tafelmusik (n) – German period music of the 16th and 17th centuries composed to coincide with dining

Theremin (n) – an electronic instrument invented around 1920, involving vacuum tubes, a fixed radio oscillator, and a variable one

Tutti (n) – a passage of orchestral music in which all instruments within a section are played concurrently

A Guide to a Few Major Catholic Beliefs

The Trinity – Catholics believe in one God existing as three bodies: the Father, the Son, and the Holy Spirit. This belief is also known as the Nicene Creed. The belief in the Trinity is also referred to as a dynamic monotheism, meaning the belief in one God in multiple forms.

Creation – Catholics believe that creation is for God's purposes, but that it is affected by Original Sin, the sin of Adam and Eve. Therefore, the Catholic Church believes that creation is good, but that humans are inherently sinful.

The Sacraments – Catholics accept seven sacraments: Baptism, Holy Eucharist, Reconciliation, Confirmation, Holy Orders, Matrimony, and Anointing of the Sick. The sacraments are believed to help individuals progress spiritually, contributing to the Church's growth as well. Not every individual receives each sacrament, but as a whole they are viewed as necessary steps to salvation.

Becoming a Saint

One might wonder, what does it take to become a saint? The answer: rigorous verification of martyrdom. On February 18, 2008, a new set of guidelines were decreed by the Vatican that set forth a rigid process to titling someone a saint.

The guidelines, titled *Sanctorum Mater*, were issued by the Vatican's Congregation for the Causes of the Saints as a response to the large number of people who have been sainted over the last few decades. Pope John Paul allowed the beautifications to nearly 1,350 people and the canonization of nearly 500 more—larger than all of the beautifications and canonizations issued by all preceding popes combined since 1588. The Catholic Church felt it was time to step in!

The Papacy

The pope (meaning "father") keeps a busy post as Bishop of Rome, spiritual leader of the Roman Catholic Church and head of state of Vatican City. In the 11th century, after the East-West Schism, Gregory VII declared the term "pope" to be reserved for the Bishop of Rome. Roman Catholics consider the very first pope to be Saint Peter, one of Jesus' twelve disciples. Since Peter, there have been 265 popes, the latest, Pope Benedict XVI, was elected in 2005.

The Process: Electing the Pope

In 1059, the electorate was restricted to the Cardinals of the Holy Roman Church, and the individual votes of all Cardinal Electors were made equal in 1179. Under present canon law, the pope is elected by those cardinals who are under the age of 80.

The election of the pope almost always takes place in the Sistine Chapel, in a meeting room called a "conclave" where the cardinals are sequestered until they elect a new pope.

Each ballot is read aloud by the presiding Cardinal, who pierces the ballot with a needle and thread, stringing all the ballots together and tying the ends of the thread to ensure accuracy and honesty. Balloting continues until a pope is elected by a two-thirds majority.

Once the ballots are counted and bound together, they are burned in a special stove erected in the Sistine Chapel, with the smoke escaping through a small chimney visible from St. Peter's Square, therefore announcing to the world the election of a new pope.

Papal Trivia

- Charlemagne was the first emperor crowned by a pope. For over a thousand years, popes have played powerful roles in Western Europe, regulating disputes among secular rulers.
- The pope has quite a few titles:
    - Bishop of Rome
    - Vicar of Christ
    - Successor of the Prince of the Apostles
    - Supreme Pontiff of the Universal Church
    - Primate of Italy
    - Archbishop and Metropolitan of the Roman Province
    - Sovereign of the State of the Vatican City
    - Servant of the Servants of God
- The formal way to address the pope is "Your Holiness" or "Holy Father."
- The longest-reigning pope was Pius IX, who served for 31 years, 7 months, and 23 days (however, according to tradition, Saint Peter headed the church for 35 years and has thus far been the longest reigning pope in the history of the church).
- The shortest-reigning pope was Urban VII, who only reigned for 13 calendar days and died before consecration.
- The youngest pope was John XII, who was 18 when he became pope.
- The first pope that wasn't canonized as a saint was Liberius.
- Only Italians held the papal post for more than 450 years until Polish Pope John Paul II was elected in 1978.
- Pope John Paul II snuck out to ski and hike in the Italian Alps more than 100 times before being discovered by a ten-year-old boy.

- Pope John Paul II met five US presidents during his papacy: Jimmy Carter, Ronald Reagan, George H.W. Bush, Bill Clinton, and George W. Bush.
- Adrian IV is the only English pope. There has not yet been an American pope.
- Since 1378, all popes have been Roman Catholic Cardinals.
- Pope John XXIII, elected at age 77, is to thank for shifting Mass from being celebrated in Latin to local languages.
- Pope Gregory XIII had one son when he was elected in 1572.
- All seven popes during the period of 1305 to 1378 were French. In fact, Pope Clement V actually moved the papal court to the city of Avignon. It was moved back to Rome in 1378.
- Pope Pius X is responsible for moving the age of which a child can receive Holy Communion from 13 to 7.
- The fruit cantaloupe was named after the commune Cantalupo in Sabina, Italy, a summer residence of the pope.
- There have been 23 popes named John and 16 named Gregory. In descending order after that were Benedict (15), Clement (14), Innocent (13), Leo (13), and Pius (12).

Fast Facts About Lent

Celebrated by most denominations of Christianity, Lent comprises the 40 days before Easter. This time is devoted to fasting and prayer, representative of the time Jesus spent resisting temptation by Satan while fasting in the desert following his Baptism.

The weeks of Lent are believed to prepare the Christian for the celebration of the Resurrection of Jesus, culminating on Easter Sunday. In most Western Christian denominations, Lent begins on Ash Wednesday and lasts through Holy Saturday, the day before Easter on the Christian calendar. The six Sundays that occur during Lent are not counted as fasting days, as most Christians regard them as mini-Easters.

The name *Lent* has origins in the Middle Ages when churches began delivering sermons in their native language instead of Latin. The English word *lent*, stemming from the Germanic root word for "spring," was adopted.

Fasting during Lent was at one time far more strenuous than it is today. During the Middle Ages fasters resisted meat, eggs, dairy products, and alcohol products while fasting. Some fasters abstained from eating until three o'clock in the afternoon, while most fasted until evening time and then allowed themselves a small meal with no meat or alcohol.

In modern times, a majority of Christians observe Lent as a voluntary sacrifice instead of an obligation. Most decide to give up a particular food, drink, or activity for the duration of the 40 days. Others take on a volunteer or charity activity.

The Holy Days Within the Season of Lent

- Ash Wednesday – the first day of Lent in Western Christianity
- Clean Monday – the first day in Eastern Orthodox Christianity
- Spy Wednesday – the Wednesday of Holy Week which commemorates the Biblical story of Judas spying on Jesus in the garden of Gethsemane.
- Maundy Thursday – the Thursday of Holy Week when Christians celebrate the Last Supper.
- Good Friday – Friday of Holy Week when Christians remember the crucifixion and burial of Christ.

Patron Saints

Many sects designate patron saints of particular causes or as one's personal saint. These saints are chosen as special protectors or guardians over the particular cause, which is often closely associated with that saint's life. These areas can include occupations, illnesses, churches, countries, disasters, or anything pertinent to human life.

Some offbeat patron saints:

- Falsely Accused: Raymond Nonnatus
- Bee Keepers: Ambrose
- Coffin-bearers: Joseph of Arimathea
- Contagious diseases: Roch, Sebastian
- Eczema: Antony the Abbot
- Haemorrhoid sufferers: Fiacre
- Insanity: Dymphna
- Misbehaving Children: Matilda
- Nighmares: Raphael the Archangel
- Death by Artillery: Barbara
- Insect Bites: Mark the Evangelist
- Ulcers: Charles Borromeo
- Rabies: Hubert, Ubald

The Pen Names of Famous Pen Holders

Author: George Eliot
Famous Works: *Silas Marner, Middlemarch*
Real Name: Mary Ann Evans

Author: Mark Twain
Famous Works: *The Adventures of Tom Sawyer, Adventures of Huckleberry Finn, The Prince and the Pauper*
Real Name: Samuel Langhorne Clemens

Author: Lewis Carroll
Famous Works: *Alice's Adventures in Wonderland, Through the Looking Glass*
Real Name: Charles Lutwidge Dodgson

Author: Voltaire
Famous Works: *Candide, La Princesse de Babylone*
Real Name: François-Marie Arouet

Author: O. Henry
Famous Works: *The Furnished Room, The Gift of the Magi*
Real Name: William Sydney Porter

Author: George Orwell
Famous Works: *Animal Farm, Nineteen Eighty-Four*
Real Name: Eric Arthur Blair

Author: Dr. Seuss
Famous Works: *Oh The Places You Will Go, The Lorax*
Real Name: Theodore Geisel

Author: J.K. Rowling
Famous Works: The Harry Potter series
Real Name: Joanne Rowling

Author: Pablo Neruda
Famous Works: *España en el Corazón, Obras Completas*
Real Name: Neftali Ricardo Reyes Basoalto

Author: Woody Allen
Famous Works: *Annie Hall, Crimes and Misdemeanors*
Real Name: Allen Stewart Konigsberg

Author Stephen King tried to fool everyone by publishing four titles under the name Richard Bachman. The writing styles of Bachman's and King's novels were compared, and it was soon revealed that Bachman was, in fact, Stephen King.

A Plot to Know: A Rose for Emily

This story, one of Faulkner's most famous, was first published in 1930 and takes place in a fictional city called Jefferson, Mississippi. The story follows an eccentric woman named Emily Grierson, who has become somewhat of an enigma of the town of Jefferson. After her father's death, Emily refused to enter the town, pay her taxes, or bother with the upkeep of her home. She is seen often with a man named Homer, who the townspeople rumor to be her lover, however peculiar. When Homer disappears, the townspeople assume that he, a transient worker, has simply left Emily. Many years later, when Emily was old and frail, she finally passed away. When townspeople enter her home, they find, astonishingly, the corpse of Homer, her former lover, lying in Emily's bed next to an impression in the mattress that suggests that Emily has, in fact, been sleeping with Homer's corpse for decades.

Hemingway vs. Faulkner

When alcohol fueled the feud between literary giants Hemingway and Faulkner, the latter claimed that Hemingway "had no courage." Later, when Faulkner said, "Hemingway has never been known to use a word that might send a reader to the dictionary," Papa retaliated: "Poor Faulkner. Does he really think big emotions come from big words? He thinks I don't know the ten-dollar words. I know them all right. But there are older and simpler and better words, and those are the ones I use." Perhaps some of those "older and simpler words" included "Old Corndrinking Mellifluous," a pet name Hemingway devised for Faulkner.

Studying and IQ

- Because IQ tests measure a person's ability to understand ideas and not the quantity of knowledge, learning new information—or studying for the test—does not automatically increase a person's IQ score.
- Studying may exercise a person's mind, which could help develop greater cognitive skills, but scientists have not fully investigated this relationship. The connection between learning and mental ability is still largely unknown, as are how the brain works and the nature of intellectual ability.
- There is evidence to conclude that intellectual ability depends more on genetic factors than on environmental factors, but environmental conditions play a role in the development of intelligence.

Breastfeeding and IQ

A 2007 study in New Zealand and Britain led researchers to discover a gene that explains why breastfed babies tend to be more intelligent than those fed bottled milk. The gene, FADS2, is found in 90 percent of people and serves to process fatty acids in the body. Babies who were breastfed and shared the genetic variant scored higher on intelligence tests than bottle-fed babies in the study.

Nurturing an IQ

There is some evidence that children who receive better nurturing and diet as babies develop higher intellectual ability, and those who have a higher degree of intellectual stimulation in preschool tend to have higher IQ scores for a few years, but this stimulus does not permanently increase IQ scores. For the most part, adult IQ scores don't significantly increase over time. There is evidence that maintaining an intellectually stimulating atmosphere—learning new skills or solving puzzles—boosts some cognitive ability, but the changes do not permanently affect IQ scores.

It is important to understand that IQ tests are simply tools for measuring intellectual ability. IQ tests don't measure creativity, social skills, wisdom, acquired abilities, or a host of other things that figure into overall intelligence. IQ tests are valuable when determining intellectual potential. There is some correlation between IQ and a person's success in school and the workplace; however, there are many times when life skills and IQ travel on different tracks.

Genius IQ is generally considered to begin around 140 to 145, representing 0.25 percent of the population (1 in 400):

- 115 to 124 – Above average
- 125 to 134 – Gifted
- 135 to 144 – Highly gifted
- 145 to 164 – Genius
- 165 to 179 – High genius
- 180 to 200 – Highest genius
- + 200 – Super genius